Asia's New Regionalism and Global Role

Agenda for the East Asia Summit

Editors

Nagesh Kumar, K. Kesavapany and Yao Chaocheng

Published by:

RIS
Research and Information System for Developing Countries
New Delhi

ISEAS
Institute of Southeast Asian Studies
Singapore

First published in India 2008 by:

Research and Information System for Developing Countries (RIS)
Zone 4B, 4th Floor, India Habitat Centre
Lodhi Road, New Delhi 110 003, India.
Tel. : 91-11-24682177-80
Fax : 91-11-24682173-74
Website: www.ris.org.in
Email: publication@ris.org.in

First Published in Singapore in 2008 for worldwide distribution outside India by:

Institute of Southeast Asian Studies (ISEAS)
30 Heng Mui Keng Terrace,
Pasir Panjang
Singapore - 119614
Tel: (65) 6870 2447 Fax: (65) 6775 6259
E-mail: pubsunit@iseas.edu.sg
http://bookshop.iseas.edu.sg

Distributed in India by:

BOOKWELL
24/4800, Ansari Road, Darya Ganj, New Delhi-110002, India
Ph: 91-11-23268786, 23257264 Fax: 91-11-23281315
E-Mail: bkwell@nde.vsnl.net.in ▪ bookwell@vsnl.net
Website: http://www.bookwellindia.com

Asia's New Regionalism and Global Role: Agenda for the East Asia Summit Edited by Nagesh Kumar, K. Kesavapany and Yao Chaocheng

ISBN: India 81-7122-098-3 Singapore 978-981-230-749-1

Printed and bound in India.

Asia's New Regionalism and Global Role

Agenda for the East Asia Summit

RIS

Research and Information System for Developing Countries (RIS) is an autonomous policy think-tank, established in 1984 in New Delhi, and specialised in trade and development issues. Its work programme focuses on multilateral trade negotiations, regional economic integration in Asia, new technologies and development, South-South Cooperation and strategic responses to globalization.

The work of RIS is published in the form of research reports, books, discussion papers and journals. For more information about RIS and its work programme, please visit its website: www.ris.org.in.

ISEAS

The **Institute of Southeast Asian Studies (ISEAS)** was established as an autonomous organisation in 1968. It is a regional centre dedicated to the study of socio-political, security and economic trends and developments in Southeast Asia and its wider geostrategic and economic environment.

The Institute's research programmes are the Regional Economic Studies (RES, including ASEAN and APEC), Regional Strategic and Political Studies (RSPS), and Regional Social and Cultural Studies (RSCS).

ISEAS Publishing, an established academic press, has issued almost 2,000 books and journals. It is the largest scholarly publisher of research about Southeast Asia from within the region. ISEAS Publishing works with many other academic and trade publishers and distributors to disseminate important research and analyses from and about Southeast Asia to the rest of the world.

Contents

Preface vii

List of Tables and Figures ix

List of Contributors xi

1. Asia's New Regionalism and Global Role: An Editorial Introduction 1

Part I: Asia's New Global Role and Regional Economic Integration

2. Economic Integration and Asia's New Role in the Global Economy
Soogil Young 11

3. Relevance of Broader Regional Economic Integration in Asia and a Roadmap
Nagesh Kumar 21

4. A Strategic Perspective on Asian Economic Integration: The Importance of Building 'One Asia'
Eric Teo Chu Cheow 47

Part II: Building Blocs of Broader Regional Cooperation

5. ASEAN's Role in Asian Economic Integration
K. Kesavapany 61

6. Japan and an Asian Economic Community
Masanori Kondo 83

7. China's Role in the Asian Economic Integration Process
Yao Chaocheng 95

8. India and the Asian Economic Integration
Mukul G. Asher and Rahul Sen 105

Part III: Trade and Investment
9. Forging an Integrated Asia-Pacific Region
Tiziana Bonapace and Mia Mikic 141
10. Welfare Gains from Regional Economic Integration in Asia: ASEAN+3 or EAS
S.K. Mohanty and Sanjib Pohit 165

Part IV: Monetary and Financial Cooperation
11. Monetary and Financial Cooperation in Asia
Ramkishen S. Rajan 185
12. Reducing Global Imbalances and Accelerating Growth: Role of Regional Financial Cooperation in Asia
Ramgopal Agarwala and Prabir De 203

Part V: Regional Cooperation for Energy Security
13. Asian Energy Outlook to 2020: Trends, Patterns and Imperatives of Regional Cooperation
Kokichi Ito, Li Zhidong and Ryoichi Komiyama 221
14. Regional Cooperation for Asian Energy Security
Vipul Tuli 247

Part VI: Epilogue
15. An Agenda for the East Asia Summit
Editors 269

Preface

This book is a sequel to two previous publications *Towards an Asian Economic Community: Vision of a New Asia* (New Delhi and Singapore, RIS and ISEAS, 2005) and *India-ASEAN Economic Relations: Meeting the Challenges of Globalization* (New Delhi and Singapore, RIS and ISEAS, 2006). It seeks to carry forward the debate started in the previous volumes on the issue of regional economic integration in Asia which is currently engaging the minds of leaders and policy makers of the region.

This books puts together the revised versions of a selection of papers presented at the High-level Conferences on Asian Economic Integration organized by RIS, in Tokyo (November 2004), Taiyuan, People's Republic of China (September 2005), New Delhi (November 2005), and Singapore (November 2006) in collaboration with ISEAS, Singapore; and with Shanxi University of Finance and Economics, Taiyuan (for the Taiyuan Conference), among other policy think-tanks. This series of High-level conferences was launched by RIS in March 2003 in New Delhi as a part of a larger research programme on Asian Economic Integration supported by the Sasakawa Peace Foundation (SPF). The research programme and the series of conferences have evolved over the past four years with the collaboration of a number of policy think-tanks and with the contribution of a number of experts. The research programme and the conference series have served to provide a forum for a continuing dialogue on the relevance, prospects and challenges for regional economic integration in Asia especially in the context of the launch of the East Asia Summit as an inclusive forum bringing together 16 major and among the most dynamic economies of Asia.

Completion of this volume gives us an opportunity to put on record our appreciation and thanks to numerous organizations and individuals for their contribution to the research programme leading to this volume. We are most beholden to the SPF for their generous support to this programme. In particular, we would like to thank Mr Akinori Seki, President and Dr. Lau Sim Yee, Senior Programme Advisor for their constant support and encouragement to the programme throughout.

We are grateful to ISEAS, Singapore for collaborating in organization of the New Delhi and Singapore conferences. Ambassador Kesavapany, director of ISEAS has lent not only his full support but has been an important source of inspiration throughout. Shanxi University of Finance and Economics co-hosted the Taiyuan Conference in September 2005. We are grateful to Professor Yuan Meisheng, Dr

Guo Ze Guang and Dr Yao Chaocheng of the University for their cooperation. Other think-tanks that have collaborated in organization of conferences in the series include the Council on East Asian Community, Tokyo; Development Research Centre of the State Council of China, Beijing; Global Security Research Institute at the Keio University, Tokyo, Malaysian Institute for Economic Research, Centre for strategic and International Studies, Jakarta; Asian Development Bank; Institute of South Asian Studies, Singapore. UNDP's Regional Centre in Colombo also supported some activities conducted on the subject.

Professor Arjun Sengupta, M.P. and Chairman, RIS has been a great source of inspiration and guidance throughout.

The research programme and the series of conferences leading to this volume have also received support from a large number of individuals in addition to the contributors. These include political leaders and parliamentarians such as Mr Koichi Kato, Mr I.K. Gujral, Mr K.C. Pant, Mr K. Natwar Singh, Mr Prithviraj Chauhan, Mr B.J. Panda, Prof. Le Bo Linh; academic experts and policy makers such as Prof. Muchkund Dubey, Ambassador S.T. Devare, Ambassador Leela Ponappa, Prof. Mohammad Ariff, Dr Hadi Soesastro, Ambassador Shashank, Dr S.L. Rao, Prof. M. Kawai, Dr Pradumna Rana, Dr Srinivasa Madhur, Sharad Bhandari, Toshihiko Kinoshita, Prof. Rodolfo Severino, Prof. Tsugio Ide, Dr Zhang Xiouji, Eisuke Sakakibara, Prof. Shujiro Urata, Prof. Fukunari Kimura, Prof. Ito Kenichi, Dr Takehiko Kondo, Mr Y. Matsuki, Dr Chan-Hyun Sohn, Dr Djisman Simandjuntak, Prof. Manoranjan Mohanty, Ambasador Aftab Seth, Dr C. Ram Manohar Reddy, Dr Isabelle Saint-Mezard, Prof. Osamu Nariai, Ambassador Rajiv Sikri, Mr. Kavi Chongkitavorn, Ambassador M.L. Tripathi, Ambassador Nalin Surie, Dr Sanjaya Baru, Dr C. Rajamohan, Ambassador Manaspas Xuto, Mr T.C. Venkat Subramanian, Ambassador Yasukuni Enoki, Ambassador N. Ravi, Dr Gloria Pasadilla, Dr Sebonti Roy-Dadwal, Mr T.K. Arun, Dr Shi Yaodong, Mr B.S. Bishnoi, Mr Sunil Jain, Mr P.S. Raghavan, Dr Rajiv Kumar, among many others, for their inspiration, contributions and inputs to the evolution of the project at various stages.

I would like to thank all the contributors for their assistance in revising the papers for the volume in a timely manner. I am grateful to Ambassador Kesavapany and Prof. Yao for their willingness to join hands in editing this volume.

Finally we would like to thank Tish Malhotra at RIS, Manmohan Singh Khurana and Ghanshyam Das Kushwaha at Bookwell, and Triena Ong and Rahilah Yusuf of ISEAS for managing this publication under a very tight schedule.

Nagesh Kumar
Director-General, RIS
New Delhi

2 November 2007

List of Tables and Figures

Tables

3.1: Proposed East Asian or JACIK Community in relation to European Union and NAFTA in 2004 — 30
3.2: Welfare Gains from Economic Integration in East Asia or (JACIK) — 31
3.3: Relative Welfare Gains from Economic Integration in JACIK and ASEAN+3 — 33
7.1: China's Economy in 2050 — 98
8.1: Macroeconomic Indicators of Selected Asian Countries, 2004 — 107
8.2: Real GDP Growth, Selected Asian Countries — 109
8.3: External Sector Indicators of Selected Asian Countries in 2005 — 112
8.4: Leading Exporters and Importers in World Trade in Commercial Services (Excluding Intra-EU Trade), 2005 — 119
10.1: Alternative Scenarios for EAS from Simulation Analysis — 170
10.2: Absolute Change in Welfare Gains from the East Asian Economic Integration — 173
10.3: Percentage Change in Welfare from the East Asian Integration — 175
12.1: Investment Deficit in Asia — 210
12.2: Income and Investment in Southern Asia — 212
12.3: Estimates of Annual Infrastructure Investment Needs in Asia — 213
12.4: Infrastructure Investments Needs in Developing Asia, 2007-2012 — 214
13.1: Major Energy and Economic Indicators — 225
13.2: World Primary Energy Consumption — 227
13.3: World Final Energy Consumption — 231
13.4: World Power Generation — 232
13.5: Primary Energy Consumption in Asia — 234
13.6: Final Energy Consumption in Asia — 235
13.7: Power Generation in Asia — 238
A 13.1: World Primary Energy Consumption (by Region) — 242
A 13.2: Primary Energy Consumption in Asia (by Region) — 244
14.1 Importance of Market Stability for Consumers: Example of China — 253

Figures

3.1: Emerging (East) Asian Community — 26
3.2: Comparative Welfare Gains from JACIK and ASEAN+3 Approaches — 33
8.1: Dynamics of Working Age Population in Selected Economies — 110
8.2: Growth in Global Working-Age Population (15-64) — 111

8.3:	Trends in India's Merchandise Trade by Region, 1987-2004	114
8.4:	Average Growth of India's Merchandise Trade by Region, 1988-2004	115
8.5:	India's Merchandise Exports with Selected Asian Countries 1987-2004	116
8.6:	India's Merchandise Imports from Selected Asian Economies: 1987-2004	117
8.7:	Relative Costs in India and Other Selected Offshore Locations in Asia	121
8.8:	Trends in India's Total Foreign Investment Flows: 1990-2004	127
8.9:	Comparisons of FDI Confidence Index for Selected Asian Economies	128
9.1:	The Noodle Bowl	146
9.2:	Bilateral Agreements among UNESCAP Members	147
9.3:	Consolidating RTAs: an Example of a Geography-based Consolidation	154
9.4:	The Need for Consolidation of RTAs in the CIS	155
10.1:	Effects of Deeper Integration on EAS	176
10.2:	Gains for the ASEAN Group in Various Scheme of RTA	177
11.1:	The Chiang Mai Initiative: Progress to Date (as of July 2007)	189
11.2:	Structure of Asian Bond Fund (ABF2)	192
14.1:	Asia: Dominant Consumer of Oil, Gas and Coal	248
14.2:	55 per cent of Asian Crude Currently Consumed within Asia, 2003	249
14.3:	More than 95 per cent Asian Gas Production is Consumed within Asia	250
14.4:	Supplying Within Asia is More Profitable: Natural Gas Illustration	250
14.5:	Balanced Approach Increases Share and Volumes	252
14.6:	Huge Investment Requirement for Complex Refining	252
14.8:	Annual Upstream Capital Investment Requirements in Supplying Countries	254
14.9:	External Funding Requirements in Supplying Countries: OPEC Example	256
14.10:	Asian Gas Market: Third Largest Margin Pool in the World	257
14.11:	Proposed Gas Projects in Asia	258
14.12:	Coal vs. Gas in Power Generation in Asia	260
14.13:	Coal Production and Consumption in Asia, 2001-2025	261
14.14:	Asian Prospective Coal Reserves	263

List of Contributors

Ramgopal Agarwala	Senior Adviser, Research and Information System for Developing Countries (RIS), New Delhi
Mukul G. Asher	Professor, Lee Kuan Yew School of Public Policy, National University of Singapore
Tiziana Bonapace	Chief, Trade Policy, TTD, United Nations Economic and Social Commission for Asia and the Pacific (UN-ESCAP), Bangkok
Yao Chaocheng	Associate Professor/Academic Dean, Faculty of International Trade of Shanxi University of Finance & Economics, Taiyuan, China
Eric Teo Chu Cheow	Council Secretary, Singapore Institute of International Affairs (SIIA) and Managing Director, Ssvoir Faire Corporate Consultants Pte. Ltd., Singapore
Prabir De	Fellow, Research and Information System for Developing Countries (RIS), New Delhi
Kokichi Ito	Managing Director, Head of the Research Directorate-General, General Manager for Energy for Energy Data and Modelling Center, Institute of Energy Economics, Japan (IEEJ), Tokyo
K. Kesavapany	Director, Institute of Southeast Asian Studies (ISEAS), Singapore
Ryoichi Komiyama	Researcher, Energy Data and Modelling Center, Institute of Energy Economics, Japan (IEEJ), Tokyo
Masanori Kondo	Associate Professor of Economics, Division of International Studies, International Christian University, Japan
Nagesh Kumar	Director-General, Research and Information System for Developing Countries (RIS), New Delhi
Mia Mikic	Economic Affairs Officer, Trade Policy Section, Trade and Investment Division, UN-ESCAP, Bangkok

S.K. Mohanty	Fellow, Research and Information System for Developing Countries (RIS), New Delhi
Sanjeeb Pohit	Senior Fellow/Chief Economist, National Council of Applied Economic Research (NCAER), New Delhi
Ramkishen S. Rajan	Associate Professor, School of Public Policy, George Mason University, USA
Rahul Sen	Fellow, Regional Economic Studies (RES), Institute of Southeast Asian Studies (ISEAS), Singapore
Vipul Tuli	Principal, McKinsey & Co., Inc., Gurgaon, India
Soogil Young	President, National Strategy Institute, Seoul, Korea
Li Zhidong	Visiting Researcher, Institute of Energy Economics, Japan (IEEJ), Tokyo

1

Asia's New Regionalism and Global Role: An Editorial Introduction

Asia has emerged as the most dynamic region in the world with the rise of China and India as engines of growth, recovery of Japan from a decade old recession, emergence of Asian middle class as source of final demand, and increasing resilience of Asian countries to external shocks such as oil price rise, etc. Asian countries count among the largest markets in the world for an increasing number of products and services from mobile phones to motor cars to jet planes. This new found dynamism makes regionalism a viable trade and development strategy. Indeed over the past decade Asian countries have integrated themselves increasingly within the region as is evident from the high and growing proportion of intra-regional trade and investments. However, Asia has lagged behind other regions in exploitation of potential of regional trading arrangements (RTAs) that have emerged in different parts of the world following the formation of European Single market in 1992. With more than 350 RTAs or bilateral FTAs at different stages of implementation in the world and around 60 per cent of the global trade being conducted on a preferential and not on MFN basis, any region can ignore formation of its own scheme of regional integration only at its peril. Furthermore, due to lack of an effective broad regional arrangement, not only Asia is not able exploit some fruitful win-win opportunities for expediting its development and address emerging challenges better but is also not able to exercise its due role in global economic governance commensurate with its rapidly growing economic weight.

Having been the faithful adherents of multilateralism till nearly the turn of the millennium, Asian countries have been slow to respond to the global trend of regionalism. Over the past few years, Asian countries have also recognized the potential of regional economic integration and have started taking steps to benefit from it. Besides sub-regional attempts in the framework of ASEAN, SAARC and BIMSTEC groupings, a number of initiatives of broader economic integration are underway to push the agenda of regional economic integration. Besides deepening the sub-regional cooperation between its 10 member states, ASEAN has also served to bring major Asian countries, viz. Japan, China, South Korea and India together as Summit-level dialogue partners who meet annually at the ASEAN Summits. A complex web of free trade arrangements linking all these countries and ASEAN countries is in progress and a virtual Asian or East Asian economic community is emerging out of this. There is need for building on these sub-regional and bilateral attempts a broader regional framework to provide a seamless market facilitating exploitation of their synergies more effectively. Different Asian leaders and statesmen had spoken of the importance of broader regional cooperation in Asia and asserting the Asian identity.

An important initiative in the direction of evolving a broader regional framework is the launch of the East Asian Summit (EAS) in December 2005 in Kuala Lumpur, Malaysia, as an annual forum bringing together ASEAN and all its dialogue partners, viz., Japan, China, India, S. Korea, Australia and New Zealand. The new forum, that is EAS, could be of far reaching consequence for promoting broader regional cooperation in Asia. By giving to the leaders of the largest and most dynamic economies of Asia a much needed annual forum for dialogue, EAS is expected to facilitate the cause of broader regional economic integration in Asia and thereby hastening the process of re-emergence of Asia as the centre of gravity of the world economy. At its second session EAS has already endorsed the launch of a Track-II study on the feasibility of a Comprehensive Economic Partnership Arrangement of East Asia (CEPEA) combining the 16 countries and launch of an Economic Research Institute of ASEAN and East Asia (ERIA).

Against that background, this volume examines the case for broader regionalism in Asia, its potential, challenges, possible approaches and roadmaps. It also examines the potential of regional cooperation in trade and investment, money and finance, and energy security. As these areas have been identified for cooperation in the EAS framework among others, this discussion hopes to provide inputs to the EAS process.

This Volume

The subject matter of the Volume is divided in four parts.

Part I raises issues regarding the emergence of Asia as the most dynamic region of the world and the role that regional economic integration could play in its growth prospects. Specifically in Chapter 2, Young argues that the existing schemes for regional cooperation in Asia such as APEC and the ASEAN-Plus-Three have failed thus far in making a tangible progress toward their stated goals. Asia should seek to provide a new leadership in the management of the global development process. Any cooperative regional scheme should seek to address threats posed by global imbalances, project Asia's development goals and interests, and make a collective effort to improve the management of the global economic system in tune with them. He argues that EAS as a new and more inclusive forum should organize itself to pursue these goals effectively and consistently. The ultimate goal in all these efforts should be to help Asia provide a new leadership role in the management of the global development process.

In Chapter 3, taking a stock of the status of regional economic integration in Asia, Kumar, finds a great interest in Asia for building on growing functional and market driven economic integration as is clear from the emerging web of FTAs linking ASEAN and its Summit-level dialogue partners, namely Japan, China, India, South Korea, Australia and New Zealand. He makes a case for building on these sub-regional and bilateral attempts a broader regional framework to provide a seamless market facilitating exploitation of synergies more effectively. This is demonstrated by findings of studies that have shown that broader regional integration in Asia has the potential of generating billions of dollars of new output and put Asia on a high growth path in a win-win manner. EAS as a Summit level forum bringing together ASEAN and its six dialogue partners is an appropriate forum for building a comprehensive economic partnership covering them. With more than a fifth of global output and trade, half of world's population and more than two thirds of foreign exchange resources, EAS provides basis of a major grouping that could be the third pole of the world economy along with NAFTA and EU. He also proposes that the regional economic integration in EAS be pursued in a manner that balances the objectives of efficiency and equity and become a role model for international economic integration. For putting the process of regional economic integration in Asia on a most optimal track, there is a role for think-tanks of the region which could contribute to it more effectively with the establishment of an Economic Research Institute of ASEAN and East Asia (ERIA).

An effective pursuit of regional economic integration in Asia, argues Teo in Chapter 4, crucially requires building of a growing Asian identity, affinities, and a common "sense of purpose and well-being" for the common people of Asia. He, therefore, makes a case for an Asian institution or a cultural foundation to promote an Asian identity or a feeling of Asianness or 'one Asia' in the region.

Four contributions in Part II discuss the role played by the major actors in the regional context, viz. the ASEAN, Japan, China and India respectively. Kesavapany in Chapter 5 reviews the role and challenges that ASEAN faces in Asian economic integration. ASEAN's experience with building an ASEAN Community will be relevant and useful to the parallel efforts to build the East Asian Community. China and India along with Southeast Asia now constitute the new growth poles of Asia, being one of the fastest growing regions in the world. Although much discussion and brainstorming to clarify ideas and processes will be needed, he finds that East Asian regionalism is here to stay. The EAS process provides for the involvement of the three great Asian powers, China, India and Japan in community building on a win-win basis and not on a zero-sum basis. Much depends on the willingness of ASEAN to be the driver of the process and providing a neutral venue.

As the largest economy in Asia, Kondo in Chapter 6, argues, that Japan can and should play a key role in integrating ASEAN and all its dialogue partners. He finds the complementarities between economies of ASEAN+3 and India and hence the prospects for a mutually beneficial economic partnership. He argues that the ability of Japan to bring together India and East Asian countries in a regional economic integration will also determine its place as a world economic power.

Yao in Chapter 7 discusses the important role that China has to play in the process of regional economic integration. Besides economic gains, he argues that the process of integration may also provide a platform for democratic exchange and peaceful resolution of conflicts between the participating countries for common good. The principles of open and inclusive regionalism and collective leadership of Asian economic cooperation scheme will also help to balance China's dominant role.

Asher and Sen in Chapter 8 find Indian economy to be far more intricately integrated with East Asia than has commonly been perceived. The merchandize trade flows fail to capture the growing interaction between Indian and East Asian economies in knowledge-based and other business services. While India and some of the other Asian countries are competing in some areas, there are also considerable opportunities for cooperation. The dynamics of India's integration with the rest of Asia has been private sector led, with market forces playing a dominant role. East Asia has an important stake in India's successful adjustment to globalization as this would contribute to Asia's stability and prosperity and provide for global risk diversification.

Part III discusses alternative approaches for trade and investment liberalization that are central to any scheme for regional economic integration. Bonapase and Mikic in Chapter 9 begin with surveying the emerging patterns of regionalism in Asia and raise a concern regarding a noodle bowl syndrome emerging in the region from multiple cross-cutting bilateral FTAs/RTAs. With mutually inconsistent provisions, these arrangements are not only fragmenting the region's trade and investment integration process but are also leaving behind the poorer countries that are effectively excluded from this process. They make a strong case for a regional framework for the consolidation of BTAs/RTAs into one region-wide and deeper WTO-consistent trade agreement.

Mohanty and Pohit in Chapter 10 present new results on the welfare gains from different scenarios of broader regional economic integration in Asia computed in the framework of a CGE model. They find that broader regional economic integration in the EAS framework will yield significantly greater welfare gains for the region compared to ASEAN+3 based approaches. They also find that a more comprehensive approach to economic integration covering liberalization of trade in goods, services and investments will be more rewarding than a shallow regionalism covering only trade liberalization. Finally they find that broader regional economic integration in Asia could be a win-win also for the rest of the world rather than a zero sum game.

Two contributions in Part IV address the potential of monetary and financial cooperation in Asia. Rajan in Chapter 11 takes a stock of major initiatives taken in the framework of ASEAN+3 since the 1997 crisis to deepen monetary and financial regionalism, viz. the Chiang Mai Initiative (CMI) and the Asian Bond Fund (ABF) and their limitations. He argues that both of these initiatives, although in right direction, need to be augmented to be effective. Over time consideration should be given to transforming CMI into a regional reserve pooling mechanism with various tiers of liquidity. The focus on upgrading and harmonizing market infrastructures and regulatory frameworks is critical if Asia can hope to successfully promote greater financial and monetary integration as a means of making the region more resilient to local and external shocks. He also emphasizes the importance of deepening India's involvement in the emerging financial and monetary institutional integration in East Asia commensurate with its growing integration in trade and investments. One way of accomplishing that would be by extending the ongoing initiatives to all the EAS countries.

Agarwala and De in Chapter 12 argue that global imbalances pose a serious threat to the world economy and that conventional approaches are quite inadequate to tackle the problem. Demand reduction in the US should be combined with a Keynesian approach focusing on global demand augmentation in addition to demand switching for correcting the global imbalances without a global deflation. They find a high level of latent demand for national and regional investments in Asia which if exploited could make a significant contribution to reducing global imbalances while accelerating GDP growth in the region. Only a fraction of the ongoing surpluses of Asia is needed to finance these investments and such a programme of regional cooperation presents a win-win-win opportunity for Southern Asia, Northern Asia and the rest of the world and the international community (in particular the US, Northern Asia and Southern Asia) should work in a concerted way to promote such cooperation.

Similarly, two contributions in Part V deal with regional cooperation for energy security. Ito et al. in Chapter 13 find strong economic growth in Asia leading to expanding demand for energy and growing dependence of the region on the Middle East for supply of oil. They argue that the energy security is more effectively dealt at a regional level than at individual country level as it enhances their bargaining power. Regional cooperation could also be fruitful for building of a shared reserve for emergencies and effective use of the existing infrastructure to deal with short-term crises such as supply suspensions, promotion of cooperative resource development and procurement inside and outside the region, and conditioning of international oil markets. Asian countries could also cooperate in pursuit of energy diversification and in responding to global environmental problems.

Tuli in Chapter 14 also finds a strong case for regional cooperation in energy in Asia. He makes a case for creating an oil and gas market in the region that will go a long way in addressing the stability concerns of both buyers and sellers. Cooperation for energy security could begin with countries sharing detailed information on demand, supply and inventory positions, to co-investing in building emergency response mechanisms in Asia through strategic reserves, and even making joint investments in oil and gas in the region. An enduring mechanism to improve energy security in the region will be to create a pan-Asian gas grid linking multiple demand and supply sources. Furthermore, for ensuring sustainability Asian countries could pursue longer term multilateral projects to strengthen cooperation, such as joint research on energy technologies relevant to Asia, jointly addressing key environmental priorities like standardizing specifications for gasoline and diesel across Asia, and broader sharing of mutual capabilities. In addition, there could be joint research on technologies for cleaner utilization of Asian coal reserves like underground coal gasification, integrated gasification combined cycle generation and coal liquefaction.

Finally, chapter 15 in Part VI summarizes a few concluding remarks on the issues raised in the volume.

Part I
Asia's New Global Role and Regional Economic Integration

2

Economic Integration and Asia's New Role in the Global Economy

Soogil Young

Introduction

The launch of the East Asia Summit in (EAS) December 2005 in Kuala Lumpur constitutes a very important step in the promotion of Asian economic integration. Against that background it is timely for us to review and evaluate the progress that has been made towards this goal and to derive lessons for the future. This chapter offers a quick assessment of the significance of Asian economic integration as well as of the contributions made by the existing regional schemes such as APEC and the ASEAN Puls Three (APT) to the furthering of this process. On the basis of this assessment, I present my view that the existing schemes should be critically reappraised and reformed in respect of their objectives and strategies, and that Asia should seek to provide a new leadership in the management of the global development process and that those reappraisals and reforms should be guided by this ultimate objective. My belief is that the EAS could and should coordinate those reforms.

Asia's Emergence as an Engine of Growth for the World Economy

One of most striking trends of recent years has been the emergence of Asia as a new, and the most dynamic, engine of growth for the world economy.

According to Martin Wolf, in the early 2000s, Asia accounted for at least 23 per cent of the world output. Given that Asian economies as a whole constitute the fastest growing region in the world, this share will, in all likelihood, continue to grow during the first half of the present century. The key fundamentals of these economies are good and strong and inflation continues to be low. Their external positions are strong, as reflected by their increasing foreign exchange reserves that exceed US$3 trillion and account for more than 70 per cent of global foreign reserves.

Asia's rise has been led by China which has been joined by India, giving rise to the so-called 'Chindia' phenomenon.

Wolf argues that the rise of Asia constitutes the fourth big transformation in relative economic powers since the Industrial Revolution. As it continues, this transformation will also continue to impact the global economic system, not to mention, the regional economic order in Asia, necessitating and forcing adjustments along the way. Therefore, a 'new Asia' is emerging, and it will also lead to a 'new world economy'.

Spread of Asian Dynamism: the Flying-Geese

Asia's rise began with the post-War emergence of the Japanese economy on the global scene. Japan was followed in this emergence by the then so-called Asian newly industrializing economies (NIEs) in East Asia during the 1970s and the 1980s, by the so-called ASEAN-4 countries in the 1980s, in a 'flying geese' pattern. East Asia's flying geese development format was interrupted by China's rapid emergence in the 1990s into a supercharged new NIE.

Given China's strong comparative advantages in labour-intensive manufacturing, as well as the closing-in on Japan by the NIEs in a growing range of technology-intensive industries, region-wide industrial supply chains have been emerging in East Asia. China has been serving as the assembly and fabrication centre in the consequent regional production network, exporting much of the final product to the rest of the world, and especially to the US and Europe. Thus, China has also become a major growth locomotive, pulling other East Asian economies.

The Asian economic dynamism began with Japan and has been spreading to the south and the west. Since the early 1990s, this sphere of has begun to spread further to the south-west, to the newer members of the ASEAN, as well as, and much more significantly, to India. Since 1991, the economic performance of India has been truly remarkable. This is especially so in view of the fact that, in terms of its population and economic size as well as in a number of other aspects, India closely resembles China.

The rise of India has, in large measure, been due to the country's engagement with East Asia. This is shown by the fact that the rise was triggered by the economic reforms which were launched under the country's 'New Economic Policy' that was launched in 1991, which included a 'Look East Policy' (LEP). Since then, East Asia has emerged as India's largest trade partner, ahead of both EU and the US. East Asia is also becoming an increasingly important source of foreign direct investment (FDI) in India. Korean investment in India, for instance, has been increasing very rapidly since the turn of the present decade, making the country the seventh largest source of investment in India.

Regional Dimension of Asian Dynamism: Market-driven Integration

Asian dynamism has been spreading through a market-driven regional integration process. FDI flows into the region, as well as within the region, have been a major contributor to this process. As to the intra-regional flows, investment has been flowing from Japan to the NIEs, and from these economies to Southeast Asia. Since the early 1990s, there has been a considerable redirection of these flows, as well as increase in their levels. As a result, China has emerged as the largest recipient of these flows. FDI into Southeast Asian economies suffered in volume for a while but, more recently, it has begun to increase again. India's share of these flows has also begun to increase.

A major role of FDI flows in Asia has been to integrate the national economies into a region-wide production network and to cause the growth of intra-regional trade in industrial parts and components, as well as inter-industry trade between manufactured goods and natural resources. A market-driven integration process has been at work, giving rise to a vertically-integrated and globally competitive production block in the region. FDI inflows into the region from outside have been reinforcing the intra-regional flows in promoting this market-driven regional integration.

What is important to note is the fact that this process has been taking place without being promoted by regional institutional arrangements. Market forces, that is, those of dynamically changing comparative advantages, as well as the drive for international competitiveness and efficiency, have contributed to this.

The process has been facilitated by two other factors. One is the geographical and cultural proximities shared by the Asian countries, facilitating cooperative business transactions among them. The other has been their adoption of outward-oriented and market- based development strategy. The successful pursuit of this strategy requires the fulfillment of several strategic elements. It is remarkable that the Asian economies have sooner or later all put these elements in place, much through learning from each other's experiences.

The Asian Development Strategy

If we examine the list of secrets to the successful adoption of an outward-oriented market-based development strategy, the importance of the following aspects may be discerned:

- an open and liberal international trade and investment regime;
- willingness to be engaged in such an international system and to face the challenges of international competition;
- high quality of labour and education;
- a market environment which fosters vibrant private entrepreneurship; and
- a government strongly committed to the promotion of high growth based on this strategy.

Of these five factors, I would like to focus on the first two— the importance of an open and liberal international system and the willingness of nations to actively engage in the same. Although there are no institutional arrangements yet to promote regional integration in Asia, two aspects of government policy have contributed to this process. One has been the steady removal of barriers to trade and investment, undertaken unilaterally or under multilateral trade liberalization agreements. The other includes various measures to facilitate international trade and investment. Market-oriented economic reforms constitute most of these measures. These measures have come to include a broad range of financial and corporate reforms as well as the exchange-rate policy reform since the Asian financial crisis in many economies. The subsequent restructuring of these economies has been a major contributor to the latest surge in trade and investment flows in the region.

Need for Institutional Promotion of Regional Economic Integration

It appears, however, that Asian economies have passed the stage when the regional economic integration process may be left to market forces alone. There has been so much discussion on these issues in recent years that it is enough to merely list them:

- The need to counter the discriminatory impact of regionalism elsewhere as well as sub-regionalism within Asia;

- Asian financial crisis has exposed a number of Asia's vulnerabilities to further crisis, calling for collaborative reactions, for example, financial market problems at home, the problem of 'contagion', and the inadequacy of the existing international financial system including that of the IMF as the lender of last resort;
- The need for other Asian countries to cope with the rapid rise of the two new giant economies in the region, that is, China and India; and finally,
- The need to facilitate cooperative resolution of politico-security tensions by promoting cooperation on economic issues.

Existing Schemes for Broader Regional Cooperation and their Limitations

There are basically two schemes in the Asia-Pacific region intended to promote institutional cooperation between governments for the purpose of facilitating economic integration in the region. These are the APEC and the APT.

APEC

The main objective of APEC has been to promote liberalization of trade and investment. The Bogor Goals of achieving free trade by the developed members by 2010 and by others by 2020 dramatize the overriding priority assigned to this objective. Two subsidiary objectives of APEC are to facilitate trade and investment, and to help the developing members build their capacities to facilitate and liberalize trade and investment. While the main APEC process is built around the work of the trade ministers, finance ministers have also been involved in a dialogue on financial and monetary issues facing the APEC region. The thrust of the APEC Finance Ministers' Process may be said to be on facilitation as well as capacity building. What makes APEC potentially powerful is that it provides for the annual meeting of Economic Leaders.

The evaluation of APEC's achievements thus far, however, may be summed up by saying that APEC is in a crisis, and is in search of a new identity. This is not to say that APEC has not played any beneficial role or has been a complete failure, but that APEC has thus far failed in accomplishing its core mission of delivering a free trade and investment environment for its members. Bluntly put, the end result of various attempts ever since the early 1990s seems to be the conclusion that the Bogor Goals are not achievable.

In the meantime, various APEC economies have been proliferating bilateral FTAs with such provisions unique to the individual agreements that a 'Spaghetti

Bowl' of mutually inconsistent FTAs has been emerging in the APEC region. This is quite contrary to the spirit of APEC's 'open regionalism', and causes fragmentation, rather than integration, of trade and investment relations in the region. APEC has also failed in pushing the Doha Development Agenda negotiations forward towards a successful and meaningful conclusion, quite contrary to the spirit of the Bogor Goals. The Doha Round is, in fact, on the verge of a collapse.

The main reason for the failure of APEC in achieving its target has been the lukewarm response of the developed members on the whole towards trade facilitation and capacity-building. The finance ministers, in particular, have never had a serious work programme that would foster cooperation on various problems with the domestic financial systems of the emerging member economies or with the international financial system. More significantly, they have thus far failed to launch or broker any effective action programme towards the resolution of the pressing problem of global financial imbalances, which has been causing a rift across the Pacific between the US on the one hand, and the East Asian economies, and especially, China, on the other.

It is possible that APEC has been pursuing a wrong roadmap. It seems to have wrongly prioritized its goals, with too heavy a focus on the liberalization goal for regional trade to the relative neglect of its other two goals, that is, facilitation and capacity building. In addition, it has taken up an overly ambitious target in pursuing the goal of free trade and investment by 2010/2020 which is made even more difficult by the principle of open regionalism. Many members have been insisting that free trade and investment, if achieved at all, should be extended to non-members as well. These difficulties have been compounded by the absence of an effective compliance mechanism. The spirit of "concerted unilateralism" has been a spectacular failure in this regard.

The second problem with APEC has been that the US has not shown serious interest with APEC-level cooperation. Its attention has been diverted by a number of factors, including Washington's priority interest in the NAFTA and FTAA, and since 9/11, its involvement in the Iraq war.

The Economic Leaders' Meeting is potentially a very powerful instrument of the APEC. However, APEC needs to re-assess and redefine its goals, as well as draw up a new roadmap towards these goals, in order to put this instrument to more meaningful use.

APT

ASEAN Plus Three (APT) has been Asia's only or primary forum for discussion on regional integration, involving important regional countries as China, Japan and Korea. One of the forces which had led to the launching of this process was the Asian financial crisis which reminded the Asian countries of the need for collective self-help with respect to their trade and financial objectives, and more generally, of the unreliability of the international economic system as one in which they can comfortably pursue their development objectives. Another motivation for launching the APT process was to respond to the emergence of the EU, the American pursuit of the NAFTA and FTAA, as well as the disappointing performance of the APEC.

Two specific goals have been guiding the work of the APT. One has been to work towards the creation of an East Asian community, which is anchored to the goal of realizing an East Asian FTA (EAFTA). The other specific goal has been to promote regional financial cooperation in two specific forms: the Chiang-Mai Initiative whose final achievement could be the Asian Monetary Fund, and the Asian Bond Market Initiative geared to the objective of creating an Asian bond market.

The assessment of the APT process thus far may be summed up, much as in the case of APEC, by saying that not much progress has been made towards its two specific goals, and that not much progress is likely in the foreseeable future. The EAFTA does not seem to be taken seriously as a goal by any member. The members are creating more and more bilateral FTAs for themselves individually, and nothing is being done to stop the Spaghetti Bowl effect of the consequently emerging assortment of FTAs in the region. Furthermore, the ASEAN countries are working on their ASEAN Community projects including an ASEAN FTA, and not on the EAFTA.

The Chiang-Mai Initiative process seems to be in a stalemate over the difficulty of agreeing to a surveillance mechanism on macroeconomic, monetary and financial policies of individual governments. The Asian Bond Market Initiative seems to be making steady but painfully slow progress and does not seem capable of yielding an Asian bond market in the foreseeable future. This is because a well-functioning bond market must be underpinned by sound financial systems at home in individual economies and it will be quite some time before such systems emerge in the region. At a more fundamental level, it is doubtful that a regional bond market so created would be able to compete effectively with the very efficient global market.

Two fundamental problems seem to be impeding progress toward these goals in APT. One is that most of the Asian economies have structural and institutional problems at home. It will take time and great effort for them to overcome these weaknesses. However, substantial progress on specific regional initiatives cannot be made unless these weaknesses are effectively addressed first. Another problem with the APT process is that no effective political leadership has emerged thus far to push towards collective goals. Political and security tensions persist between members, and the problem of rivalry between the two largest members has, if anything, been getting worse rather than better. Trust is lacking and without this, the participants will not be able to push the process forward.

Towards a New Role in the Global Economy: Need for a New Approach

It appears from the above review of the existing schemes that they have failed thus far in making any tangible progress towards their stated goals, or addressing the concerns which have motivated the Asian economies to undertake institutional cooperation for regional integration in the first place. The agenda has been partly inadequate, and the roadmap has been inadequate, too. In addition, there has been no mechanism to coordinate these processes—the APEC, APT and ASEAN, in particular. As a consequence, there has been no effective coordination.

My conclusion, therefore, is that the existing schemes to promote regional integration in Asia should undergo a critical re-appraisal as to their goals and processes. This process should start with the correct identification of threats to the current market-driven regional integration in progress in Asia. The most serious threats to the continuation of Asian economic integration are posed by those that threaten the stability of the open and liberal global economic system, viz. proliferation of FTAs with the spaghetti bowl effect, threatened failure of WTO negotiations and continued stalemate over the issue of global payments imbalances. Any cooperative regional scheme should seek to address these threats. The second and third threats identified here would call for collective efforts by Asian countries to improve the management of the global economic system. Accordingly, a priority objective of Asian cooperation should be to project Asia's development goals, interests and due influences in this management.

In addition, Asian economies should seek a region-wide FTA of their own. This, however, should be consistent with the global objectives stated above. This consideration calls for a region-wide FTA which is open to accession by any other member who is willing to participate in the FTA on a reciprocal basis. The spirit here would be that of open regionalism but one subject to the terms of conditional MFN. All existing bilateral FTAs involving

Asian economies should be subjected to the same terms and thus made to converge toward an Asian FTA.

There is another very important threat to the continuation of Asian dynamism. This comes from within each economy: domestic structural imbalances and institutional and human capital weaknesses. There is a need for mutual development cooperation to address these weaknesses.

Finally, I would like argue that the EAS as a new and more inclusive forum should organize itself to pursue these goals effectively and consistently. The ultimate goal in all these efforts should be to help Asia provide a new leadership role in the management of the global development process. Asia should exercise its influence in the global economy that is commensurate with its rapidly growing weight.

3

Relevance of Broader Regional Economic Integration in Asia and a Roadmap

Nagesh Kumar

Introduction

Regional economic integration has been adopted as a strategy for development in different regions of the world over the 1990s, following the formation of a single market by the European Union (EU) and of North American Free Trade Agreement (NAFTA) by the North American countries. With the growing worldwide popularity of regional economic integration, more than half of world trade is now conducted between members of regional trading arrangements (RTAs) (viz., on preferential basis) and not on most favoured nation (MFN) basis. Regional integration has also become an important factor in shaping the global patterns of production and investment.

Having been the faithful adherents of multilateralism till nearly the turn of the millennium, Asian countries have been slow to respond to the global trend of regionalism. However, over the past few years, Asian countries have also recognized the potential of regional economic integration and have started taking steps to benefit from it. Besides sub-regional attempts in the framework of ASEAN, SAARC and BIMSTEC groupings, a number of initiatives of broader economic integration are underway to push the agenda of regional economic integration. Besides deepening the sub-regional cooperation between its 10 member states, ASEAN has also served to bring major Asian countries viz.,

Japan, China, South Korea and India together as Summit-level dialogue partners who meet annually at the ASEAN Summits. A complex web of FTAs' linking all these countries and ASEAN countries is developing and a virtual Asian or East Asian economic community is emerging from this.

An important initiative is the launch of the East Asian Summit (EAS) in December 2005 in Kuala Lumpur, Malaysia, as an annual forum, bringing together ASEAN and all its dialogue partners. The participants at the EAS comprise ASEAN and the four dialogue partners including India and even Australia and New Zealand. In due course, the EAS is likely to launch the process of formation of an East Asian Community (EAC) combining the ASEAN10, Japan, China, India, S. Korea, Australia and New Zealand.

Against this backdrop, and drawing upon the work done as a part of the ongoing research programme, this chapter[1] briefly summarizes the relevance of broader regional economic integration in Asia; it highlights the gains from such integration and outlines an approach for broader or pan-Asian economic integration. In the last section a few concluding remarks are made on the priorities for the agenda of future EAS.

Stimulus for Regional Economic Cooperation in Asia

The successful experience of industrialized countries in Europe and North America with regional economic integration since the mid-1980s has prompted Asian countries to adopt economic integration strategies. The RTAs such as EU and NAFTA pursued a deeper type of integration covering preferential free trading arrangements complemented by strong rules of origin and mobility of capital (and some times even labour) across the region. The level of economic integration was progressively deepened and the coverage of RTAs expanded over time. Thus, EU progressively evolved into an economic union and then a monetary union with a single currency while expanding membership to cover 27 countries. NAFTA is expanding southwards into a Free Trade Area of the Americas (FTAA). As a result, more than 50 per cent of the world trade began to be conducted on preferential rather than on MFN basis. This prompted other regions to form their own RTAs; for example, MERCOSUR and Andean Pact in South America, and COMESA, SADC and SACU in sub-Saharan Africa. Currently some 350 RTAs or bilateral FTAs are at different stages of implementation in the world. Major Asian countries such as Japan, South Korea and India, among others which had remained faithful adherents of multilateralism till the turn of the century also began to rethink the role of regional economic integration in their trade policy. Japan conducted a review of its trade policy towards the end of the 1990s and decided to assign an important role to regionalism. To some extent, the slow progress of the multilateral trade negotiations and its inability to live up to the expectations of Asian countries or to discipline the trend of regionalism has also contributed to the importance attached to regionalism by Asian countries.

A more important stimulus for regionalism seems to have come from the emergence of Asia as the centre of final demand. With the emergence of the large populous economies—China and India—as powerful growth drivers of the world economy and recovery of the second largest economy in the world, viz. Japan from a decade–long recession, Asia is quickly becoming the centre of gravity of the world economy. For many products, from jet planes to motor cars to mobiles, the biggest markets of the world are in Asia. As a result, more than 55 per cent of Asia's trade in now intra-regional thus making regional economic integration an increasingly viable trade strategy. Global investment banks such as Goldman Sachs are projecting China and India to be the two largest economies in the world by 2050.[2]

Further, regional economic integration could also help Asia exploit the profound synergies that have developed between economic structures of the Asian economies. For instance, Japan and South Korea's growing scarcity of labour is complemented by labour abundance in other Southeast and South Asian countries. Similarly, some Asian economies have specialized predominantly in manufacturing and hardware capabilities and others could complement them with their capabilities in software and services. Regional economic integration could help in exploitation of these synergies for mutual benefit. Although regional production networks have begun to be developed across Asia to exploit the synergies between economies through vertical specialization, regional economic integration can help in exploiting the potential of such rationalization or restructuring more completely as well as in expediting their development.

Finally, regional economic integration will assist Asia in the restoration of economic, political and cultural links that had existed for centuries before being disrupted during the colonial period. It has been documented by an RIS study that the Asian region has a distinct Asian identity shaped by history and cultural exchanges over several centuries. There have been vibrant flows of goods and services as well as labour and capital amongst Asian countries, sustained over several centuries. In ancient times, the famed Silk Routes provided the channels for such exchanges. Marco Polo's tales are just one of many such descriptions. During the 19th century, the colonial powers provided the framework for extensive and liberal trade within Asia in goods and services as well as massive movements of labour and capital. Assisted by the rise of Japan, trade was brisk. Even during the first half of the 20th century, the intra-regional trade ratio was over 50 per cent. These trade and investment flows were disrupted by political and military factors during the colonial period and in post-war Asia. Along with trade, there was also a vibrant exchange of ideas. Chinese scholars visited India and visa versa. Ideological influences spread across nations binding, them in ties of religion. Hinduism and with it the art of governance of Chanakya found its way across to much of Indonesia, Malaysia and Thailand. The sweep of Buddhism is well known. Religion has been a strong unifying factor because with religious beliefs, comes a way of life and as religious influence spread so did the cultural ties. Pagan, Borobudur and Angkor Wat are but a small testimony to the vast trading and cultural network that Asia had in ancient times.[3]

Trends in Regional Economic Cooperation in Asia

Asian developing countries had made a number of attempts at regional economic cooperation in the 1970s with the initiative of UN-ESCAP. These include the Bangkok Agreement of 1975 which covered exchange of tariff concessions between five member governments viz., Bangladesh, India, Lao PDR, South Korea and Sri Lanka. In 2000, China also joined the Bangkok Agreement. The Asian Clearing Union with seven members in the region, that is, Bangladesh, India, Iran, Myanmar, Nepal, Pakistan and Sri Lanka, came into being in 1974. It is generally agreed, however, that these early experiences have not been very successful. The reasons for the results not coming up to expectations have been varied. For instance, the Bangkok Agreement has suffered from its limited coverage of membership as well as products covered, preference margins not being deep enough and its scope not extending to non-tariff barriers (NTBs).

Although it was set up in 1967, ASEAN had limited cooperation in economic areas until 1992 when it decided to set up the ASEAN Free Trade Area (AFTA). Similarly, SAARC came into being in 1985, but it adopted a programme of economic cooperation on its agenda only in 1991 with the formation of the Committee on Economic Cooperation (CEC). It has since created a SAARC Preferential Trading Arrangement (SAPTA) in 1995. In 2004, it eventually agreed to create a SAARC Free Trade Agreement (SAFTA) to be implemented over a period of ten years from July 2006. Besides regional economic integration, bilateral free trade agreements between India and Nepal and between India and Sri Lanka have also speeded up economic integration in the South Asian sub-region. Another notable initiative in Asia is BIMSTEC (Bay of Bengal Initiative for Multisectoral Techno-economic Cooperation) involving five South Asian countries, viz. Bangladesh, Bhutan, India, Nepal, and Sri Lanka and two Southeast Asian countries, viz. Myanmar and Thailand. Hence, it is seen as a bridge between South and Southeast Asia. BIMSTEC also adopted a framework agreement for an FTA to be implemented within ten years at its first Summit held in Bangkok in July 2004.

The East Asian Crisis of 1997 highlighted the importance of regional economic cooperation and provided a much needed stimulus for regional economic integration in the region. The ASEAN countries expedited the programme of implementation of AFTA from 2008 to 2002 and moved on to further deepen the economic integration. The crisis also led to the launch of several regional initiatives such as the Chiang-Mai Initiative which involves ASEAN+3 (Japan, China and South Korea) countries. Besides this, the ASEAN's policy of engaging key Asian countries—Japan, China, India and South Korea —as dialogue partners has provided the much needed cohesion in the Asian region, as is clear from the numerous schemes of regional and bilateral free trade arrangements that are at different levels of implementation. China, Japan, India, South Korea (and Australia and New Zealand) are all engaged in negotiations of free trade arrangements with ASEAN. Besides this, the dialogue partners are also evolving FTAs among themselves.

To sum up, therefore, the initiatives towards regional economic integration include the following:

- Sub-regional attempts such as those by ASEAN (and SAARCT and BIMSTEC) to form FTAs and further deepen their economic integration
- FTAs or comprehensive partnership arrangements between ASEAN and its dialogue partners, Japan, China, India and South Korea. ASEAN is also negotiating an FTA with Australia – New Zealand CER (closer economic relations)
- FTAs or comprehensive arrangements between individual ASEAN countries and ASEAN dialogue partners, for example, Japan-Singapore, India-Singapore, India-Thailand, etc.
- FTAs or comprehensive arrangements between the dialogue partners for example, India-Japan, India-South Korea, India-China (under study).

Figure 3.1 shows how a virtual Asian grouping seems to be emerging from this complex web of trading arrangements, with almost every pair of

Figure 3.1: Emerging (East) Asian Community

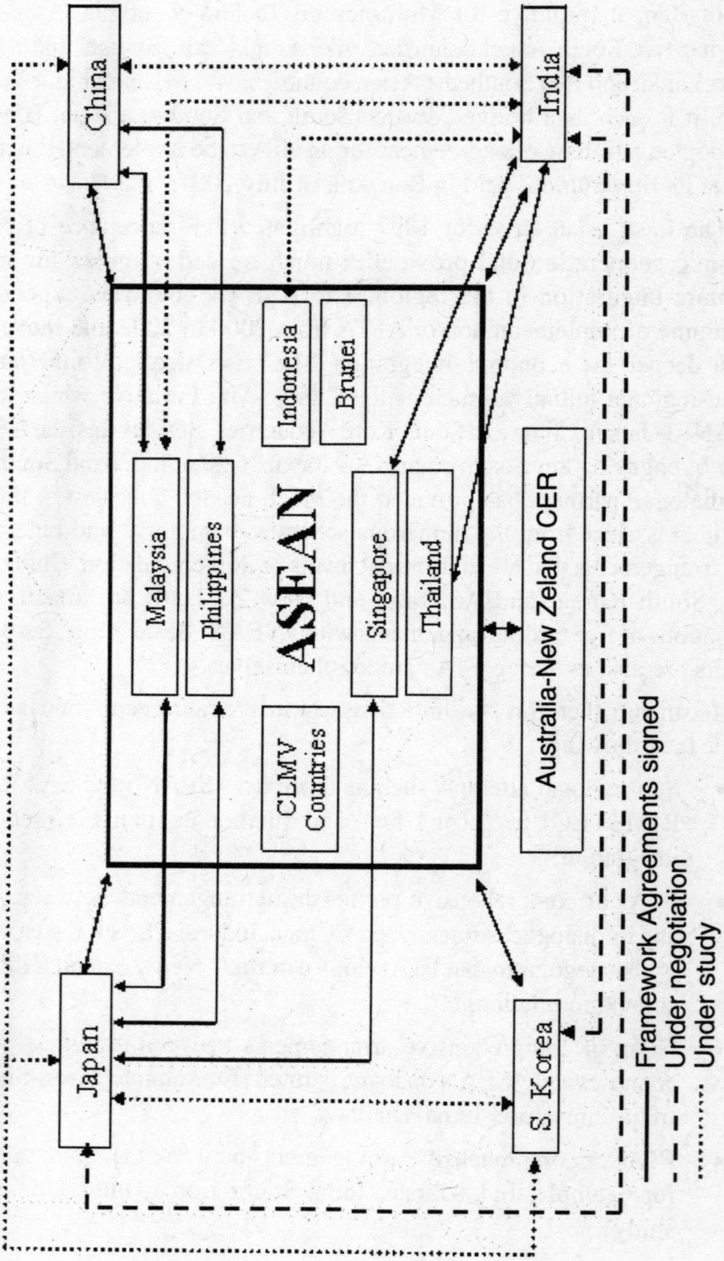

Source: RIS.

countries between ASEAN and its dialogue partners being involved in an FTA or studying one. However, it can be argued that the sub-regional or bilateral attempts at regional cooperation that have been initiated, such as those under the framework of ASEAN and SAARC or the dialogue partners, while desirable are unlikely to exploit the full potential of regional economic integration in Asia and hence are sub-optimal. This is because the extent of complementarities is limited at sub-regional levels because of similar factor endowments and economic structures within a neighbourhood. This is clear from the fact that the trade of ASEAN or SAARC countries with East Asian countries is much larger than their intra-subregional trade. It is for this reason that the success achieved so far from sub-regional or bilateral attempts at cooperation has been meagre. At the broader Asian level, on the other hand, the diversities in the levels of economic development and capabilities are quite wide thus providing for more extensive and mutually beneficial linkages. The diversity in the economic structure provides its own indigenous capacity and markets for dynamic industrial restructuring within the region on the basis of 'flying geese' patterns. Hence, Asia needs an overarching Asia-wide scheme of economic integration to fully exploit the full potential of efficiency-seeking industrial restructuring or to exploit the synergies that exist in the region. Among other factors the twin scourges of regional natural disasters (such as SARS or Tsunami) and terrorism have also promoted East Asian regionalism.[4]

There is now growing recognition in Asia of the importance of regional economic integration for generating growth impulses from within.[5] There have been initiatives for functional regional cooperation, for instance, the launch of the Asian Cooperation Dialogue (ACD) by Thailand in 2002 at Cha-Am. Similarly, China launched the Boao Forum for Asia in 2001 at Boao, in Hainan province of China, as a pan-Asian economic forum. Asian energy ministers met in January and December 2005 in New Delhi to advance cooperation in this area.[6] Some thinking on pooling information technology (IT) capabilities and resources for addressing the common needs of the region is also on, as Asian IT Ministers met in Hyderabad, India in early 2004.[7]

The Prime Minister of India Dr Manmohan Singh has been making a case for an Asian Economic Community combining Japan, ASEAN countries, China, India and South Korea as an 'arc of advantage across which there would be large-scale movement of people, capital, ideas and creativity.... Such a community would release enormous creative energies of our people'.

In that context, the launch of the EAS in December 2005 in Kuala Lumpur bringing together leaders of ASEAN10 and their dialogue partners, viz. Japan, China, South Korea, India, Australia and New Zealand, is an important initiative.

It is, therefore, clear that there is a widespread recognition in Asia of the relevance of broader regional economic integration.

Approaches to Broader Asian Economic Integration

It is clear from the previous section that the ongoing attempts in Asia towards regional cooperation at sub-regional and bilateral levels are unlikely to enable the region to exploit the full potential of regional economic integration. The multiple attempts at sub-regional and bilateral levels that are underway in the region do suggest, however, that there is now growing recognition of the importance of intensive economic integration at the pan-Asian level in the region and of the opportunity cost of not engaging in the same. There is the realization that stimulus for future growth in the region has to increasingly come from within, given the trend of formation of regional trading blocs in rest of the world as also the emergence of Asia as a centre of final demand. Substantial complementarities exist between Asian economies that remain to be exploited for their mutual common benefit. For instance, while the region has economies that are surplus in capital resources, there are also economies which have inadequate domestic savings for rapid development. The region is similarly characterized by complementarities in the demand and supply of other resources such as technology and skilled manpower. Regional cooperation by generating intra-regional demand could supplement the external demand and reduce the vulnerability of the region due to over- dependence on outside regions. Regional cooperation could also help in exploiting the existing capacities in the region fully. The lost output because of underutilization of capacity in the Japanese and Korean construction and engineering industries could be of the order of 10-15 per cent of the GDP of the region or about a trillion dollars a year.[8] A more intensive cooperation for matching the underutilized capacity in some countries of the region with un-met demand in others could go a long way in putting the region on a high growth trajectory and help Asia to re-emerge as a centre of gravity in the world economy that it was until 1800.[9]

The Asian region combines some of the fastest growing economies in the world. Together they make up a huge market that is growing faster than any other region in the world and could form a vibrant regional grouping that would be roughly of the size of the EU in terms of GDP, have larger magnitude of trade than NAFTA and greater international reserves than those of EU and NAFTA put together. The formation of a broader Asian grouping will also help the region to play a more effective role in shaping the emerging world trading and financial system so that it is more responsive to its needs. The broader regional grouping will also formalize a high level of functional integration that has taken place in Asia, especially between ASEAN and its dialogue partners.

An Approach to Integration

The approach towards the process of broader regional economic integration has to take into consideration the process of cohesion in Asia brought about by ASEAN. As argued earlier, ASEAN has helped to bring together four major economies of Asia as its annual Summit-level dialogues partners, that is, Japan, China, South Korea and India. These countries meet annually at the ASEAN+1 Summits and also at ASEAN+3 (Japan, China and Korea) Summit. It has been observed that ASEAN+1 approaches have become more attractive compared to ASEAN+3 as is clear from the FTAs being evolved by China, Japan, India and Korea with ASEAN [10]. FTAs between Japan, Korea and China and those between India-China, India-Korea and India-Japan are being negotiated or studied. In other words, ASEAN and the four dialogue partners, Japan, Asean, China, India and Korea (JACIK), are all engaged in evolving FTAs between their different pairs, as shown in Figure 3.1. Through this complex web of FTAs a virtual JACIK or an East Asian FTA is emerging. In case the AFTA-CER FTA (Australia-New Zealand) is included, then JACIK-AN countries are all part of a complex web of interlinking FTAs. However, these bilateral or sub-regional FTAs do not allow full exploitation of the potential of regional economic integration due to substantial complementarities in factor endowments and levels of development. Hence, a vision for Asian economic integration is to begin by coalescing these multiple FTAs between JACIK (or JACIK-AN) countries into an overarching East Asian RTA.[11] A broader overarching framework alone will allow optimal utilization of Asia's resources and synergies for their mutual common benefit. As one observer has pointed out, without some form of overall regional framework within which to work, capital, human and natural resources may all be deployed at less than their optimal value.[12]

The East Asian RTA combining JACIK economies could become the core of an EAC which could be expanded later to include other Asian countries into an Asian Economic Community. This approach is supported by a number of Asian leaders including former Singapore Prime Minister Lee and the Indian Prime Minister.[13] President Arroyo of the Philippines has observed that 'the emerging ASEAN+3+India … will be a formidable regional grouping that can negotiate then with the European Union, the Americas, Africa and such regional groupings'.[14]

Combining fourteen of the largest and fastest growing economies of Asia with vast complementarities, East Asian or JACIK trade bloc is a potential third pole of the world economy. For instance, it combines a population of 3 billion or a half of the world population (see Table 3.1). In terms of purchasing power parity, the JACIK grouping will have a gross national income of US$16 trillion, much larger than either NAFTA or EU. JACIK's exports will add up to US$1.66 trillion compared to US$1.48 trillion of NAFTA. The combined official reserves of the JACIK economies at US$1.6 trillion in 2003 are much larger than those of the US and the EU put together. In fact, the latest estimates suggest that foreign exchange holdings of JACIK countries are nearly US$3 trillion. Therefore, the region would have a sufficiently large market as well as financial resources to support and sustain expedited development of the region's economies.

As the East Asia Summit brings together all the JACIK countries and CER countries (Australia and New Zealand), a beginning of the broader regional integration can be made in the EAS forum. The Japanese Minister of Economy, Trade and Industry (METI), at the Economic Ministers Meeting of the EAS countries held in August 2006, proposed initiating a study on a Comprehensive Economic Partnership in East Asia (CEPEA) covering the EAS countries and a research institute to provide intellectual inputs to assist economic integration, viz. Economic Research Institute for ASEAN and East Asia (ERIA).[15] The Second EAS held in Cebu on 15 January 2007 has endorsed the preparation of the track-II feasibility study of a CEPEA involving the 16 EAS participating countries and setting up of ERIA.

Table 3.1: Proposed East Asian or JACIK Community in relation to European Union and NAFTA in 2004

(billion US$)

Parameter	EU	NAFTA	JACIK (14)	EAS Members (16) (JACIK-AN)
Gross National Income, PPP (in Purchasing power parity)	10137	12847	16058	16716
% of World total	20.14	25.53	31.91	33.22
GDP	10505	12431	7262	8198
% of World total	29.37	34.76	21.24	22.92
Exports (2002)	3523	1486	1657	1757
% of World total	46.50	19.62	21.88	23.20
International Reserves	285	170	1657	1757
Population (millions)	381	425	3065	3089
% of World total	6.12	6.83	49.27	49.65

Source: RIS based on World Bank, *World Development Indicators 2005,* CD-ROM; IMF, *International Financial Statistics 2004.*

Gains from JACIK or EAS Economic Integration

The studies conducted by RIS have found considerable evidence of complementarities between the production and trade structures of the JACIK countries.[16] Formation of an RTA may help in exploitation of these complementarities for mutual advantage. Furthermore, trade policy liberalization needs to be accompanied by additional measures such as freer capital mobility, harmonization of customs procedures and product standards and mechanisms to ensure an equitable distribution of gains. RIS studies conducted in computable general equilibrium (CGE) model framework have shown that a trade liberalization in the framework of an RTA in JACIK could produce efficiency gains worth US$147 billion (see Table 3.2). However, when an RTA is combined with investment liberalization and mobility of skilled manpower, the gains from integration add up to US$210 billion—representing more than 3 per cent of the combined GDP of JACIK economies. What is

Table 3.2: Welfare Gains from Economic Integration in East Asia or (JACIK)

	Estimated welfare gains in US$ million		
	Scenario I (Trade liberalization)	Scenario II (Trade and Investment liberalization)	Scenario III (Trade, Investment and mobility of skilled workers)
Japan	107626	111807	150695
Korea	13043	13317	14076
China-HK	6327	7100	16328
ASEAN (5)	13451	13553	19405
India	6971	7379	9937
JACIK	147418	153156	210441
Rest of the world	-27293	-45306	109916
World	120125	107849	320357

Source: RIS Simulations. See Mohanty et al (2004) for details.

more, all the JACIK countries benefit from integration. Interestingly, the welfare of the rest of the world also improves by US$109 billion in the Scenario III, suggesting that Asian economic integration will be Pareto optimal. Further, the creation of regional institutional infrastructure to mobilize even a moderate proportion of the region's considerable reserves of about US$3 trillion for investment in the creation of regional public goods such as transport infrastructure, gas and oil pipelines, satellites and broadband cables has the potential to generate additional output and welfare effects that could add up hundreds of billions of dollars (in view of substantial underutilized capacity in Japan, Korea and other Asian countries in engineering and construction industry).

The above findings have been corroborated by a recent study conducted by the Asian Development Bank (ADB).[17] Using GTAP 6 database with a version of World Bank's Linkage model, the ADB team generated projections of income and trade for 2025 with different scenarios to examine the relative relevance of regional integration vis-à-vis global trade liberalization. The findings suggest that 'regional trade and integration offer Asia great potential for rapid and sustained growth'. The ADB study finds that much of Asia's benefits from global trade liberalization can be realized by regional initiative alone. Significantly, it finds that the combined gains from removing tariff and structural barriers to Asian trade far outweigh those of global tariff abolition. Hence, regionalism should be very high priority for Asia. The study also finds that regional integration can promote Asian economic convergence, raising average growth rates and benefiting poorer countries. In particular, greater regional integration will propagate commercial linkages and transfer the stimulus of Asia's rapid growth economies, particularly China and India, to their neighbours. Asian economic integration increases trade and incomes for the rest of the world. Thus, it could be a win–win or the 'arc of advantage' for the region and the world!

EAS vis-à-vis ASEAN+3 based East Asian Economic Integration

There is some debate on whether ASEAN+3 (APT) is a better forum for evolving a broader scheme of economic integration in Asia than EAS. However, the research has shown that EAS has greater potential to generate welfare gains for all the partners than ASEAN+3. The CGE simulations conducted to examine the potential gains from Asian economic integration reported earlier were repeated for ASEAN+3. The simulation results as summarized in Table 3.3 clearly bring out the fact that welfare gains for each participant in EAS or JACIK are much higher than those in an APT framework. Significantly, welfare gains in JACIK or EAS framework are higher by US$48 billion compared to APT. The explanation for considerable difference in welfare gains between EAS and APT based approaches is possibly the increased diversity due to inclusion of additional countries such as India with complementary strengths. India's software and services dominated economy complements well with the hardware and manufacturing driven economies of other East

Asian countries. Obviously India's inclusion is welfare enhancing for all the partners and creates a win–win situation for Asia.[18]

Table 3.3: Relative Welfare Gains from Economic Integration in JACIK and ASEAN+3

	Estimated welfare gains in US$ million (Scenario III)		Gain from India's inclusion
	JACIK	Asean+3	
Japan	150695	124065	26630
Korea	14076	11683	2392
China-HK	16328	10810	5517
ASEAN (5)	19405	14585	4821
India	9937	972	8965
Asia	210441	162115	48326

Source: RIS simulations

Figure 3.2: Comparative Welfare Gains from JACIK and ASEAN+3 Approaches

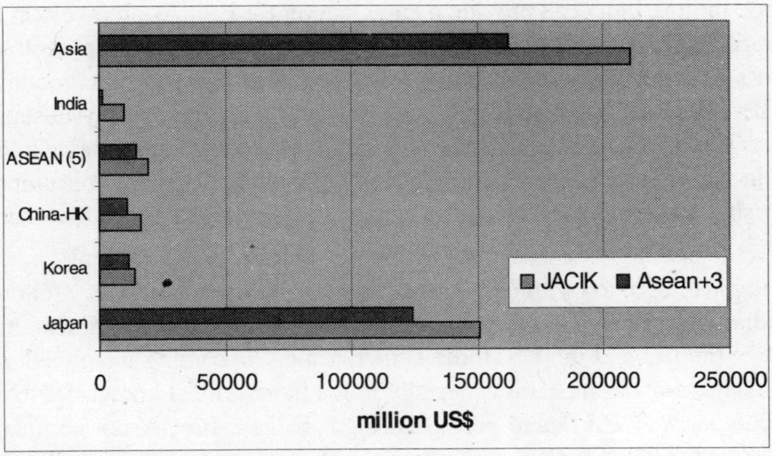

Source: RIS simulations.

Furthermore, EAS will be able to benefit from the dynamism and other strengths of India, Australia and New Zealand for mutual benefit. India with a US$1000 billion economy growing at 9 per cent per annum and a 300 million strong middle class is emerging as the second largest economy in the world.[19] With foreign exchange reserves of over US$230 billion, one of the best performing stock market in Asia,[20] low rates of inflation, market-determined exchange rates, abundant human capital and entrepreneurial resources, rapidly growing industry and services and a prudently managed financial system,[21] India is attracting attention for its strong macro-fundamentals. India has recently been ranked among the top two investment destinations in the world by AT Kearney in terms of FDI Confidence Index recently.[22] India is seen as having the potential to show the 'fastest growth over the next 30 and 50 years'.[23] Another study by IMF finds India poised to sustain about 7 per cent growth rates for over the next 30-40 years with very few downside risks.[24] According to IMF, India is contributing nearly 10 per cent of the global growth and 20 per cent of Asian growth.[25] With the growing economic integration of the Indian economy, this growth is spilling over to the other economies as well. With two major dynamos viz. China and India propelling regional growth, the Asian dream will be realized faster.[26] With booming demand for infrastructure investments that are projected to be over US$500 billion, India can provide a huge market for East Asian investors and underutilized construction and engineering capacities. It can help neutralize any loss of demand in Asia resulting from the US trying to curb its mounting trade deficit. Malaysian companies, among others, have already won substantial projects in roads construction in open competitive bidding. The booming middle class in the country is increasingly becoming a source of final consumption with rising income levels. India, for instance, has emerged as a major market for high spending tourists for a number of countries in East Asia.

Rapid integration with East Asia as a part of the Look East Policy followed by India since 1991 has made the region the largest trade partner of India ahead of the EU and the US. India is increasingly becoming integrated with East Asian production chains especially in the more critical knowledge-based segments such as R&D and product design. Indeed, East Asian companies have begun to exploit India's strengths in R&D, software and design by locating their global R&D centres in India. For instance, Samsung's R&D Centre in India, recently announced the successful development of a hybrid mobile phone that works across GSM and CDMA environments. China's Huawei Technologies, like many others, employs hundreds of engineers involved in chip design or embedded software development in Bangalore. Hyundai uses its Indian operations as a sourcing base for compact cars. Toyota is sourcing gear boxes from its Indian plant for Southeast Asian markets. Furthermore, these production networks not only include those belonging to Japanese or Korean companies but also those being developed by Indian enterprises. For instance, Daewoo Trucks has become linked with the production chain of Tata Motors with its acquisition by the latter. Several Indian companies have also begun to take advantage of cheaper manufacturing costs for hardware in China and other East Asian countries by rationalizing their production. This trend is likely to be more firmly entrenched as the emerging free trade arrangements between India and East Asian countries come into effect. India is already evolving an FTA with ASEAN (besides individual countries such as Singapore and Thailand), South Korea and Japan, is studying FTA with China and is hence very much a part of the growing web of FTAs linking the East Asian countries. There are also complementarities in the demographic trends of East Asia and India. Just as East Asia is about to enter a phase of demographic burden, implying lower share of working age population, and higher median age of workers, India is entering a demographic gift phase, with higher share of working age population. Through IT, an India integrated into Asia could help address East Asia's demographic challenges.[27] With its excellent trading and transport links and emerging preferential trading arrangements with South Asian countries, GCC and other West Asian countries, India could act as a bridge for East Asia with markets in South, West and Central Asian countries. Finally, it can be argued that an EAS based grouping will be more balanced than an APT based grouping.

The growing economic integration of East Asia and India and its potential is catching people's imagination. A survey conducted by the World Economic Forum and Taylor Nelson Sofres at the World Economic Forum's New Asian Leaders (NALs) Retreat held in Seoul in June 2003, covering all participants and invitees and other Asia-based Global Leaders for Tomorrow revealed that over 37 per cent of New Asian Leaders view an extended Asia—Asean+4, including China, Japan, India and Korea—as the most desirable model of economic integration, with only 26.8 per cent preferring Asean+3.[28] Former Singapore Prime Minister and Minister Mentor Lee Kuan Yew has argued that 'India should join in, as there is nothing to be lost. It will expand the market, force more specialization, division of labour, and India has some thing to contribute in economic, political, diplomatic as well as the security field. So I believe it is to the advantage of the ASEAN countries that any such East Asian Community should include India'.

Priority Areas of Cooperation in EAS Framework

The above discussion has shown that the EAS RTA or CEPEA would be highly welfare enhancing for not only the participating countries but also for the rest of the world. There are a number of other areas of fruitful cooperation such as monetary and financial cooperation and cooperation for energy security, science and technology, among others. Some of the areas identified for cooperation within the EAS framework are as follows.

EAS RTA or a Comprehensive Economic Partnership of East Asia

EAS at its second session agreed to launch a track-II feasibility study on comprehensive economic partnership of East Asia covering all EAS countries. The EAS comprehensive economic cooperation arrangement could target to liberalize regional trade and investment regimes in a phased manner by 2020 with provisions for safeguards for sensitive products, special and differential treatment for countries at different levels of development and dispute resolution. Agricultural trade liberalization should be attempted on a separate track from that of industrial goods to allow supremacy to considerations of food security and livelihood issues. Care must be taken in designing the programmes of regional economic integration in such a manner that they keep equity, employment generation and necessary social transformation and social safety nets for the vulnerable sections of the society at their heart and represent regionalism with an 'Asian Face'. By balancing the interests of efficiency and equity, the Asian arrangement could well emerge as a role model for trade liberalization in multilateral as well as regional contexts for the whole world.[29]

Monetary and Financial Cooperation in Asia

Combined foreign exchange reserves of JACIK countries now add up to nearly US$3 trillion and comprise the bulk of such reserves in the world. It has been argued that because of a lack of a regional framework for their deployment in Asia, these funds have been invested in low yielding US treasury bonds and are able to contribute to the Asian development more meaningfully. This is matched by a substantial deficit for investments in Asia with infrastructure development needs of underdeveloped parts of Asia running into trillions of dollars. India alone has a requirement of US$500 billion for infrastructure development over the next five years.

The objective of the financial cooperation in Asia should be to leverage the combined strength of foreign exchange reserves of EAS countries for their mutual benefit. There is a growing consensus that Asia needs a regional institution for mobilizing its foreign exchange resources for its own development, for achieving stability of real effective exchange rates and also for an orderly response to external shocks. Even conservative commentators such as Martin Wolf now acknowledge the importance of Asia for having its own regional monetary and financial institutions.[30] Studies have shown that there is growing macroeconomic interdependence between Japan, Korea and ASEAN. Such interdependence is likely to include China and India, and Australia and New Zealand with ongoing reforms, liberalization and market opening.[31]

A number of important initiatives have been taken in the area of monetary and financial cooperation in Asia over the past decade including the Chiang-Mai Initiative and the development of Asian Bond Funds. However, these initiatives need to be deepened, scaled up and broadened to cover all the EAS member countries to become more effective.

Asia also needs a unit of account to facilitate its growing intra-regional trade which has approached nearly 55 per cent of Asia's trade. East Asia has also emerged as India's largest trading partner ahead of North America and the EU. One area of cooperation is the creation of a regional unit of account, viz. Asian Currency Unit (ACU) that could bring about a relative stability of intra-regional exchange rates. In due course, the ACU could begin to emerge as a parallel currency.

In view of the sizeable resources of Asia and massive needs for bridging the demand-supply gaps in infrastructure financing in Asian countries, we believe that a more ambitious attempt needs to be made towards regional financial cooperation. There is a need for a regional monetary and financial institution to foster cooperation in Asia in these spheres. In a similar vein, Datuk Seri Abdullah Ahmad Badawi, Prime Minister of Malaysia has suggested that Asian countries could use 'a fraction' of their massive foreign exchange reserves as capital for a fund, which would invest in basic economic infrastructure including super highways and super railways linking and binding the East Asian community. Asia has the resources to set up an institution with a large capital base which would enable it to undertake funding of infrastructure development, offer balance of payments support to member countries and create an ACU as a unit of account to begin with for facilitating the growing intra-regional trade and to emerge as a parallel currency in due course. Even a small fraction of the foreign exchange reserves of EAS countries invested in such an institution could create an institution with a massive capital base. Besides providing a mechanism for exchange rate stability, and facilitating trade transactions within the region, the Asian monetary and financial architecture would also provide a channel for funding development of regional public goods and other huge infrastructure development projects without putting pressure on the government budgets in the member countries.[32] The borrowers could be regional companies (such as Channel Tunnel Company for the UK and France) jointly owned by governments and private sector in the region. Similarly, there is also substantial potential for bond market development in Asia and some steps have already been taken in this regard.[33] This will help in creating demand for the underutilized construction capacity in parts of Asia (as observed earlier). Among other possibilities for monetary and financial cooperation in Asia are the development of an Asian Bond Market for which a couple of initiatives have been taken, or the setting up of an Asian Investment Bank to facilitate infrastructure financing and cooperation between the national exim banks of the region.[34]

The EAS held at Cebu in January 2007 identified finance as one of the areas of cooperation and has sought proposals from officials for consideration at the third Summit in Singapore.

Cooperation for Energy Security

Major countries of Asia namely Japan, China, India and South Korea among others are highly dependent upon oil and gas imports and could benefit from mutual cooperation in the area. The regional cooperation in the area of energy could cover, for instance: ensuring security and sustainability of energy supply, overseeing efficient utilization of natural energy resource in the region, managing energy demand in a rational manner, with due consideration of the environment, establishing policy framework and implementation modalities for setting up of energy networks in the region such as region-wide oil or gas grids and coordinating, managing and monitoring the implementation of such a network. One of the target areas of Asian energy cooperation could be to build an Asian Strategic Petroleum Reserve (SPR) and to create an Asian Emergency Response System. An Asian SPR would be like a global energy security insurance policy. The Asian SPR would be a safeguard against OPEC's ability to raise oil prices and would prevent any market failure, by enabling governments to provide supply liquidity in an emergency situation. Asian countries have some ongoing cooperation in the area as joint exploration or oil equity sharing by Japanese, Korean, Chinese and Indian oil companies in exploration projects in third countries within the region such as in Myanmar and Vietnam and outside the region as in Sudan. Japan, Korea, China and India have begun to coordinate their positions in their negotiations with OPEC with respect to the Asian premium that is being charged by the Middle East countries on their supplies to Asian countries.[35] The cooperation could also extend to cover the joint patrolling of the sea-lanes through which the bulk of the oil and gas supplies for the region pass through, for example, Malacca Straits, to prevent piracy. Finally, JACIK countries could contemplate building an Asian gas/oil pipeline connecting them. Asian energy ministers met in January 2005 in New Delhi to advance cooperation in this area.[36] There is a need to create an Asian Energy Dialogue combining the Asian energy enterprises and other stakeholders to take the initiative of energy cooperation on a continuous basis. The Cebu Summit of EAS has identified energy security as an important areas of its work and issued a Cebu Declaration on Asian Energy Security.

Cooperation in Core Technologies for Addressing the Digital Divide and Nutritional and Health-related Issues

The Asian region's substantial capacities in hardware and software areas could be pooled together to address the digital divide to empower poor to benefit from the fruits of new technologies. This would require joint development of cheaper hardware and development of software in local languages and graphic interfaces, and would call for the pooling of complementary strengths of East Asia and India in hardware and software, respectively. Similarly, cooperation in biotechnology could focus on nutritional and health needs of the poor in Asia. Appropriate regional institutional mechanisms need to be created to facilitate a pooling of resources and capabilities from different member countries for these tasks. Some thinking on pooling resources for addressing the common needs of the region is already on (as Asian IT Ministers met in Hyderabad, India in early 2004).[37]

Global Governance, Peace and Security

Regional economic integration is also likely to strengthen Asia's role in global economic governance. Although Asian countries hold two- thirds of the world's foreign exchange reserves, the decision-making powers in the Brettonwoods institutions, for instance, are dominated by the western countries. By forming credible schemes of regional economic integration, Asia will be able to seek its due place in global economic governance and contribute to building a more democratic and multipolar world economy. Asian economic integration by increasing the interdependence of countries in the region, will ensure peace and stability. That is why Prime Minister Dr Manmohan Singh has argued that the Asian economic community would constitute an 'arc of advantage and prosperity and stability and closer economic integration' and would release enormous creative energies of its people.

Concluding Remarks

Developments of the past few years have led to an Asian resurgence with the emergence of China and India as engines of growth, recovery of Japan from a decade-old recession, rise of the Asian middle class as a source of final demand, and increasing resilience of Asian countries to external shocks such as oil price rise etc. Over the past decade Asian countries have also integrated themselves within the region as is evident from a high and growing proportion of intra-regional trade and investments. Besides the growing economic interdependence, Asian countries also face shared vulnerabilities to external shocks and natural disasters such as Tsunami.

To sum up the above discussion, it is clear that there is great interest in Asia to build on growing, functional and market-driven economic integration, and the emerging web of FTAs linking ASEAN and its Summit-level dialogue partners namely Japan, China, India and South Korea and possibly Australia and New Zealand.

ASEAN has played an important role in evolving a framework for broader cooperation by bringing together major Asian countries like Japan, China, India and South Korea as dialogue partners. These dialogue partners are all working on ASEAN+1 FTAs. China, Japan, Korea and India are also studying bilateral FTAs between themselves. Through the emerging web of FTAs a virtual Asian economic community is evolving. There is a need to build on these sub-regional and bilateral attempts for a broader regional framework to provide a seamless market that would facilitate exploitation of synergies more effectively. Studies have shown that broader regional integration in Asia has the potential of generating billions of dollars of new output and putting Asia on a high growth path. Further, it has been shown that Asian economic integration will benefit the rest of the world as it implies trade creation rather than trade diversion. Hence, it is a case of win-win for Asia as well as for the world economy. Regional economic integration is also likely to bring about convergence in the levels of development and hence could be an important instrument in region's fight against poverty.

Different Asian leaders and statesmen have spoken of the importance of broader regional cooperation in Asia asserting the Asian identity. However, Asia lacked a forum for dialogue for such cooperation. The launch of the EAS in Kuala Lumpur on 14 December 2005 attended by the leaders of ASEAN10, Japan, China, South Korea, India, Australia and New Zealand provide a forum for such a dialogue to the region. The second session of EAS held in Cebu in January 2007 agreed to launch a feasibility study of a comprehensive economic partnership covering all EAS countries. EAS members together account for more than a fifth of global output and trade, half of the world's population and more than two- thirds of foreign exchange resources. The EAS provides the basis of a major grouping that could be the third pole of the world economy after NAFTA and EU. By providing a seamless market to the EAS (or Asian) businesses and industry such an arrangement will help in efficiency-seeking restructuring of Asian industry and could emerge as an engine of growth. Such a comprehensive partnership, once evolved and consolidated, could be subsequently expanded to include other Asian countries to create a truly Asian Economic Community which could be an 'arc of advantage, peace and shared prosperity' in the words of the Indian Prime Minister, Dr. Manmohan Singh.

It has also been shown that EAS-based integration has considerably higher potential for welfare improvement than ASEAN+3 integration besides being a more inclusive and balanced framework. It would also enable the grouping to benefit from the dynamism and complementary resources and capabilities of economies such as India and Australia. In particular, with a US$1000 billion economy growing at 9 per cent per annum., a sizeable large middle class and strong macro-fundamentals, India will be able to contribute meaningfully to the East Asian integration in a mutually beneficial manner.

The other adjuncts of the EAS comprehensive economic cooperation arrangement could include an Asian monetary and financial architecture of EAS countries for facilitating intra-regional trade and exchange rate stability within the region by pooling reserves, creation of an ACU as a unit of account, setting up of an Asian investment bank, and also an Asian Energy Forum to pursue regional cooperation for energy security.

To support these initiatives Asia needs think-tanks to brainstorm on the policy challenges for regional economic integration and provide a roadmap for the official processes. In that direction, the Japanese proposal for an Economic Research Institute of ASEAN and East Asia (ERIA) has been endorsed by the EAS at its Cebu Summit. ERIA is expected to foster analytical capability building in the EAS region through cooperation with national think-tanks in these countries. It could also coordinate different networks of think-tanks such as the New Asia Forum coordinated by RIS and NEAT (Network of East Asian Think-tanks), among others, to assist the policy process in a more effective manner. Finally, EAS could take initiatives for greater people-to-people exchanges, cultural interactions and educational and media exchanges to allow an Asian identity or 'Asianness' or 'One Asia' to take hold.[38]

Endnotes

[1] This chapter has evolved over time with valuable feedback received at different conferences and seminars in New Delhi (March 2003), Beijing (April 2003), Tokyo (July 2003), Singapore (February 2004), Manila (July 2004), Tokyo (November 2004), Washington, DC (June 2005), Kuala Lumpur (July 2005), Taiyuan, China (September 2005), Goa, India (October 2005), New Delhi (November 2005), Singapore (November 2006), Beijing (January 2007), among other places.

[2] See Wilson and Purushothaman (2003).

[3] See Shankar (2004) for more details.

[4] See Teo (2005).

[5] See the writings of Yamazawa (1998, 2001a, b), Alatas (2001), Shinawatra (2001), among others, for arguments for closer economic cooperation in Asia.

[6] India hosted a Meeting of Asian Energy Ministers in New Delhi in early 2005 to discuss issues of mutual concern. See *New Asia Monitor,* January 2005 for details.

[7] See *New Asia Monitor*, March 2004 for details.

[8] See Agarwala (2002) for more details.

[9] See Madison (2000); also see RIS (2004).

[10] See Bonapace and Mia Mikie, this volume.

[11] Experts who have favoured such an approach include Wei (2004), Yao this volume and Bonapace this volume.

[12] Rowley (2004).

[13] See for instance, the address of Singapore's Mentor Minister, Mr Lee Kuan Yew at the Foreign Correspondents Association of Singapore reported in *The Straits Times*, 22 December 2004. Prime Minister Dr Manmohan Singh has envisioned an Asian Economic Community evolved using a building bloc approach to begin with Japan, ASEAN, China, India and Korea at the Laos Summit in November 2004.

[14] See speech delivered at the ASEAN Business Summit, Vientiane, Laos, 28 November 2004.

[15] See Kitamura (2006) for more details.

[16] See Sinha-Roy et al. (2004)

[17] Brooks, Ronald-Holst and Zhai, (2005). See also Mohanty and Pohit, in this volume for more uptodate estimates.

[18] See Mohanty and Pohit, in this volume, for a more update analysis of the two approaches finding EAS based integration to be considerably more productive than APT.

[19] See Wilson and Purushothaman, op.cit.

[20] India's capital markets are highly developed with world-class electronic settlement system and rapidly improving corporate governance systems. Over 6000 companies are listed on India's stock exchanges next only to NYSE. India topped the MSCI index for Asian countries in terms of stock market returns for September-December 2004 period as reported in *Financial Express*, 17 December 2004.

[21] Ratio of non-performing assets to GDP is just 3 per cent compared to China's 41 per cent, Japan's 11 per cent and Thailand's 9 per cent.

[22] http://www.atkearney.com/shared_res/pdf/FDICIOct_2004_S.pdf

[23] See Wilson and Purushothaman.

[24] An IMF Working Paper (04/118) projects India's growth rate to 2025 at 7% 'with more upside potential than downside risks'.

[25] see 'Is India becoming an Engine for Global Growth?' in IMF (2005) *World Economic Outlook*, September 2005: 36-7.

[26] Kesavapany (2005) has used the metaphor of dynamo: 'one can ask why we should deny ourselves the benefits to be derived from one of the two major dynamos propelling regional growth'.

[27] See Asher and Sen (2005).

[28] *Source:* The World Economic Forum, Press Release, 18 June, 2003.

[29] See RIS (2006).

[30] See Wolf (2004), among many others.

[31] See Kawai (2004); also see Saksena (2003).

[32] See Agarwala (2004).

[33] See presentation by Ambassador M. Xuto at the High-level Conference on Asian Economic Integration organized by RIS in Tokyo, 18-19 November 2004.

[34] See Rajan (2006), this volume.

[35] See Ito et al. (2005) for more details.

[36] See endnote 6.

[37] See *New Asia Monitor*, March 2004 for details.

[38] For more detailed analysis, see Teo this volume.

References

ADB (2005) *Asian Economic Cooperation and Integration: Progress, Prospects and Challenges,* Manila: Asian Development Bank.

Asher, Mukul and Sadhna Srivastava (2004) 'India and the Asian Economic Community', in Nagesh Kumar (ed). *Towards an Asian Economic Community: Vision of a New Asia,* New Delhi and Singapore: RIS and ISEAS: 91-108.

Asher, Mukul and Rahul Sen (2005) 'India's Integration with East Asia: Win-win for Asia', RIS Discussion Paper #93, available at *www.ris.org.in*

Agarwala, Ramgopal (2004) Reserve Bank of Asia: An Institutional Framework for Regional and Monetary Cooperation in Asia, in Nagesh Kumar ed. *Towards an Asian Economic Community: Vision of a New Asia,* New Delhi and Singapore: RIS and ISEAS: 177-203.

__________, (2002) Towards and Asian Economic Community: Monetary and Financial Cooperation, RIS Discussion Paper #33, New Delhi, available at *www.ris.org.in*

Alatas, Ali (2001) *'ASEAN Plus Three' Equals Peace Plus Prosperity*, No. 2, Institute of Southeast Asian Studies, Singapore.

Bergsten, Fred (2000) 'Towards a Tripartite World', *The Economist*, July 15: 20-22.

Bonapace, Tiziana (2005) Regional Trade and Investment Architecture in Asia-Pacific: Emerging Trends and Imperatives, RIS Discussion Paper #92, New Delhi: Research and Information System for Developing Countries.

Brooks, Douglas, David Roalnd-Holst and Fan Zhai, (2005), 'Growth, trade and integration: Long-term scenarios of developing Asia', Manila: Asian Development Bank, July.

ESCAP (1994) *Infrastructure Development as Key to Economic Growth and Regional Economic Cooperation*, Economic and Social Commission for Asia and the Pacific, New York: UN.

JBIC (2000) 'Special Issue: Infrastructure for Development in the 21st Century', *JBIC Review, No. 3, Japan Bank for International Cooperation*, Tokyo, Japan.

Kawai, Masahiro (2004) 'Prospects for Monetary Cooperation in Asia: ASEAN+3 and Beyond', Presentation at the High-level Conference on Asian Economic Integration: Vision of a New Asia, organized by RIS, Tokyo, 18-19 November 2004. *www.ris.org.in.*

Kesavapany, K. (2005) A New Regional Architecture: Building the Asian Community, public lecture delivered in New Delhi on 31 March 2005, excerpted in *New Asia Monitor*, April 2005: 1.

Kitamura, Toshiaki (2006) 'Japan's New Deal for Asia', *Far Eastern Economic Review,* 169(7), September: 41-44.

Kumar, Nagesh (2004) (ed.) *Towards an Asian Economic Community: Vision of a New Asia,* New Delhi and Singapore: RIS and ISEAS

__________(1998) 'Multinational Enterprises, Regional Economic Integration, and Export-Platform Production in the Host Countries: An Empirical Analysis for the US and Japanese Corporations', *Weltwirtschaftliches Archiv*, 134 (3): 450-483.

__________ 2001, 'Flying Geese Theory and Japanese Foreign Direct Investment in South Asia: Trends Explanations and Future Prospects,' *Journal of International Economic Studies*, 15: 179-192.

__________ (2002) Towards an Asian Economic Community: Relevance of India, RIS Discussion Paper #34.

Madison, Angus (2000) *The World Economy: A Millennial Perspective*, OECD

Mohanty, S.K., Sanjib Rohit and Saikat Sinha Roy (2004) 'Implications of Economic Cooperation Among JACIK Economies: A CGE Modelling Approach', in Nagesh Kumar (ed.) *Towards an Asian Economic Community: Vision of a New Asia,* New Delhi and Singapore: RIS and ISEAS: 109-122.

RIS (2006) *Regionalism with an 'Asian Face': An Agenda for the East Asia Summit,* RIS Policy Brief #28, available at *www.ris.org.in*

__________ (2005) *Towards an Asian Economic Community: An Agenda for the East Asia Summit—Reflections from Asian Think-tanks Dialogue on Broader Asian Economic Integration,* New Delhi and Singapore: RIS and ISEAS.

__________(2004) *South Asia Development and Cooperation Report 2004,* New Delhi: RIS. available at www.ris.org.in

__________(2002) *South Asia Development & Cooperation Report 2001/02*, New Delhi: Research and Information System, available at *www.ris.org.in*

Rowley, Anthony, (2004) Asian Integration needs and overarching framework, *The Business Times, Online Edition 7* January 2004, excerpted in *New Asia Monitor,* March 2004: 6.

Saksena, Sweta C. (2005) 'India's Monetary Integration with East Asia: A Feasibility Study', RIS Discussion Paper # 64-2003, available at *www.ris.org.in*

Shankar, Vineeta (2004) Towards and Asian Economic Community: Exploring the Past, in Nagesh Kumar (ed.) *Towards an Asian Economic Community: Vision of a New Asia,* New Delhi and Singapore: RIS and ISEAS: 13-42.

Shinawatra, Thaksin (2001) 'Asian Cooperation Dialogue', Speech Delivered in New Delhi on 28 November 2001, excerpted in *RIS Digest*, December 2001: 3-5.

Sinha Roy, S. (2004) Complementarities and Potential of Intra-regional Transfers of Investments, Technology and Skills in Asia, in Nagesh Kumar (ed.) *Towards an Asian Economic Community: Vision of a New Asia,* New Delhi and Singapore: RIS and ISEAS: 123-155.

Teo, Eric Chu Cheow (2005) 'Strategic Relevance of Asian Economic Integration', RIS Discussion Paper #90. New Delhi: Research and Information System for Developing Countries. available at *www.ris.org.in*

Wei, Li (2004) 'A Road to Common Prosperity: Relevance of an FTA between India and China', in Nagesh Kumar ed. *Towards an Asian Economic Community: Vision of a New Asia,* New Delhi and Singapore: RIS and ISEAS: 75-90.

Wilson, D. and Roopa Purushothaman (2003) *Dreaming with BRICs: The Path to 2050. Global Economics* Paper #99, Goldman Sachs, available at *www.gs.com.*

Wolf, Martin, (2004). 'Asia Needs the Freedom of Its Monetary Fund', *Financial Times*, 19 May 2004, excerpted in *New Asia Monitor*, July 2004: 6.

World Bank (2000) *Trade Blocs*, The World Bank Policy Research Report, New York: Oxford University Press.

Yamazawa, Ippei (1998) 'How to Get Over the Asian Currency Crisis: A Proposal for an East Asian Stable Currency Group', Discussion Paper No.6, APEC Study Centre, Columbia University.

__________(1999) 'APEC After Ten Years: How Much Has Been Achieved in Liberalization and Facilitation' in *Towards APEC's Second Decade: Challenges, Opportunities and Priorities*, APEC Study Centre.

__________ (2001a) 'Asia-Pacific Regionalism and Japan's Strategy', *Japan Review of Internal Affairs,* 203-221.

__________(2001b) 'How will Asia and Japan survive the Globalization Challenge?', *Asahi Shimbun,* October 2, 2001.

Yao, Chao Cheng (2005) 'China's Role in the Asian Economic Unification Process', RIS Discussion Paper #89. available at *www.ris.org.in*

4

A Strategic Perspective on Asian Economic Integration: The Importance of Building 'One Asia'

Eric Teo Chu Cheow

The Rise of Asian Regionalism Through Market-driven Economic Integration

Thanks to increasing people-to-people contacts and the freer movement of goods, services, tourists and expatriates across the whole region, the longer-term goal of an East Asian Community (EAC) may already be crystallizing much faster than was envisaged thought.[1] In fact, Asian regionalism (East Asia plus India) has increased in recent years, thanks not only to the three waves of changes and transformations, but also to three other economic and financial regional facts, as follows:

- Firstly, intra-regional trade has substantially increased for East Asia-13, from 36.1 per cent in 1985 to about 50 per cent in 2000 and further to more than 55 per cent in 2004, especially as China becomes a greater trading partner for all the Asian economies; India's trade with the rest of Asia, though still small, is increasing rapidly.
- Second, in Asia's trade, current account surpluses of the 13 nations amount to more than US$300 billion per year, this is despite a shift towards more domestic-led growth in Asian economies, thereby

signifying a trend towards more mature economies in the region; if India is added to the 13, this surplus would increase even more. These economies have also become more important competitors amongst themselves, besides being increasingly important markets for their neighbours too. Deflationary trends do exist across Asia (besides Japan), as over-capacity may constitute a growing problem in many of the East Asian economies, although China, India, South Korea and most ASEAN countries are currently experiencing some doses of rising inflation. Moreover, China and India are also showing ASEAN the way in stressing the need for greater re-distribution of wealth and equity in order to secure socio-economic sustainability in the longer term, as Beijing ensures 'upliftment' of its 900 million peasants amidst a booming economy[2] and India caters to rural infrastructure, education and health urgently.

- Last, Asia (that is ASEAN, China, Japan, India and South Korea) has become an enormous pool of foreign reserves— estimated at some US$3 trillion or more than 50 per cent of the world's total reserves. China's and Japan's foreign reserves are now estimated at more than US$ one trillion each; India has surpassed the US$200 billion foreign reserves mark at the beginning of this year. Asians are, therefore, the world's top savers (which is clearly recognized by Asians themselves too), although a big chunk of these reserves are currently sustaining the US deficit through Japanese (and increasingly, Chinese) purchase of American T-bonds. In a way, this Asian wealth is unfortunately 'parked' outside Asia and thereby, not necessarily helping to build East Asia itself.

Attempts at regional coordination and cooperation had in fact begun timidly. Although Malaysian PM Dr Mahathir Mohamad's East Asian Economic Grouping/Caucus idea was shot down in the early 1990s, this grouping has been de facto created, thanks to efforts of coordination on the Asian side during preparations for the Asia-Europe Meeting or ASEM. Since then, this grouping of East Asia (thirteen states) has been dubbed 'ASEAN+3' and is evolving as a regional framework. In turn, the habit of coordination and cooperation amongst the thirteen is facilitating a freer flow of ideas, and even in unofficially adopting an 'appropriate' economic model for Asia, as Asian policy-makers exchange notes on and discuss the 'best' socio-economic model for Asians. India has been progressively drawn into this group, as its economy takes off and economic interaction increases with ASEAN+3 economies.

The East Asia Summit (EAS) launched in December 2005 in Kuala Lumpur, has brought India, Australia and New Zealand to join this regional entity, after the two countries Down Under signed the ASEAN Treaty of Amity and Cooperation (TAC). India already has a growing trade with ASEAN and Northeast Asia; Australia and New Zealand also have important investment and trade relations with both ASEAN and Northeast Asia. The EAS could, therefore, create a new Asian Economic Community or AEC as a region-wide economic cooperation entity; Asian regionalism is on the rise, as 'intellectually' shown by the High-level Conferences on Asian Economic Integration.[3]

In fact, in economic integration terms, there is already a slow shift away from the 'flying geese model of vertical East Asian economic integration', which was centred on Japan (vertically) through capital flow, technological transfer and supply of manufacturing parts and based on market exchange and a clear regional division of labour and production networks (thanks primarily to the expensive cost of production in Japan and the strength of the Yen after the Plaza Agreement). According to an ADB Institute Research Paper,[4] this regional model appears to be shifting towards that of "bamboo capitalism" or "parallel development", based on FDI flows in the region, which create intricate intra-regional production networks, based on the exchange of parts, components and other intermediate products, and hence a "horizontal network of trade and capital", with China at its core. This FDI-driven supply chain has indeed created diverse and vibrant local industries around the Asian region, and the further these supply chains are decomposed and extended geographically, the faster and the more profuse would be the proliferation of new entreprises and FDI flows across Asia. Similarly, India is playing an increasing role as the hub for regional services and outsourcing, just as China is at the centre of the region's manufacturing chains. There is, therefore, a new division of labour, production and services across the whole of Asia.

As a region and for the creation of a future AEC, it is believed that there are currently **three 'regional integration models',** which are being discussed. East Asian economic integration could either be implemented through:

- first, **knitting or weaving a web of existing bilateral free trade areas (or FTAs) together region-wide to create a huge pan-Asian FTA;**
- second, finding the means to **effectively use the mass of 'unproductive' Japanese savings more efficiently** (now the centre of the controversial postal reforms, championed by former PM Junichiro Koizumi, instead of letting them remain 'fallow' in the banks with sub-zero interest rates or 'lie' massively in T-bonds in the United

States) in urgently developing the weaker economies of Asia through a sort of 'Japanese Marshall Plan for Asia', although the latter should also create conditions for fruitful and sound investment in the weak economies; and

- last, **creating an integrated Asian region, centred on growing China and India, and their enormous potential economic development,** through trade (in both goods and services) and investments both ways (China/India—rest of Asia, as well as rest of Asia—China/India), as well as through a new integrated China-centred production chain-cum-demand network in the whole region or an India-centred services outsourcing hub-and-chain; the current ASEAN-China and ASEAN-India FTAs could be "expanded" both geographically (and intellectually) to eventually include Japan and Korea too, as well as "deepened" beyond a mere FTA to a regional comprehensive economic agreement, if need be.

Lessons from Recent Referenda in Europe for Asian Regionalism

The recent referenda in Europe could probably offer a few lessons[5] in what Asians should not do or forget, in pursuing the goal of Asian regionalism. Recent referenda in both France and Netherlands dealt a big blow to European integration, as the French and Dutch people overwhelming rejected the proposed EU Constitution 55-45 per cent and 64-37 per cent, respectively. Nine countries, including Germany, Spain and Italy, had already approved the same via the parliamentary process; Britain, Denmark, Luxemburg and Poland had then decided to postpone their referenda.

This surprising popular opposition to the EU Constitution, which had taken months to negotiate, has inevitably set back EU integration, weakened the EU economically (as shown by the Euro's plunge on world markets in the aftermath of the French and Dutch rejections) and diminished the credibility and reputation of the Union, especially after the Summit in Luxemburg collapsed in open dissensions amongst European leaders over the referenda as well as over the socio-economic model to adopt in the future. Key European leaders, such as Germany and France have, however, vowed to press on with the agenda for uniting Europe, although the European budget for the next eight years lies in shambles and the future of European architecture has become mired in profound controversy.

What lessons can Asia draw from this European debacle and malaise? How can Asians avoid a similar debacle in future?

There appear to be at least four lessons, which Asian leaders could learn from recent European events and developments.

First, the massive rejection by the French and the Dutch appears to be linked to the growing malaise that European integration is no more in the hands of the people, but solely in the hands of the elite of Europe (leaders, parliamentarians, political parties and most importantly, the European Commission bureaucracy in Brussels). The grouse against the Brussels Commission is particularly strong, as the French and Dutch feel that it is not chosen by them, but solely nominated by governments out of political compromise, and hence it is no longer accountable to the European people.

The massive rejection of the French and Dutch could be attributed to a rejection of the European Commission or the Euro-bureaucracy, which they deem not to be accounting sufficiently to the European populace. The "European project" is thus seen to be elitist and no longer "connected" to the common people of Europe.

The fundamental lesson for Asia is the importance of building its regionalism closest to the people, with the majority of them being involved in the formation of the economic, social, cultural and political pillars of the grouping. A Brussels-type regional bureaucracy, aloof from the feelings and needs of the people, must be avoided, as Asians also seek greater accountability and good governance. A 'progressive' institutional framework for Asia would thus be preferable.

Second, as the French and Dutch were among the six founder members of the Union, it is significant that this enlargement was rejected by them; many reminisced the days when they were a small and tightly-knitted entity. The new EU Constitution is thus perceived to be a "political project", with which the French and Dutch population can hardly associate any more, especially when they see it as a political means of encompassing the maximum of Central and Eastern European states (in the Post-Cold War Scenario) without necessarily any real benefits for them.

This brings to mind another lesson for Asia, viz. a small and limited entity may be better than a vast and massive grouping, for which the people of the region feel no common bonding. Starting the EAS with a massive grouping may have the advantage of "power-projection" to the rest of the world, as it is touted to comprise one-third of the world's population (with China and India included), but it remains to be seen if the member countries of the future EAC could create popular affinities amongst the future grouping's peoples.

Third, nationalism must be reduced, just as a regional identity evolves progressively; this, in turn, would reduce pressure from nationalistic forces.

In fact, a European identity has already been successfully evolving in parallel with individual national identities, even in a 'nationalistic' country such as France. What is probably most telling is that the majority of the French still openly say that they believe in Europe, although they reject the proposed Constitution and the type of Europe that is developing today. In a way, a European identity has successfully taken root, even in France.

On the other hand, Asians, especially Northeast Asians, would have enormous difficulties trying to mould a "common Asian identity" today; this goal is even more difficult between China, the two Koreas and Japan, thanks to the current feuds between Tokyo and its neighbours. Founded on history, territorial and politico-strategic disputes, nationalism is riding high in these countries, as the latest feuds have illustrated. Under these circumstances, it would be almost impossible to mould a Northeast Asian identity, not to mention an Asian one, when so much divides rather than unites them. The situation may not be necessarily better in Southeast Asia, given the vicious conflicts in the past few years between Thailand and Cambodia, and the present stand-off between Indonesia and Malaysia over disputes in the Sulawesi Sea.

Fourth, regional integration is always easier during good economic times, as the grouping's people normally accept regional projects better without feeling threatened by other members in the grouping. The adverse socio-economic situation in France had a lot to do with the 55 per cent of 'non' vote, as unemployment rose to the fore of concerns. As cheaper Polish, Hungarian or Slovak labour could potentially threaten French employment, farmers and labour unions expressed their worries and concerns openly. The Dutch feared wanton immigration and a threat to their interests by bigger European powers—France, Britain and Germany.

The last fundamental lesson for Asia is undoubtedly to choose the "correct" moment to launch its regional project and proceed decisively during good times. More must be done to reduce the economic or political threat perceptions of bigger or more powerful nations on the smaller Asian countries. This should then increase the acceptability of regional integration and allay concerns, in times of economic slowdown or in moves, which could be seen as security threats.

Of crucial importance is moulding an Asian identity progressively; this process of 'a growing commonality and affinities' cannot be forced upon the peoples of Asia politically. Hence, Asia should draw useful lessons from the difficulties which Europeans face in their integration process, as we organize the EAS in order to build the AEC of tomorrow.

Creating an Asian Identity and Affinity Should Be the Principal Strategic Approach of the AEC

Just as I had elaborated on the utmost necessity of building the future Asian regional entity on the premise of an overriding strategic goal, viz. the securing of peace and stability in Asia after years of mistrust, suspicions and conflicts,[6] as the Europeans have done (rather successfully), the strategic approach should be based on building an Asian 'commonality and affinities', especially in identifying Asians with 'one Asia'.

Building an Asian identity would indeed pose the main challenge to the future of the AEC or any other Asian regional entity, because without an Asian identity or affinity, any attempts in Asian regionalism would undoubtedly fail in the longer term.

There are no doubts that the region's economists (and from without) have all seen the "coming together of Asia" through regional trade and investments; in fact, the level of interdependency within Asia has increased through these economic linkages, as well as Asia's own common vulnerability in natural disasters and diseases, as stated earlier. The case is clear that Asian inter-dependence in all areas has increased tremendously over these past few years.

However, as the recent experiences of Europe have shown, moulding this 'common identity and affinities' may be more difficult, yet more crucial, for as long as the people do not 'feel' bound together, no amount of trade, investment and interdependency arguments can bind a region together, which must be built on a sense of 'common purpose and well-being'. This is indeed the quintessential prerequisite of 'building a common Asian house', that has been much talked about as the overriding goal for Asia tomorrow.

How could the region then build this "common identity and affinities" through a "sense of common purpose and well-being"? How could the two be intrinsically linked together to ultimately build the "common Asian house"?

A few measures could be envisaged in a pragmatic and progressive way to accompany the growing economic and financial ties, which could indeed be attributed to market forces alone. The political and cultural ties would have to built up by governments and the peoples of Asia themselves, as they mould their "common purpose and well-being" for the future.

First, Asian governments, in heeding the voice of the peoples, either in democracies or socialist forms of government, must increasingly speak of "moulding a common Asian region" in their speeches, declarations or policy formulations. A deliberate effort must be taken from a communications and PR point of view to set the stage for such an enterprise, especially by highlighting the positive spin-offs to the people of such an enterprise. This approach should be well-coordinated across the region to ensure consistency of message and PR marketing of this 'common identity and affinities' and Asia's 'common sense of purpose and well-being', would indeed be a very powerful message, if well delivered jointly to the peoples of Asia.

Second, no efforts must be spared in highlighting the common prosperity of a region, if we take-off together, not from an economist's vision of increasing trade and investment flows, but based on how this common well-being would affect ordinary people in the streets when their everyday well-being would be improved by a common economic purpose in Asia. This should be the message, as it is addressed to the common people, and not only to the elite or the businessmen of Asia.

Third, understanding each other more and better in Asia could be the theme of this campaign of "togetherness", as Asians are only beginning to discover each other. Tourism promotion and intensifying people-to-people relationships, thanks to the advent and take-off of budget airlines in Asia, as well as common cultural programmes in the growing media of Asian societies, should help lower suspicion levels and promote deep people-to-people understanding. Asians must ultimately feel that they belong together and can live together as one big family in a "common house" and under a "common roof".

Last, as institutions are being built to serve the region (but not huge faceless bureaucracies as in Brussels), they must be in tandem with a savvy PR exercise to promote region-wide people-oriented policies, and not just promote converging trade and investment policies, which may not mean much to the common man. As democracy takes root in Asia across all the participating countries, the common people in Asia must clearly identify themselves with this common task and perceive the advantages of being bonded together, otherwise Asian regionalism would fail as it would be an empty shell with no cohesive bonding for Asians.

An extremely important learning from the recent European experiences is the necessity for a monumental regional PR exercise; if there is only one aspect which could be 'centralized' as a regional institution, it should be an Asian PR institution, which could work towards uplifting the 'common identity and affinities' in Asia. It should be a media-cum-cultural exercise to promote 'one Asia', even before building the appropriate institutions or common regulations and policies. There must, therefore, be a 'democratic uplift' for this 'one Asia' enterprise across the whole region for Asia to be truly a worthwhile investment in the future.

Hence besides the market forces, which have coalesced Asian economies together through trade and investments, people-to-people understanding, rapprochement and entente must be at the crux of a common and *volontariste* approach of Asian governments to mould this "one Asia", with a strengthening Asian identity, affinity and sense of purpose and common well-being across the continent for the future of this regional entity, in whatever form, it ultimately takes off.

What Should then be the Process and the Real Issues in Asian Economic Integration?

A number of issues need to be addressed by the EAS or the new "Group of Sixteen", such as the following:

- Is this entity (AEC) purely economic, although it is becoming less and less obvious to organize a purely economic entity nowadays, as APEC's evolutionary process has clearly shown?
- Would this "Group of Sixteen" be based on open regionalism, especially if its main and primary function is economic, viz. based primarily on trade and investments, and ultimately converging the fiscal and monetary policies of Asian economies in the long run?
- What would the new grouping's relations be with the existing ASEAN+3, whose developments and relations have intensified in the last ten years? Basically, how do we structure the concentric relationships of ASEAN, ASEAN+3 and 'Group of Sixteen', or should the last grouping simply supersede ASEAN+3 altogether, whilst maintaining ASEAN as a core organization (as it celebrates 40 years of its existence) of the 'Group of Sixteen'?
- Could the "Group of Sixteen" be termed the AEC of tomorrow, as it could probably form the core entity of the 'new Asia'? What would be the terms of reference for its future expansion, especially if it were to be expanded to eventually include Mongolia and North Korea in the North, Timor Leste in Southeast Asia, the Pacific Islands in Oceania (which are closely linked to Australia and New Zealand) and the other members of SAARC, which would increasingly grow in affinity, and have stronger economic relations, with India on a sub-regional basis?

Some have argued that there is an inherent logic of totally dismantling 'ASEAN+3' or fusing 'ASEAN+3' completely into the new 'Group of Sixteen' or the future AEC, if the Group caters to economic issues alone. It could be synonymous with the European experience, except that the latter followed a progressive expansion from the initial 6 countries to the 27 today.

Second, just as the 'ASEAN+3' experience has proven, it may not be that easy to restrict the future entity to economic and financial issues alone, as socio-economic interdependency increases in Asia and as socio-economic issues 'explode' more and more on the Asian scene, with increasing impact and repercussions for all Asians. As in 'ASEAN+3', the AEC or 'Group of Sixteen' may have to enact growing cooperation in harmonizing social, environmental, health and educational policies, besides trade and investments alone. Furthermore, there is a need to perhaps extend the Chiang-Mai Agreement on financial cooperation to India, Australia and New Zealand, as future participants in the AEC; however, these three countries have already been inducted into the Asian bond market and could thus already take their rightful place in the common Asian financial landscape today and tomorrow.

In fact, in terms of goal and agenda, this 'Group of Sixteen' or AEC could work towards the ultimate convergence of economic, trade, investment, as well as fiscal and monetary policies, just as was seen in Europe with its economic community and then, in its community and then, union expansion and 'deepening', a four-step approach over some 45 years. However, Asia is today taking only its first and initial steps in regional cooperation, not to mention, ultimate integration, although this could be inscribed as its long-term principal goal (of ultimately achieving the AEC). More importantly, as stated earlier, is the urgent need to boost efforts to create public and mass awareness of the 'one Asia' concept and the PR institution which would help develop a region-wide marketing PR of Asia's 'commonality and affinities' and its 'sense of common purpose and well-being', thus building ultimately 'a common Asian house' together for all Asians.

Perhaps, it is also incumbent for the EAS to state clearly Asia's cherished goal of open regionalism (in the AEC), and not create an Asian protectionist trade bloc, which would principally be detrimental to Asia's growing trade and investment links with the rest of the world, especially with the US and Europe. The future grouping's economic relations with these two principal trading partners in the world would also need to be clearly discussed and stated (as a principled commitment) in the final communiqué of Kuala Lumpur, especially to allay fears and suspicions of both the US and EU in their future economic relations with Asia. An 'inclusionist', and not exclusionist, policy must be stressed, and a policy of an ultimate expansion (or not) of this new grouping must also be clearly laid down for the intention and attention of future members of this "Group of Sixteen".

Finally, a name must be selected for the grouping to reflect the process ahead as well as the goals and parameters of this 'Group of Sixteen'. The AEC is a sound fundamental choice if its main goal is purely or initially economic, but it would also limit its scope of cooperation, if the name is taken at face value. Again, Europe could provide inspiration as it had expanded from Coal and Steel Community to European Economic Community (or EEC), and then to the European Community (EC), and finally to the European Union (with a common European currency and the successful convergence of economic and social policies today).

The AEC could thus be a first regional take on a long road to Asian cooperation and integration; but it must be accompanied by efforts to lessen nationalistic feelings amongst the peoples (and especially the young) in the three Asian giants China, India and Japan (and also South Korea). More importantly, learning from the European experiences of France and Germany, these three countries must urgently institute youth exchange programmes among themselves to reduce suspicions of each other, especially among the youth. These can derive inspiration from the 1963 Elysees Accord signed in Paris by French President Charles de Gaulle and German Chancellor Konrad Adenauer which established a youth exchange office, and has since brought at least a million French and German youth to stay in each other's countries. This is especially useful for Beijing, New Delhi and Tokyo (as well as Seoul) to begin with just as ASEAN intensifies its own internal exchange programmes, as well as those with the other Northeast Asian countries, India, Australia and New Zealand.

Conclusion

The EAS should squarely tackle the issues of the name, process, scope and goal of Asia's future entity. It must acknowledge Asian rapprochement through trade, investments and its growing interdependency, but it should also learn from recent European experiences and lessons on what to avoid in building its own regionalism, cooperation and integration. Building a growing Asian identity, affinities, and a common 'sense of purpose and well-being' for the people of Asia remain key and crucial to this common Asian endeavour.

It will be useful to engender a democratic debate on how Asian leaders perceive the future direction of this "one Asia" and come out with clear answers to the four fundamental issues outlined above, whilst creating, as Asia's primary strategic approach at this stage, a PR institution that could build this commonality progressively in line with the market forces, which are building the economic and financial pillars of this "new Asia".

The task of building the possible AEC of tomorrow is enormous, as the feeling of "Asian-ness" still eludes the majority of Asians today. Trade and investments may help, but efforts to promote this "one-ness" within Asia cannot be spared, as Asian governments must now pronounce clearly "as one" the people's desire to unite; Asians must be brought together progressively, by moulding a common "Asian identity and affinities" and with a common "sense of purpose and well-being", which must filter down to as wide a cross-section of the Asian population as possible.

Endnotes

1 Eric Teo, *Japan Times*, 13 February 2004 & 31 December 2004, *China Daily*, 10 February 04 & PACNET#8, 20 Feb 04.

2 Eric Teo, *China Daily*, 19 Mar 04 on 'Healthy Growth Key to Political Stability'.

3 Eric Teo Chu Cheow, *China Daily*, 21 December 2004 on 'Bigger Steps Towards Asian Integration.'

4 ADB Research Paper, January 2003, published by the ADBI, Tokyo

5 Eric Teo Chu Cheow, *The Japan Times*, 25 June 2005 on EU Lessons for East Asian Regionalism.

6 Eric Teo Chu Cheow, RIS Discussion Paper, RIS-DP #90, March 2005, after a paper presented at the High-level Conference on Asian Economic Integration in Tokyo on 18-19 November 2004.

Part II
Building Blocs of Broader Regional Cooperation

5

ASEAN's Role in Asian Economic Integration

K. Kesavapany

Introduction

The process of launching and sustaining Asian economic integration is as much a political as an economic initiative and effort. Political leaders provide the vision, bureaucrats provide the legwork and flesh out the vision in negotiated agreements and businesses undertake the actual transactions. Asian economic integration can take various forms, such as formal economic agreements for examaple, free trade areas (FTAs) or it can be market driven, like production chains set up by multinational corporations (MNCs). Thus, it is a joint effort between political leaders and businesses that has launched and sustains, Asian economic integration.

The mechanisms that are used in building Asian economic integration are well-known, so we shall allude to them briefly. These include:

- A network of bilateral and multilateral FTAs that link the Asian economies, with ASEAN serving as the hub through its FTAs—at various stages of negotiation or implementation—with China, India, Japan, South Korea and Australia and New Zealand;
- Production chains set up by MNCs which bring together inputs from several Asian countries for final assembly in one Asian location;

- Cross-country FDI from Asian countries into other Asian economies, with a tide of Indian and Chinese FDI supplementing the traditional investors, Japan, Korea, Taiwan, Singapore and Hong Kong;
- Intra-Asian trade, boosted by economic locomotives, now including China and India.

Certain preconditions are necessary for Asian economic integration to become a reality. These are:

- The need for the very idea of an Asian community to be articulated and conceptualized in detail by leaders and officials;
- The example of an actual, thriving community within Asia, namely ASEAN, which has existed and cooperated well for 40 years;
- The rules, norms and practices of running a community; here again ASEAN has set some precedents, such as the "ASEAN Way";
- The willingness of ASEAN to be the driver and neutral venue;
- The involvement of the three great Asian powers, China, India and Japan in community building on a win-win basis and not on a zero-sum basis.

Did ASEAN leaders have a conscious game plan for Asian economic integration? Probably so, and the starting point was the Kuala Lumpur meeting in 1997 that launched the ASEAN+3 process. The Asian financial crisis opened the eyes of many leaders to the need for Asian economic cooperation, when they saw that the US and the IMF were reluctant to help the Asian victim economies. In December 2005, they launched an even more inclusive forum of the East Asia Summit (EAS), bringing together ASEAN plus six countries namely China, Japan, South Korea, India, Australia and New Zealand.

Founding the ASEAN Community

To start with, we look at the ASEAN initiatives in community building. Apart from the historic 1967 Bangkok Declaration which established ASEAN itself, the points of origin of the process of building the Asean community, or the founding documents, are the Bali Concord II of October 2003 and the ASEAN Vision 2020 statement issued at the 1998 ASEAN Summit. Since its foundation in 1967, ASEAN has concentrated on economic cooperation (especially after 1976), but after the invasion and occupation of Cambodia (1979-89), ASEAN increaased political cooperation in order to achieve a peaceful settlement of the Cambodian conflict. ASEAN has played a crucial role in maintaining regional peace and security and in enhancing Asian regional economic cooperation. Immense challenges, such as the Asian financial crisis and the SARS epidemic, have kept ASEAN very busy and forced it to embark on new directions in cooperation, specifically, to start building an ASEAN Community by 2015 and to help build an ASEAN economic community. As Singapore holds the ASEAN Chairmanship during the 40th anniversary year, 2007-08, there is some anticipation of new directions from Singapore. Put in another way, Singapore is the current pilot of the ASEAN ship, and the passengers hope for some inspired helmsmanship.

The ASEAN 2020 Vision

In October 2003, the Summit in Bali was regarded as a milestone in giving ASEAN renewed impetus and new directions, at a crucial time when most of its members had just recovered from the Asian financial crisis (1997-98), when it was facing serious economic challenges from India and China, and there were great security challenges from international terrorism, the unilateral behaviour of the US in Iraq and Afghanistan, and from the new security doctrines, such as pre-emption, of the Bush Administration. It was felt necessary to focus on new goals which would provide ASEAN members with renewed cohesion within a cooperative framework— an impetus to strive towards higher objectives. These aims have been set out in the ASEAN Vision 2020 statement:

'A concert of Southeast Asian nations, outward looking, living in peace, stability and prosperity, bonded together in partnership and dynamic development, and in a community of caring societies'.

In a globalized world, trade liberalization and market integration have become *de rigeur* policy agendas for nearly all countries, including ASEAN countries. Thus at the 9th ASEAN Summit in Bali in October 2003, ASEAN leaders agreed to establish the ASEAN Economic Community (AEC). Its aim was to set up a single market and production base with free flow of goods, services, investments, capital and skilled labour. To accelerate the liberalization process, 11 priority sectors, later increased to 12, were fast-tracked so that a single market could be formed by 2010. Measures to implement this include: imposing zero tariffs; removal of non-tariff barriers; faster harmonization of product standards; mutual recognition of test reports and certification, faster customs clearance and simplified customs procedures.

In November 2004, implementation measures for the AEC were laid down in the Vientiane Action Programme, or VAP. This document contained clearer goals and strategies for achieving the AEC. It also prescribed a monitoring and evaluation system.

What Exactly is a Community?

Before proceeding further, we need to elaborate on the concept of 'community'.

According to Amitav Acharya, the key attributes of a community include the following:

- The importance of trust, friendship, complementarity and responsiveness;
- A regional association may grow into a community through an evolutionary process of socialization and identification;
- A community can be socially constructed through socialization, building norms and symbolic identity-building;
- The need to build a sense of collective identity, to define who is in and who is out.[1]

What observers will note is the stress on socialization and identity building. Are these processes at work in ASEAN? It does not seem so to observers. People in ASEAN countries still define themselves as nationals/citizens of individual countries, after 40 years of the existence of ASEAN. The reason could be that they do not see any benefit of claiming ASEAN identity: no ASEAN passport; no economic benefits; no prestige. They do not see visible Asean institutions, such as an ASEAN Parliament, an ASEAN Court, an ASEAN University, a central bureaucracy or common policies, unlike the EU which has the Brussels institutions and a common EU Foreign and Security Policy, a Mr EU in the form of the President of the EU Commission, and free and easy movement across EU borders.

It would thus appear that ASEAN needs to put in more efforts over the next few decades to strengthen its socialization and identity-building endeavours. A good start has been made but much more needs to be done. For instance, the legal basis of ASEAN needs to be strengthened: In the efforts to build an East Asian community (EAC), the legal basis of this proposed community also needs to be clarified and institutionalized. The formal adoption of the ASEAN Charter in November 2007 at the Singapore ASEAN Summit will help to resolve this problem.

If the ASEAN experience is to be useful to the process of building an EAC, then what ASEAN is trying to do in building the three ASEAN communities should be of interest to the EAC building process, which has barely started.

The Three ASEAN Communities

The Bali Concord II document sets out the goal of achieving an Asean Community by 2020, based on three 'pillars': security; economic, and socio-cultural. All three communities are linked inextricably, and weaknesses in one could weaken the others. However, achieving the ASEAN Community by 2015 (the January 2007 Asean Summit in Cebu advanced the target year) will be a challenging task, given the cultural diversity, different levels of economic development and different strategic orientations and external linkages among Asean's members. The same differences are seen in the East Asian region.

The ASEAN Security Community (ASC)

This is a form of cooperative security. It is not a defence pact or a military alliance. Security communities have developed a long-term habit of war-avoidance, a sense of common purpose and a "we-feeling". The ASC is thus a community in which members regard their security as fundamentally linked to one another, are bound by common perceptions of security threats, and are united by common objectives in addressing these threats—relying exclusively on peaceful means of settlement. The Bali Concord II spelt out five areas for greater political and security cooperation. These are setting norms and common values, maritime security, counter-terrorism and transnational crime, defence cooperation and weapons of mass destruction. An Action Plan on the ASC was adopted at the Asean Ministerial Meeting in July 2004 in Jakarta.

The ASEAN Economic Community (AEC)

The concept of AEC is clearer. It was approved at the Phnom Penh ASEAN Summit in 2002 and will be based on the ASEAN Free Trade Area (AFTA), the ASEAN Framework Agreement on Services (AFAS), the ASEAN Investment Area (AIA), and the Hanoi Plan of Action. The target date is now set as 2015. The aim of the economic community is to strengthen ASEAN'S competitiveness and, of course, to increase ASEAN prosperity as well. Under AFTA, tariffs on almost all products traded among ASEAN'S first six members had already come down to 0 to 5 per cent by 2003. Vietnam did this in 2006. Laos and Myanmar are committed to achieve this level by 2008, and Cambodia by 2010. To help the newer members, ASEAN has set up the Initiative for ASEAN Integration (IAI). At the Phnom Penh Summit, ASEAN approved a six-year (2002-08) work-plan with 54 projects in order to implement the IAI. Concrete aid from the six older members takes the form of training, equipment and experts. The priority areas, originally four, have now been expanded to seven: human resource development, infrastructure (mainly transport and energy), information and communications technology, promoting regional economic integration, tourism, poverty and quality of life and general coverage projects.

The ASEAN Socio-cultural Community (ASCC)

The aims of the ASCC include: ensuring equitable access to opportunities regardless of race, religion, language, or socio-cultural background; ensuring that human potentials are nurtured to the fullest; addressing issues of poverty and equity, and taking special care of vulnerable groups; protecting the environment and natural resources for sustainable development; enhancing civil society, and looking after the health and harmony of ASEAN citizens. In short, the ASCC is focused on poverty eradication and human development. The ASCC agenda has four key elements:

- Building caring societies to address issues of poverty, equity and human development;
- Managing the social impacts of economic integration via education and ensuring social security;
- Enhancing environmental sustainability and governance;
- Strengthening the foundations of regional social cohesion.

Implementation modalities include national initiatives, regional activities and regional mechanisms or standards. Member countries shall prepare individual action plans for the period 2005-10, consistent with national policies, priorities, capacity and budgetary resources. Self-reliance, shared responsibility and ownership are the principles that guide the implementation of ASCC projects. It is hoped that the ASEAN Foundation will play an active role in implementing the ASCC.

Lessons from the Community Building Process in EU

Comparing ASEAN with other community-building efforts, we should discuss why this process succeeded in the EU. Several important factors could help explain this:

- First, the members were mature nation-states that were prepared to pool their sovereignty for the common good and to help achieve common goals;
- Second, they shared similar culture and histories and were not too dissimilar in terms of size, population, resources and levels of development;

- Third, they were all developed states which had the capacity to engage in community-building;
- Fourth, there was Germany, which was prepared to play the role of financier and bear the burden of budget payments;
- Fifth, the EU had visionary leaders such as Jean Monnet, Charles de Gaulle and Konrad Adenauer, who understood the need for building a European community in order to avoid a repeat of the World Wars.

In contrast, ASEAN consists of a group of developing countries which are zealous about protecting their independence and sovereignty, and whose diversity is amazing. Three of the ten ASEAN members are least developed countries; two are experiencing severe economic problems, plus separatism and terrorism threats. Singapore is too small and too frugal to act like Germany. Thus we should not be surprised if the effort to build an ASEAN Community encounter meet serious problems. No other group of developing countries has embarked on such an ambitious project. Perhaps, after a few years, as in 2010, ASEAN should review whether the target date is achievable.

The Genesis of Economic Cooperation within ASEAN

The steps towards economic integration in ASEAN started with the establishment of the AFTA and the signing of a Common Effective Preferential Tariff (CEPT) Scheme in 1992. The aim was to eliminate tariff barriers among Southeast Asian countries and to integrate the ASEAN economies into a single production base and regional market. Over time, regional economic integration has been extended to include other areas of economic cooperation apart from merchandise trade. These include the AFAS (signed in 1995), for liberalizing trade in services within ASEAN, and the AIA (signed in 1998), for liberalizing investment flows within the region.

This section reviews the state of economic integration in ASEAN by analysing the developments in each of these components of regional integration involving merchandise trade, services trade and investment flows, respectively. It also analyses the trade facilitation measures undertaken to support these components and the ways in which these can promote greater economic integration among the ASEAN economies.

Merchandise Trade

The CEPT under AFTA was fully implemented in 2003 with the first six members (Malaysia, Singapore, Indonesia, the Philippines, Thailand and Brunei) complying with the Agreement on the CEPT Scheme, which requires that tariff rates on products traded within the region, with a few exceptions, be reduced to between zero and 5 per cent. Some of the earlier targets for newer ASEAN members have been advanced in the light of rapid changes in the global economy. Thus, Vietnam was expected to reach its tariff elimination target in 2006, Laos and Myanmar in 2008 and Cambodia in 2010. Among the new members of ASEAN, Vietnam was expected to maximize the number of tariff lines in the 0-5 per cent range by 2003, while the deadline for Laos and Myanmar was 2005.

The above indicates that there has been significant progress on CEPT implementation, with the intention of achieving an FTA among all ASEAN members much earlier than planned. In September 1999, ASEAN Economic Ministers (AEM) went further to realize the regional FTA by signing an agreement to adopt a target of zero tariffs by 2015 for the ASEAN-6 countries and by 2018 for the newer ASEAN member countries. Hence, the full implementation of the CEPT across all ASEAN members by 2010 and the target of close to zero tariffs by 2018 would be important building blocks for regional economic integration.

Services

The AFAS is an ASEAN agreement to liberalize regional trade in services. Signed at the Fifth ASEAN Summit on 15 December 1995, the AFAS aims at reducing restrictions on intra-regional trade in services beyond those already undertaken under the General Agreement on Trade in Services (GATS).[2] In other words, the AFAS is meant to be GATS-plus.[3] Under the AFAS, initial negotiations focused on financial services, transport, telecommunications, tourism and professional business services.

The AFAS has completed four rounds of negotiations, resulting in five packages of commitments in seven service sectors, adding construction and maritime transport services to its initial list of five sectors. The initial package of commitments was endorsed during the 29th AEM meeting on 16 October 1997 in Kuala Lumpur, Malaysia. A second package was concluded at the 30th AEM on 7 October 1998 in Makati City, Philippines. A third was approved during the 7th ASEAN Transport Ministers meeting in Kuala Lumpur, Malaysia in October 2001. The third round of negotiations was launched during the 33rd AEM at Hanoi, Vietnam, starting from 2002 and ending in 2004, covering all service sectors and all four modes of service provision. The fourth round took place in 2005-06, culminating in the fifth package of commitments.

The AEM have considered that for the third round of negotiations—with the view to accelerating progressive liberalization—member countries adopt the 'like-minded countries approach' (also known as the 'ASEAN minus-X principle') wherein agreements could be concluded by those countries that were ready, while others could accede at a later time.

Thus, over about eight years since AFAS was signed, four rounds of negotiations have taken place. However, an analysis of the commitments made by individual ASEAN countries indicates that not much progress has been achieved. Indeed, if one compares the specific AFAS commitments offered by the ASEAN economies, the content of services trade liberalization in most of these countries can at best be termed as 'weak'. The common trade barriers as reflected in these commitments, are mainly in the form of restrictions on equity participation, on the type of commercial establishment that is allowed to be set up by the foreign company (that is, joint ventures, representative offices, branches or wholly foreign— owned), and on the movement of natural persons (mode 4). These are common for other categories of services trade as well. These barriers continue to affect the efficiency and competitiveness of the service sectors in these countries, but are retained since they serve domestic business interests.

One of the key challenges facing AFAS is the accommodation of the uneven levels of development among the ASEAN economies, gaining technical expertise in the legal and sectoral aspects of services trade liberalization, and at the same time ensuring that the process of liberalization proceeds smoothly. Some analysts argue that AFAS should have a multi-track approach wherein some industries that are growing more rapidly be liberalized faster than others. This indicates that in the context of broader economic cooperation, it is the area of services trade liberalization among ASEAN economies that would be the most challenging to implement, especially as it would affect the domestic interests of each member country in a different manner.

Investment

ASEAN Ministers signed the Framework Agreement on the AIA on 7 October 1998 in Manila. The AIA aims to make ASEAN a competitive, conducive and liberal investment area. The privileges offered by the AIA in investment, market access and the granting of national treatment, take immediate effect for ASEAN investors, with the exception of those sectors in the list of exclusions for each country—the Temporary Exclusion List (TEL), the Sensitive List, and the General Exception List. Under the AIA, Brunei Darussalam, Indonesia, Malaysia, Myanmar, the Philippines, Singapore and Thailand had until 1 January 2003 to phase out their Temporary Exclusion Lists for the manufacturing sector. The newer members of ASEAN—Cambodia, Laos and Vietnam—have until 1 January 2010 to do so.

The AIA is expected to have important implications for investment strategies and production activities in the region. For instance, the AIA will encourage investors to think increasingly in regional terms, adopt regional investment strategies and form networks of operations. It is thus expected to provide greater scope for division of labour and industrial activities across the region, creating opportunities for greater efficiency and cost competitiveness. Current and potential investors are expected to benefit from the AIA arrangements through: greater investment access to industries and economic sectors; national treatment as ASEAN investors, greater transparency and a more liberal and competitive investment regime; and lower transaction costs for business operations across the region.

The Ministerial-level ASEAN Investment Area Council oversees the implementation of the Framework Agreement. This Council is assisted by the ASEAN Coordinating Committee on Investment. There are currently three programmes that constitute the building blocks for the AIA: a) the Cooperation and Facilitation Programme to strengthen ASEAN's competitiveness and to provide investors with an efficient and low-transaction cost investment environment; b) the Promotion and Awareness Programme to promote ASEAN as a single investment destination and to give investors a better understanding and awareness of the region's investment opportunities; c) the Liberalization Programme to open up investment regimes throughout the region by eliminating investment barriers, liberalizing investment rules and policies and granting national treatment.

The AIA programme is supported by the industrial cooperation scheme—ASEAN Industrial Cooperation (AICO)—which was initiated in 1996 to encourage companies across ASEAN economies to cooperate in the manufacture of selected products, which could enjoy the ultimate preferential tariff levels in the CEPT scheme as well as other privileges.

Thus, through the AIA and AICO, ASEAN economies already have a framework agreement in place for regional industrial and investment cooperation, which, once fully implemented, would be an important element of a more economically integrated ASEAN. This would not only help in attracting foreign investments into the ASEAN economies but would also help in fostering greater intra-regional investment within ASEAN. However, since commercial presence through foreign investment is a major mode of service provision, the success of the AIA would critically depend upon the pace and extent of services trade liberalization within ASEAN.

e-ASEAN

The ASEAN leaders, at their summit meeting in Manila in November 1999, endorsed the e-ASEAN initiative. This aims to develop a broad-based and comprehensive action plan, including the physical, legal, logistical, social and economic infrastructure needed to promote an ASEAN e-space, as part of an ASEAN positioning and branding strategy; e-ASEAN would cover the economy, society and government. A high-level e-ASEAN Task Force comprising government and private sector representatives has been working on concrete ways to realize the initiative. While focusing on encouraging and facilitating the growth of e-commerce, e-ASEAN would also include prescriptive measures to narrow the digital divide within the region.

This is a bold initiative that needs to be explored in greater detail, in order to integrate it with other initiatives on regional trade and investment cooperation. The proposed ASEAN e-space, as envisaged by this initiative, would be vital for efficient networking and coordination within the ASEAN.

Trade Facilitation

Trade facilitation measures constitute a vital support framework for ensuring the success of any regional trade and investment programme. In this context, it is important to note that an ASEAN Agreement on Customs (AAC) was signed in 1997, which is aimed at enhancing customs cooperation and the harmonization of procedures and ensuring efficient administration and expeditious clearance of goods. This would, in turn, facilitate the flow of trade and investments among ASEAN countries. Another objective is to ensure the consistency, transparency and fair application of customs laws and regulations, procedures and other administrative guidelines within each ASEAN member state. This has been established as part of the broader ASEAN Customs Vision 2020.[4] ASEAN member countries established a dispute settlement mechanism in November 1996 in Manila to strengthen the rules and disciplines of the CEPT programme. An ASEAN Harmonized Tariff Nomenclature has also been adopted.

Two other important developments have taken place in this area. The first relates to the harmonization of product standards. ASEAN has identified 20 priority sectors, mainly electrical and electronic products, whose product standards would be harmonized. The second relates to the development of Mutual Recognition Arrangements (MRAs) between ASEAN members. A

Framework Agreement on MRAs was signed in December 1998. Under the MRAs, products traded between ASEAN members need to undergo tests only once—tests by the exporting country would be recognized by the importing country. So far, MRAs have been concluded for electrical and electronic products and for cosmetics. Those for pharmaceuticals and a number of other products are being worked on.

Challenges for ASEAN Economic Integration

In an increasingly globalized economy, it has thus become critical for Southeast Asia to stay competitive in order to remain an important growth pole in Asia, along with the emerging market economies of China and India. For ASEAN countries, this would involve the restructuring and integration of their economies. Clearly, an economically integrated ASEAN with a combined population of more than 550 million could make the region more competitive vis-a-vis China and India, while at the same time strengthening economic linkages with them. It is in this context that at the ASEAN Summit on 4 November 2002 in Cambodia, ASEAN leaders agreed to transform ASEAN into an AEC. Although the concept of an AEC and how this would be achieved were not elaborated during the Summit, it undoubtedly involved fostering closer economic cooperation and expediting the current economic integration process within ASEAN.

The analysis of the present state of economic integration programmes in ASEAN suggests that most of the programmes for achieving regional economic integration through trade and investment are already in place, with most of the components, with the exception of AFAS and e-ASEAN, having a deadline for implementation by 2010. In other words, most of the building blocks for the proposed AEC (by 2020) already seem to be in place. However, there are serious challenges faced by both ASEAN as a single entity as well by its individual member countries, in order to realize the goal of the AEC.

First, with the implementation of the CEPT on target for all ASEAN economies by 2010, services trade liberalization under AFAS needs to be accorded top priority. It is expected that the current round of negotiations as well as the future ones would yield more substantial commitments for market access in important service sectors, namely telecommunications, energy services, financial services, travel and transport, which are essential for enhancing the competitiveness of ASEAN countries in an increasingly knowledge-based and rapidly globalizing world. Although the ASEAN-minus-X principle is useful in this regard to allow faster members to liberalize earlier, it is important to ensure that slower members are able to 'catch up' faster in this area. Establishment of deadlines for implementation of negotiations under AFAS is critical to provide a sense of urgency in this respect. Thus (as mentioned earlier), rapid progress and implementation of services trade liberalization would be central to the early realization of the proposed AEC.

Second, it is important to note that for the above to be successful, many of the individual member countries within ASEAN would have to focus on domestic reforms, and would need to enhance their competitiveness in these sectors. This is particularly true in case of the financial services sector, which was most affected during the 1997-98 crisis. Some ASEAN countries, such as Malaysia, have made important progress in these directions, but others have fallen back on the pace of domestic reforms and would need to step up the pace.

Finally, it is important to note that although individual programmes and framework agreements for regional economic cooperation are in place, they are inadequate for achieving the proposed AEC. They require the establishment of a stronger institutional structure with a better enforcement mechanism. There is thus a need to streamline, strengthen and enhance coordination among the existing institutions, as well as design better enforcement mechanisms, in order to facilitate the creation of an economic community as envisaged by the proposed AEC. Creation of new regional institutions may be required in this context, with the powers of the existing ASEAN Secretariat being strengthened.

Therefore, if individual ASEAN member governments can commit themselves to the speedy implementation of the component programmes, particularly in services and investment liberalization, successfully implement a zero-tariff AFTA and achieve better trade facilitation across borders, then with a proper institutional framework in place, the ASEAN would be able to consolidate itself as a regional market in the form of the proposed AEC by 2015.

ASEAN and the Broader Asian Community

ASEAN felt that it was necessary to expand regional cooperation, as it would help the region to engage and cooperate, especially after the end of the Cold War divisions; and that the region should organize itself in response to the EU and NAFTA blocs, as argued by Indonesian economist and current Trade Minister, Mari Pangestu. Some ASEAN members such as Malaysia and Thailand had actively promoted various ideas for greater East Asian regional cooperation. Malaysia had for some time since 1990 promoted its EAEC concept, whilst

Thailand had launched its Asian Cooperation Dialogue and BIMSTEC (Bangladesh, India, Myanmar, Sri Lanka and Thailand Economic Cooperation) concept as well as setting up the Asian Bond Fund in June 2003 with US$1 billion. ASEAN'S bid for ASEAN-led regionalism began in the 1990s, with the launch of the ARF in 1994. This was followed in 1997 by the APT.

Japan helped ASEAN as it wanted to assist the Asian countries which had suffered from the Asian financial crisis. In August 1997, Japan organized a conference in Tokyo, sponsored by the IMF. The IMF decided to set up a fund of US$17.3 billion, of which $4 billion came from Japan. The US persuaded Japan to support the Manila framework or emergency loan, in November 1997.

The first APT summit was held in Malaysia in December 1997, in the midst of the financial crisis. ASEAN has insisted that it should be at the core of the EAC, as it has concerns about being dominated by Northeast Asia. This EAC concept was proposed by Japanese Prime Minister J. Koizumi in January 2003. In December 2003, at an ASEAN-Japan meeting in Tokyo, ASEAN formally supported the EAC concept. At the sub-regional level, ASEAN countries have organized various schemes, such as BIMP-EAGA (Brunei-Indonesia-Malaysia-Philippines East ASEAN Growth Area), the Emerald Triangle among Cambodia, Laos and Thailand, and the Economic Cooperation Strategy among Cambodia, Laos, Myanmar and Thailand. In 2005, another, even more inclusive, forum that is, EAS was launched which included APT countries and India, New Zealand and Australia.

At the cross-Pacific level, there is APEC, but the 1980s rhetoric of building a Pacific community seems to have dissipated in the new century. The APEC process is likely to slow down because of US domestic pre-occupation with 2008 presidential politics, and because the triangular relations among the US, Iraq and Iran are now centre-stage (in mid-2007).

For ASEAN itself, its expansion into ASEAN-Plus activities has helped it to remain relevant amidst rapid changes. However, the greater challenge for ASEAN is how to ensure its own institutional relevance and distinctiveness within the larger Asian context.

Rise of China and India

ASEAN leaders have been concerned about the growing competitive challenge from China. According to the United Nations Conference on Trade and Development (UNCTAD), China is now the largest recipient of FDI flows in the Asia-Pacific region. There are acute concerns that China's rise would divert FDI inflows from ASEAN towards China and intensify export competition in third markets in products where both China and ASEAN enjoy strong comparative advantage, thus affecting ASEAN's competitiveness.

Concurrent with China's rapid growth, the Indian economy is also emerging as a potential challenger to Southeast Asia. However, India also provides economic opportunities for cooperation with a growth of more than 9 per cent per annum. Thus, China and India along with Southeast Asia now constitute the new growth poles of Asia, being one of the fastest growing regions in the world. Bilateral trade growth has increased among these three entities in recent years, with ASEAN-China trade growing at about 30-50 per cent per annum, ASEAN-India trade growing at about 30 per cent per annum, and a 52-fold increase in China-India trade over a decade, albeit from a significantly low base. Such trends are indicative of an emerging economic network among these three growth poles.

Japan's Role

Japanese were the pioneers of Asian regionalism in the 1980s. Why Japan and not others? South Korea was absorbed in national economic development and with catching up with Japan. China was busy with domestic reforms and was isolated after the Tien An Men incident. ASEAN was busy at the sub-regional level of cooperation and involed with the Cambodian issue, later it was weakened by the Asian financial crisis. The Japanese had long felt isolated and were bothered by identity crises: were they Asians or westerners by virtue of OECD membership? They wanted to belong to some group but felt rejected by their immediate neighbours, which had suffered from Japanese colonialism, occupation and World War II aggression. Japan thus turned its attention southwards to ASEAN, which welcomed its trade and investments. Another reason why the Japanese turned to Southeast Asia was to consolidate goodwill with neighbours and to relocate their factories, which suffered from the appreciation of the Yen in 1985. Upon their election, Japanese Prime Ministers have made customary visits around the ASEAN capitals and invariably announced in one of the capitals some doctrine (usually named after themselves), accompanied by offers of aid as goodwill. Aid also enabled Japanese investments to operate efficiently with the improvement of infrastructure and human resources through ODA. By the late 1980s, Japan decided to revive the concept of Asia-Pacific regionalism and helped to launch APEC in 1989, which was the first formal, multilateral organization for the broad Asia-Pacific. Japan's interest in Asian regionalism coincided with the proposal of Malaysia's Prime Minister Mahathir Mohamad to set up an East

Asia Economic Group—later watered down to an East Asia Economic Caucus—which would have been the East Asian counterpart of the EU and NAFTA. Although the US had criticized Japan for not doing enough to help the countries afflicted by the Asian financial crisis, Japan had contributed US$44 billion by October 1998, whilst the US gave only US$4 billion. Later, Japan announced the New Miyazawa Initiative, a US$30 billion capital support package. Critics noted that the schemes were repackaging of old funds, not new money. At the second APT Summit, Prime Minister Keizo Obuchi offered a US$20 million Japan-ASEAN solidarity fund, which has been administered by the ASEAN Foundation. In May 2000, at Japan's urging, the second APT Finance Minister's meeting was held in Chiang-Mai, and resulted in the Chiang-Mai Initiative. Thus through the Asian financial crisis and because of Japanese attempts to help the afflicted countries, Japan became more involved in East Asian regionalism. Another factor was the failure of the Early Voluntary Sectoral Liberalization scheme of APEC, partly because of Japan's opposition.

In January 2002, Prime Minister Junichiro Koizumi announced that Japan was willing to conclude an FTA with ASEAN, called the JACEP or Japan-ASEAN Comprehensive Economic Partnership, to be realized by 2012, although there are known difficulties over agricultural trade. In January 2002, Japan proposed the Initiative for Development of East Asia (IDEA) and also called for the creation of an EAC. Both proposals need to be fleshed out. The future of Japan's role in East Asian regionalism is uncertain because of Japanese difficulties with FTAs, especially with regard to agricultural trade liberalization.

At the January 2007 EAS, Japan proposed a Comprehensive Economic Partnership for East Asia (CEPEA) and an Economic Research Institute for ASEAN and East Asia (ERIA), something similar to the OECD. In 2007, Japan made strenuous efforts to cultivate relations with India and Australia, which were seen as part of the attempt to counter-balance China, at the same time that the US was promoting its Democratic Four concept, also seen as a similar effort to counter-balance China.

China's Role

There are several possible interpretations concerning China's role in promoting East Asian regionalism. First, that China wants to build a bloc which it can dominate and lead, and use it as a power base to challenge the US; the problem, of course, is that some East Asian countries such as South Korea and Japan will not accept this. Another theory could be that China wants to co-opt its neighbours, which might be negatively affected by its rising economic power, and extend its influence. A third version is that China may be trying to exclude the US by helping to build an Asians-only club; but again this might not work because there are some states which would like the US to continue playing a security and economic role in the region. Last, China might be trying to construct an East Asian club in which it has legitimacy and seniority. History will show which theory will prove to be correct. The possible reactions of regional states to China's efforts to build an EAC, might be divided into: (a) neutral position, adopted by states that do not wish to be pressured by either the US, Japan or China; (b) supportive position, adopted by those who see profit in doing so; and (c) negative, by states that fear, for various reasons, that a China-led East Asia might not suit their national interests.

China has launched its concept of its peaceful development, as a way to reassure its neighbours that its rise will not cause any upsets, as it needs a peaceful external environment for its domestic economic development. Chinese General Cai Bing Kui stated at an ISEAS forum in June 2004 that: 'China will not create obstacles or threats to anybody. It does not seek hegemony now, nor will it seek hegemony after it becomes powerful in the future'. China has also taken other measures to reassure ASEAN, for example, by agreeing to issue with ASEAN the Declaration on the Conduct of Parties in the South China Sea, offering to double ASEAN-China trade, becoming the first ASEAN Dialogue Partner to sign the Treaty of Amity and Cooperation in Southeast Asia, negotiating the ASEAN-China FTA, and becoming ASEAN's first 'strategic partner'.

India's Role

The implosion of the Soviet Union and the end of the Cold War created the basis for New Delhi to embark on a Look East policy (LEP). The domestic economy, too, moved towards a new realism when India embraced economic liberalization in the 1990s to take advantage of the opportunities opening up in the global market place. The period since India adopted this new economic paradigm and the LEP has witnessed a substantial transformation of its global relations, including with the ASEAN, East Asia and Australasia. This shift has occurred primarily because of the recognition of India's increasing capacity to address its developmental challenges, and the potential of its US$1000-billion economy, growing currently at 9 per cent, to provide substantial commercial opportunities.

Goh Chok Tong, Singapore's former Prime Minister and now Senior Minister, once likened India and China to the two wings of ASEAN's fuselage. This metaphor will come true sooner, I think, than most people anticipate. By adding the Indian market to the already large Chinese, Japanese, Korean and

ASEAN markets, three billion people attract global attention and FDI. India adds a healthy and constructive element to the reform processes underway in Asia, and thus inspires laggards to take heed and join the competition or be left behind. The Asian boom has attracted investment, trade and tourism interest in the oil-rich Gulf states, and India is part of this Asian story. India is beginning to transit from being focused on South Asia and the West to looking more towards the East is thus, emerging as a more active regional player, interacting more with China, Japan and ASEAN.

A recent Goldman Sachs report projects that India's future potential or sustainable growth rate would be about 8 per cent per annum until 2020, driven by productivity growth in manufacturing and services. India is also well positioned to reap the benefits of favourable demographics, including an 'urbanization bonus' and a further rise in capital accumulation, in part from an upsurge in FDI. However, this potential will turn into reality only if the current risks to growth—political risk, including a rise in protectionism; supply-side constraints, including business climate, education and labour market reforms; and environmental degradation—are properly managed by the policy makers.

The EAS Process

The EAS, which was inaugurated in Malaysia in 2005, is very different from the original 1990 proposal for an East Asian Economic Caucus. That original proposal, dubbed a 'legendary caucus without Caucasians', was one that the US, Japan, Australia and other countries countered with a proposal for APEC. The EAS, with ASEAN in the driver's seat, includes the major powers and significant players that will determine East Asian outcomes in the coming decades, including China, Japan and India. Widening the original idea of an East Asian grouping by inviting India, Australia and New Zealand reflected realities on the ground: the presence of emerging patterns of trade, investment and diplomacy that are going to make a material difference to the lives and security of the people of this region. Attempts to relegate New Zealand, Australia and India to the level of second-tier countries, at the periphery of an EAS led by 'apparently' core countries; failed. This failure paved the way for the EAS to become an inclusive and, therefore, meaningful process.

The rationale of the EAS is interesting. In one view, Chinese perceptions of declining American power, caused by Washington being sucked into the 'war on terror', made Beijing see an opportunity to 'steer East Asian multilateralism' along the lines of the Shanghai Cooperation Organization, 'to serve Beijing's strategic goals and further weaken US influence in East Asia'. However, there are countries that 'remain wary of becoming divided into

Chinese and American blocs in East Asia' and their 'alarm prompted a campaign to include India, Australia and New Zealand and to ensure that ASEAN remained central to any future East Asian Community'.[5] Chinese sources, though, are at pains to emphasize that Beijing is not practising a 'Chinese Monroe Doctrine', with or without the 'Roosevelt Corollary', of seeking absolute influence over East Asia.[6] In any case, although Washington has not been invited to join the grouping, it is not without influence in it. Five of the democracies in the EAS—Australia, Japan, South Korea, Thailand and the Philippines—are treaty allies of the US; India and Singapore have strong defence relationships with Washington; and Canberra has declared that it will not sign anything that affects its defence relationship with Washington.

India's presence is not meant to contain China's influence—an impossible objective, in any case—but to include China and incorporate its legitimate interests in an organization that reflects the normative and practical goals of Asian multilateralism. India is being courted by great powers such as China, Russia, Japan, the EU and the US. One strong signal is the US-India civil nuclear cooperation and the US statement that Washington will help India to become a great power. Visits by Chinese leaders planned for 2007 also attest to rise in India's regional and global standing. Prime Minister Manmohan Singh's visit to japan in December 2006 was reciprocated by Prime Minister Abe's visit to Delhi in August 2007. Japan is increasingly courting India and the launch of negotiations on a bilateral FTA, is perceived by Tokyo as a means to balance China. However, all three countries have common economic imperatives to improve relations. So, could India act as bridge-builder between China and Japan? Is it possible to create a New Order that has room for all powers and may be based on concepts such as cooperative security?

The answer will turn at least partly on the way that two recent developments play out. The first is India's strategic dialogue with Japan, whose outlines became clearer when Indian Foreign Minister Pranab Mukherjee met his Japanese counterpart, Taro Aso. Press reports said that the meeting 'set out the roadmap for a new geopolitical alignment in Asia', with Japan's vision of an 'arc of freedom and prosperity' fitting neatly with India's vision of an 'arc of advantage and prosperity'.[7]

Conclusion

ASEAN has begun building an ASEAN Community. The vision is bold; the road is long and difficult. Its experience will be relevant and useful to the parallel efforts to build the EAC. However, there are many obstacles as a majority of ASEAN states are either least developed states or are trying to cope with serious socio-economic problems. They thus lack the capacity to engage in community building. ASEAN members will find these processes very demanding, as many are still re-building their economies and societies in the aftermath of the Asian Financial Crisis, and they have been gravely weakened. They are also trying to cope with the insistent demands of modernization, globalization and terrorism. Not all can cope with so many tough demands at the same time.

Economic changes within the Asean countries formed a push factor in favour of market liberalization. The influx of FDI into ASEAN consequently re-oriented their economies towards export of manufactured goods. This process created new economic elites and new sets of economic policies that favoured market liberalization. Two other push factors were the rise of competitors such as China and India, and globalization.

There is still much conceptual misunderstanding about the structures and processes involved. There are also misgivings about the roles and influence of the big powers, viz. Japan, China and India, and how the balancing of interests would be achieved. China and India along with Southeast Asia now constitute the new growth poles of Asia, also being one of the fastest growing regions in the world. Much cooperation, discussion and brainstorming is needed to clarify ideas and processes. It is clear that East Asian regionalism is here to stay. The EAS process provides for the involvement of the three great Asian powers, China, India and Japan in community building on a win-win basis and not on a zero-sum basis. Much depends on the willingness of ASEAN to be the driver of the process and to provide a neutral venue.

Endnotes

1 See Amitav Acharya (2001) *Constructing a Security Community in Southeast Asia: Asean and the Problem of Regional Order,* (London Routledge: and 2000) *The Quest for Identity: International Relations of Southeast Asia,* Oxford:OUP.

2 The GATS is the service element of the WTO. The agreement which came into force in 1995 is negotiated by the government themselves and consists of multilateral rules covering international trade in services.

3 This sort of preferential treatment in services trade among regional groupings is permitted under WTO rules, provided that the agreement covers 'substantially all' sectors, and eliminates discrimination among members to a substantial extent as well.

4 The theme of the ASEAN Customs Vision 2020 is: *An ASEAN customs partnership for world class standards and excellence in efficiency, professionalism and service and uniformity through harmonized procedures, to promote trade and investment and to protect the health and well-being of the ASEAN Community*. See Joint Press Statement on the Fifth ASEAN. Brunei Darussalam, 22-23 May 1997 (www.aseansec.org)

[5] Malik Mohan, 'The East Asia Summit: More Discord than Accord', *YaleGlobal*, 20 December, (yaleglobal.yale.edu/display.article?id=6645)

[6] Suryanarayana, P.S. 2005 'Political haze over East Asia vision', *The Hindu*, 20 December.

[7] Bagchi, Indrani, 2007 'India-Japan Strategic Talks Begin', *Times of India*, 23 March.

6

Japan and an Asian Economic Community

Masanori Kondo

Introduction

This chapter examines the Japanese trade policy, focusing its recent development in free trade agreement (FTA) and its relationship with India as well as China. It also examines the role of Japan in building an Asian Economic Community (AEC), which includes India. First, it reviews the status of Japanese FTAs with other countries. Japanese FTAs are already in place with Singapore and Mexico, and some more negotiations are underway with various Asian countries. This chapter also compares the Japan-Korea-China economic bloc with other economic blocs. Lastly, it examines the future prospects for JACIK (Japan, ASEAN, China, India and Korea), presenting some examples of such attempts, like the Japanese investment into India via Singapore, or Indian investment into China via Singapore to explore the Japanese market.

Japan's Bilateral Trade Negotiations in Asia

Economic Partnership Agreements (EPAs) have become extremely important for Japanese policy makers in the past few years. Looking for greater progress beyond a mere FTA, the Japanese government has been actively negotiating EPAs with other countries. There are several reasons why Japan prefers an EPA over an FTA. As pointed out by Kinoshita (2005a), FTAs can help economic development but cannot solve income disparity problems. Proactive steps to correct such discrepancies are necessary for further economic integration. Recognizing this important fact, the Japanese government has proposed EPAs rather than FTAs to its neighbouring countries.

Few question the importance of successful negotiations of FTAs and EPAs by Japan with its Asian neighbours. Asia is not only the region that accounts for the greatest percentage of Japanese exports of goods and services, but it also has the highest tariff rates across regions where Japanese companies do business. Therefore, it is reasonable to conclude that successful Asian FTAs and EPAs have the greatest potential to boost Japanese exports and strengthen Japan's overall economy.

In the past few years, quite a few EPAs have been under negotiation between Japan and other Asian countries. This reflects increased momentum for regional integration in Asia. So far, an EPA with Singapore is being implemented, and an EPA with Mexico has finished the negotiation stages. Besides, the negotiations for EPAs with Malaysia, Philippines and Thailand have been completed in principle. While there is some more way to go for Korea and ASEAN, joint study or negotiating groups have been set up for India, Indonesia and Australia. The following is an overview of Japanese EPAs with Asian nations.

Singapore: Singapore and Japan's close political and economic ties made them a near perfect match for an early FTA. Since the early 1970s, Japan has consistently been one of Singapore's top three trade partners and the number one investor country. Out of nearly 5000 multinational corporations (MNCs) operating in Singapore, over 1700 are Japanese firms. Since 2000, the amount of Japanese investment has topped US$14 billion. As stated earlier, Singapore was the first country with which Japan singed an EPA. Because the two economies were already liberally open to trade in most products, the FTA concentrated mostly on investment and opening up of sectors such as service, finance, information technology, and transportation. The fact that Singapore does not export agricultural commodities, allowed Japan to dodge its most sensitive trade issue and gain easy internal support for the agreement.

Philippines: Japan reached an agreement in principle on the major elements of an EPA with the Philippines in November 2004. It dealt mainly with the areas of industry, agriculture and services. One of the major issues on the admittance of Philippine workers into Japan was the reason for several road blocks in the negotiation process. While the Philippine Government desired an increase in the admittance of lawyers, health workers and nurses, Japan was extremely reluctant towards any kind of fast increase in foreign workers, especially, nurses and health care workers. It was agreed that Philippine nurses would have to pass the Japanese language examination. While the numerical quota or goal on how many nurses were to be admitted was not initially identified, it would be included in ongoing negotiations. However, for the first year, one hundred nurses will be sent to Japan.

Malaysia: The two governments confirmed the agreement in principle on major elements of the Japan-Malaysia EPA negotiations at the EAS held in Kuala Lumpur in December 2005. Though lowering of tariffs with regard to steel, automobiles, and plywood were the most difficult points in the negotiating process, an agreement has been reached that targets a 10-year plan for the gradual phase-out of Malaysian tariffs on Japanese exports in the steel and automobile sectors.

Thailand: In principal, an agreement has been made between the two countries. Trade matters relating to agriculture were agreed on first, and then issues relating to steel, auto parts, services and investments were discussed. After the progress made on industrial goods in June 2005, a general agreement was reached in September 2005. Thailand's extremely high automobile tariff of 80 per cent will be gradually lowered by 5 per cent each year for cars above 3000cc until it reaches 60 per cent in 2010. It was agreed at the time that the Japanese and Thai governments will then renegotiate how the further liberalization of automobiles should proceed. The Japanese government has expressed a desire for the total elimination of automobile tariffs in 2010. Thailand will gain an elimination of tariffs for vegetables, fruits, cooked chicken, processed shrimp, textiles, and jewelry exports to Japan.

Korea: Japan is actively working for an FTA negotiation as per the Japanese view point, but the Korean government has not been very keen to enhance the policy dialogue. Six meetings have already been held, however, and a major part of the negotiations is expected to be completed soon. An FTA with Korea would be a great boon to Japanese exports, especially with respect to auto parts and industrial machinery sectors. However, the talks are threatened to be stalled by the South Korean Government's strong request to exempt automobiles from the tariff cuts—currently at 8 per cent. South Korea fears an influx of Japanese cars would cause great damage to its domestic automobile industry.

Indonesia: A joint group was set up to study the impact of FTA/EPA, similar to the Joint Study Group between India and Japan. The first round of negotiations has started, and subsequent rounds are to continue every two months. Currently, the framework for the negotiations is nearly complete, and both sides expect to be able to start substantive talks soon on various areas including market access, investment, trade in services, personnel transfer, energy and bilateral economic cooperation. Japan is seen to be particularly interested in the development of energy resources in order to gain access to the much-coveted Indonesian oil deposits. Both sides have expressed a strong desire to complete a deal within two years.

ASEAN: The first meeting among all the countries was held in Tokyo in April 2005. There were several points of contention, especially with regard to how an FTA with ASEAN would be related to bilateral FTA negotiations and how the rules of origin would be defined. When the two sides met for a ministerial meeting in September 2005, there was no leeway on either side to overcome these issues. The representatives from ASEAN strongly lobbied with Japan to drop its plans to start concrete trade negotiations for a broad ASEAN agreement until all the individual bilateral FTAs have been concluded. The ASEAN ministers also expressed their disappointment at the slow pace and lack of progress in the meetings with Japan.

Meanwhile, Japan has started independent bilateral negotiations with Cambodia, Laos, Myanmar, Vietnam, and Brunei, and plans to eventually link them together into one larger ASEAN FTA. The two sides have agreed to full trade liberalization by 2012, which is behind the China-ASEAN agreement for 2010 and the South Korea-ASEAN agreement set for 2009.

India: A joint study group to assess the prospects and impacts of EPA was set up and upon its successful conclusion and adoption of its report by the two Prime Ministers in December 2006 in Tokyo, the CEPA negotiations were launched. The two sides have spoken positively about the possibility of an FTA. It is likely that an India-Japan EPA will boost Japan's direct investment in India. On the trade front, export of Indian mangoes has been one of the main issues. The double-taxation issue for Indian software exports to Japan will be settled soon. Japan has also proposed a US$ 90 billion Delhi-Mumbai Dedicated Freight and Industrial Corridor during the visit of Prime Minister Abe to New Delhi in August 2007.

Australia: A feasibility study on the impact of FTA/EPA has been initiated, where Japan has finally agreed to a study that includes agriculture. Japan's growing interest towards Australia for importing natural resources could help move the process along. However, Australia's large agricultural sector and its desire to gain further entrance to Japan's market will almost certainly prove to be a difficult, sticky point to overcome. Japanese agriculture industry also fears that countries such as Canada may follow, if Japan imports more agricultural commodities from Australia under the FTA.

China: China is Japan's most important economic partner in Asia. According to a 2005 Mizuho Research Institute study, 37.5 per cent of the Japanese companies that were surveyed, chose China as the most desirable FTA partner, followed by the United States (18.7 per cent). China also appears to be showing a great deal of interest for an FTA with Japan in order to boost its exports. The Japanese market is seen as having great potential for Chinese agricultural exports. However, pressure from Japanese agriculture as well as Chinese high-tech firms, fearing competition, makes progress towards an FTA politically very difficult. Questions concerning faithful compliance from the Chinese government in regard to intellectual property and service sector commitments are also an issue.

While the Japanese corporate climate, especially the manufacturing industry, for the most part appears eager and ready for an FTA with China, there are still many forces at work that prevent Japan from moving forward on negotiations. The first of such factors is Japan's desire not to even begin talks about an FTA with China until the tri-lateral investment treaty including South Korea is successfully concluded. This treaty is set to replace bilateral investing treaties that are currently operational between the three countries.

Another potential problem relates to Japanese resistance to a potential flood of Chinese agricultural products into its market. While many experts point out that increasing demand for agricultural products within China and the advantage of high quality Japanese food products such as rice would offset much of the pain from liberalization, there still remains a great deal of fear in this area. The Japanese Government must also undertake more research into what possibilities a China FTA would entail. There is also a great deal of discussion on how to deal with China's intellectual property problems and WTO commitments, and whether issues such as these should be tethered to bilateral free trade negotiations. Lastly, the recent icy political relationship between Japan and China has not helped to encourage a spirit of cooperation.

Taiwan: The economic relationship between Japan and Taiwan is strong, especially in the electronics industry. Because Taiwan is treated as a separate economic entity, an FTA would have to take place separately from any negotiation with Bejing. However, given the fact that Taiwan already has very low tariffs on Japanese exports, there is little motivation for an FTA between the two countries.

Sino-India-Japanese Relations

Developments towards a Change in the Sino-Japan Relationship

The compatible aspects of the Chinese and Japanese economies have resulted in an explosive growth of trade and investment between the two countries. Given the factors of Japan excelling in high-level technology research and development and having the world's second largest consumer market, and China being a geographically close haven of inexpensive labour as well as its possibility for becoming a desirable consumer market in the future, Sino-Japan trade and investment have continued to develop to the point where China has surpassed the US in becoming Japan's number one trading partner. In 2004, the trade between Japan and China increased by 25.7 per cent to become almost US$167.9 billion. There are 9.2 million Chinese workers employed in Japanese factories within China, and taxes paid by Japanese companies comprise 9.1 per cent (US$5.9 billon) of all of the total tax revenue from foreign firms operating in China. With both economies expected to grow at substantial rates in the upcoming years, this economic relationship is expected by many economic experts to grow and develop further.

However, despite these close economic ties, recent political relations between the two countries have been deteriorating at a rapid pace. China is increasingly being viewed as becoming more aggressive in asserting its authority in East Asia, causing concern among many Japanese and others because of its more aggressive stance towards Taiwan with its recent "anti-secession law" that confirms China's right to use "non-peaceful means" to reunite Taiwan with the mainland. In 2005, China participated in a joint military exercise with Russia, and one of the exercises involved using an amphibious assault in order to take island territory. Many consider this to be a warning to Taiwan.

China has been seen as using its new found political influence in East Asia to oppose Japan's bid to become a permanent member of the United Nations Security Council. There are also several territorial disputes between Japan and China, including the Senkaku Island Chain located south of Japan's Okinawah as well as a disputed deep sea oil field, which lies in an overlapping area of Japan and China's exclusive economic sea zones. Japan accuses China of being an unfaithful negotiating partner by not suspending exploration and development of the zone, while it continues to send military naval units into the disputed area. China has criticized Japan's negotiation of development rights of the underwater oil field to several Japanese energy companies.

There is also the long standing historical Sino-Japanese dispute, specifically concerning Japan's past military actions in Asia. China has decried the Tokyo Board of Education's recent authorization of new textbooks which gloss over Japan's wartime aggression over China (along with South Korea). China has also strongly protested Japanese Prime Minister Junichiro Koizumi's repeated pilgrimages to Yasukuni Shrine, where several class A war criminals were buried. The most recent visit took place in October 2005, shortly after Koizumi's party won a heavy victory in the September 2005 parliamentary election. Koizumi claims the visits are personal in nature and has made several statements in his trips to Asia stating condolences and regret over Japan's past actions.

With the Japanese population observing a large amount of media coverage of recent anti-Japanese riots in China, more and more of the Japanese people are beginning to see China less positively and the number of those who consider China a trustworthy partner in international affairs has decreased rapidly, especially in the past years. The combination of these factors and others is prompting the Japanese leadership to seek new ways to deal with its growing rivalry with China. Quite a few Japanese argue that one of these is to seek a new economic and political partnership with India.

Indo-Japanese Relations: New Possibilities and Challenges

In April 2005, two weeks after Chinese Prime Minister Wen Jiabao took part in a historical China-India Summit in New Delhi, Japanese Prime Minister Junichiro Koizumi also visited Inddia and met many government officials, where he made the statement: 'We are now in an era in which Asia is currently experiencing a process of transformation and India, too, is changing, thus elevating the importance even further of India and Japan cooperating as true global partners.' Japan and India are also currently cooperating towards United Nations Security Council reform, in which both are attempting to gain permanent Security Council positions.

While there seems to be much promise in the political realm as Japan eagerly desires to counterbalance China's growing influence and India seeks to grow in diplomatic influence as well, the economic relationship between the two countries is still quite underdeveloped. Indo-Japanese trade remained stagnant at around US$4-5 billion per annum for the past decade. Many Japanese companies do not find India a very attractive investment location and Japanese average annual direct investment into India has been only around US$200 million. Overall, both in terms of trade and investment, the volume of the Japanese economic relationship with India is merely 3 per cent of that with

China. Some of the reasons attributed for the same by the Japanese include: the lack of investment in India, such as poor infrastructure, pro-labour laws, intellectual property problems and cultural differences.

While Japanese business remains stagnant in India, Korean firms have been investing heavily in India, and companies such as LG, Samsung and Hyundai have succeeded in capturing a large market share in India. More recently, Sino-Indian trade and investment have seen explosive growth. In 2004-05, China became India's second largest trade partner and market for Indian products. China is a major importer of Indian iron ore, textiles, plastics, steel and chemicals. For India, trade with China is seen as a vital catalyst for growth.

Koizumi and other Japanese officials have made statements that Indo-Japan trade can easily be increased to US$10 billion within three years, and more Japanese companies are taking a second look at investment opportunities in India. While there are some positive indicators, many remain skeptical that Japan can create an economic relationship with India that rivals China. A big question mark remains whether Japanese political ambitions can prompt a cautious business community into strengthening its position in India.

JACIK (ASEAN+4)

While many Japanese experts see the future of Asian economic integration as ASEAN+3 (ASEAN along with Japan, South Korea and China), the growing economic presence of India cannot be ignored. For the past 15 years, India has continued to grow at an astonishing rate of 6 to 8 per cent per annum, and its extremely large population is predicted to increase its average consumption per capita by a multiple of 2.6 before 2020. The International Energy Agency (IEA) also predicts that India will become the greatest consumer of energy in Asia by 2020.

India is starting to look eastward with regard to forging new economic partners. As stated above, India has recently made great strides to increase trade and investment with China and Korea. Korean companies such as LG, Samsung and Hyundai have been extremely successful in India. India-ASEAN trade has also been booming. With India's growing political and economic importance in Asia, it would be a grave mistake to attempt to exclude India from any plans for Asian economic integration. It should only be a matter of time before the idea of 'ASEAN+4' is realized by the major players in the Asian economy.

Japan's Roles for Future Integration of JACIK

JACIK as a New AEC

In the past decade, ASEAN has been struggling to compete with China in its export market, especially as compared to the US or Europe. Although the Chinese currency was devalued, it is still not enough to allow ASEAN to compete with China. Meanwhile, trade between ASEAN and India has also surged, and Indian policy makers have been shifting their focus more towards East Asia. Under the circumstances, it is not surprising that India has been added to ASEAN+3.

Among ASEAN countries, Singapore seems to be particularly active towards working for JACIK, trying to balance the two Asian superpowers. The importance of India for Singapore (and vice versa) can be confirmed by the recent Comprehensive Economic Cooperation Agreement (CECA). Under the agreement, Singapore intends to be a hub for a third party country, such as Japan for investment in India. Already, several MNCs are considering investment in India via Singapore.

Motives and Strategies

While Singapore is actively working for JACIK, the motivation to promote JACIK for Japan is somehow more political and less economic than for JCK. In Japan, many people want to include India in the EAC as it can be a counterbalance to China. However, with the improvement of India-China economic relationship, this is less important for India. As we have seen in JCK, market forces will be more important than political considerations. Some people are afraid that with so many countries very little may be decided by JACIK.

Many Japanese consider ASEAN as an Asian partner for economic reasons, but India for political reasons. However, if Japan thinks India is more important in its business, this can be a strong driving force for JACIK, as Japan already has close ties with ASEAN+3. Japan can play a leading role to combine China, Korea, ASEAN and India, rather than considering only China, Korea and ASEAN as its economic partners.

Since it is an economic matter, the main driving force will be Japanese companies, rather than the government, as has been the case in ASEAN. One good example is Toyota, which has decided to make its Indian plants a global export base of transmission to its factories in other Asian countries. Another good example is Canon, which invested in India not from Japan but from its subsidiary in Singapore. The CECA between India and Singapore will also bring more Japanese investment in India via Singapore. The other example is that of TCS, the leading Indian IT firm, which invested in China via Singapore, partly considering working from China into the Japanese market. In its China office, a Korean engineer who speaks Japanese is employed, and this is a good example of JACIK cooperation. The other examples are Sony and Daikin, both exporting their products from Thailand to India.

Conclusions

The key role that Japan can play for Asian economic integration is clear: it is to integrate ASEAN+3 and India through trade and investment. Until recently, many Japanese companies were only comfortable manufacturing in ASEAN and China to export back to Japan. Conversely, not many Japanese companies have made serious efforts to do business with India. Many Japanese still look at Asian economic integration only as the relationship among ASEAN, Japan, China and South Korea. However, as detailed in Kumar (2004) and Brooks et al. (2005), it is quite clear that if India is included in the Asian economic integration, Japan will gain large economic benefits.

Further, an important factor that will increase the economic importance of India is its labour supply. In the near future starting with Japan, many of the countries in East Asia are anticipated to experience economic effects from declining birthrates and an ageing society. Yet, much more important than the massive numbers of workers in India is the increase of skilled technicians and managers. American firms have done well to tap this resource, and as a result, the country has seen a large measure of success in fields such as IT. As other countries in Asia begin to face labour shortages, the labour pool in India will become indispensable in supporting the continuing economic growth in Asia.

Whether or not Japan can contribute to the momentum of economic integration among India and other East Asian countries is a deciding factor in whether Japan can maintain its place as a world economic power. As shown in this chapter, Toyota, Canon and Sony understand this important trend. While India is often seen in Japan as a country where it is difficult to do business, the 'East looking' India is seen very differently by other Asian countries. Whether Japan can make positive advancements towards the development of JACIK will be the key not only for its East Asian strategy, but also for its global strategy. The expectations for Japan's economic contributions towards Asia remain very high.

References

Brooks, Douglas, David Roland-Holst, and Fan Zhai. 2005. 'Asia's Long-term Growth and Integration: Reaching beyond Trade Policy Barriers' (ADB Policy Brief No.38.
http://www.adb.org/Documents/EDRC/Policy_Briefs/PB038.pdf

Japanese Ministry of Economy. 2005. Trade and Industry 'Japan's Policy on EPAs/FTAs'.
http://www.meti.go.jp/english/information/downloadfiles/FTAprogress200503.pdf.

Japanese Ministry of Foreign Affairs (homepage):
http://www.mofa.go.jp/mofaj/area/singapore/kyotei/pdfs/honbun.pdf.
http://www.mofa.go.jp/region/asia-paci/philippine/joint0411.html.
h*ttp://www.mofa.go.jp/region/asia-paci/malaysia/joint0505.html.*
http://www.mofa.go.jp/region/asia-paci/thailand/joint0509/index.html.

Kinoshita, Toshihiko, (2005a) 'Economic Integration in East Asia and Japan's Role' (Conference Paper, Washington DC: January). *http://www.glocom.org/opinions/essays/20050131_kinoshita_economic/index.html.*

____________. (2005b) 'Regional Economic Grouping in Asia: Opportunities and Challenges' (Conference Paper, New Delhi: March)
http://homepage3.nifty.com/tkinoshita/research/pdf/2005/050316e.pdf.

Kondo, Masanori. (2005) 'Why has Some MNCs Are More Successful Than Others?' (Paper Presented at India-Japan Joint Study Group Meeting).

Kumar, Nagesh (2004) *Towards an Asian Economic Community: Vision of a New Asia*. New Delhi: RIS and Singapore: ISEAS.

__________ (2002) *Globalization and the Quality of Foreign Direct Investment*. New Delhi: Oxford University Press.

Saxena, Sweta Chaman. (2003). 'Trade Complementarities and Potential for a Single Currency in JACIK', New Delhi: RIS.

7

China's Role in the Asian Economic Integration Process

Yao Chaocheng

The Emerging Asian Economic Integration Process

Asia has 49 nations and regions, with a population of 3.513 billion and a territory of 44 million square km, taking 60 per cent and 29.4 per cent of the world total, respectively. The rapid economic growth rate of 7 per cent, in recent years, in the Asian region has laid a solid material foundation for pan-Asian regional cooperation.

China and the ASEAN signed a free trade area (FTA) agreement in November 2002 to establish a free trade zone by 2010. This future free trade zone comprising 10 ASEAN countries and China (referred to as ASEAN+1) will be the third largest in the world with 1.7 billion consumers and a trade volume of $1.2 trillion annually, next only to the NAFTA and the EU. On 7 October 2003, China, Japan, Korea and the ASEAN also agreed on a plan of setting up a bigger free trade zone by 2020, embracing the region currently referred to as the ASEAN+3.[2]

India, the largest economy in South Asia, is also actively taking steps to join East Asia's economic integration movement. In September 2003, a free trade plan (including 2.5 billion consumers and comprising 75 per cent of the total Asian population) was reached by the ASEAN, China, Japan and India, at Jakarta in (Indonesia). It is reported that the plan shall be gradually implemented between 2012 and 2017.[3] It is quite likely that the set-up will evolve into ASEAN+4 (ASEAN and China, Japan, Korea and India).

Also, on 23-24 December 2003, members of the Expert Committee of the SAARC held a meeting in New Delhi, India, for a final assessment and approval at of the proposed programme of setting up a South Asia Free Trade Zone.

In addition, it is expected that Asia will witness more bilateral FTAs leading up to various other larger regional agreements. The Bangkok Agreement is another notable regional trade arrangement in Asia that includes six countries: three from East Asia (China, Korea and Laos) and three from South Asia (India, Bangladesh and Sri Lanka). The significance of the agreement lies in the fact that it might serve as a platform to link Eastern Asia and South Asia into a broader regional trade agreement.[4]

In December 2005, in Kuala Lumpur, Malaysia, two non-Asian nations, Australia and New Zealand, were invited to participate in the East Asia Summit (EAS), showing a larger scale economic cooperation scheme in an idea of open regionalism.

The Asian Development Bank plans to launch an Asian Currency Unit (ACU), a weighted index of a basket of Asian currencies as a benchmark to monitor moves in the values of currencies in the region, according to a senior bank official, Masahiro Kawai, economic adviser to ADB President Haruhiko Kuroda.

The above facts show that Asian nations have already entered the primary stage of economic unification. Chapter VIII of the Charter of United Nations also encourages regional, social and economic cooperation. The UN has set up the Economic and Social Commission for Asia and the Pacific (UNESCAP), the main function of which is to promote economic and social development through regional and sub-regional cooperation and integration. The ASEAN is playing an important role as the centre axle of the Asian economic unification process with its well-developed political and market mechanisms.

The ongoing regional economic unification shall make Asia the fulcrum of economic activity in the world and contribute substantially to global security in the 21st century. Even though Asia is too large and beset with complicated differences in terms of culture, political systems, economic strengths, as well as religious diversity, the continent's nations can cooperate with each other by developing a consensus on the basis of mutual respect towards the existing differences. Also, the maximum danger will not be from the 'fault-lines', but from the ignorance of the policy makers who are not working positively on the issue.

The Rise of China

In the 21st century, three trends are clearly visible: shifting population and economic centres; pervasion of advanced production methodology and political and social structures; and the changing international political order. These three trends reveal that a few non-Western nations might be emerging as world superpowers. Amongst these, China has the maximum potential.

A report by the UN Trade and Development Council, *The World Economic Situation and Prospect in 2003*, commented: 'Twenty five years ago, China cautiously and firmly had taken steps on the new long march of opening and reform. Today, China has replaced the US and Japan in Asia becoming the locomotive of Asian economy'.

The outcome of China's opening and reform, an economic miracle greater than the one achieved by the 'Four Dragons', has drawn the attention of the world. In his book, *Will China Be Number 1?* (May 2002), Paul Bracken, an American professor from the Yale Business School, reminisces, 'Five hundred years ago, China was the world's sole superpower. When many Europeans were living in mud huts and scratching the soil with sticks, China was the greatest economic and military power on earth. Now, with a growing economy and a young population, the nation is again rising to superpower status—with the US as nemesis'.

Another American scholar, Angus Maddison, in his book *Reviewing the World for 200 Years*, elaborates that in the year of 1820, China's GDP was the highest, followed by India, France, and UK. Due to well-known historical reasons, China lagged behind in the following centuries. US GDP took the world leading position only in 1895 when China lost Taiwan in the Jiawu War with Japan. Japan's GDP overtook China and became the second largest in the world, as late as 1968 when China was plunged into the 'Cultural Revolution'. China's pragmatic opening up and policy reforms since 1978 has made its economy recover quickly.

Maddison also predicted that assuming China's growth rate persists at 7 per cent and of the US at 3 per cent, China would once again be the largest economy in the world by the year 2020, based on calculations made through purchase power parity (PPP) method. China has not yet agreed to the PPP calculation. According to China's own calculation, it is currently the sixth largest economic power in the world and by 2020 it will be one of the three biggest economies in the world with its GDP doubled to US$4 trillion.[5]

Since 1985, China's GDP has been growing annually by 9.7 per cent on an average and reached US$1 trillion in 2003, becoming the second largest in

Asia. It can be extrapolated that within 15 years China's GDP will overtake Japan and by the middle of the 21st century, it will match that of USA, assuming the similar growth rates persist as the following calculation shows, assuming growth rates of 7.5 per cent for China, 2.5 per cent for Japan and 3 per cent for the US.

Table 7.1: China's Economy in 2050

	2001	2025	2030	2040	2050	
China	1000	5672	**8114**	16785	**34595**	(in billion USD)
Japan	3881	7019		**7942**		
USA	8000	16262	16749	25336	**34049**	(in billion USD)

In his book, *Reoriented: Economic Globalization in Asian Age*, Professor Andre Gunder Frank, points out, "The center of the world economy is once again moving to the Middle Kingdom of China."

It is not for the first time that the world is facing a rising nation. However, a rising China should be different. The US had a population of only about 30-40 million and Japan of 100 million when they rose to power. China, on the other hand, has a population of 1.3 billion. It is indeed the first time that the world is witnessing such a populous nation rising.

China's Role in Asian Economic Unification

Being a beneficiary of economic globalization, China took the strategic decision to deepen domestic economic reforms, to open further to the world and to positively participate in the Asian economic unification process. On 8 October 2003, China formally signed the ASEAN Treaty of Amity of Cooperation (TAC) becoming the first member nation outside Southeast Asia. China has played leading roles in the FTA programmes of ASEAN+1 and ASEAN+3. Meanwhile, China is also negotiating FTAs with Thailand, Malaysia and Philippines. The FTA plan with India is under study. In October 2003, China also put forward a four-points proposal in the meeting of ASEAN+3 to deepen economic cooperation in eastern Asia, viz. doing a feasibility study on the Eastern Asian Free Trade Zone; boosting cooperation in financial and monetary sectors; setting up 'Asian Bonds Market'; strengthening political and security cooperation; and expanding the social, cultural and technological cooperation.

In the year 2002, trade volume between China and 26 Asian nations increased by 21.59 per cent. The exports and imports increased by 16.74 per cent and 25.81 per cent, respectively. In the last two years, while the world economy was in recession and the markets of US, Europe as well as Japan were hardly expanding, China's trade volume, particularly the imports from neighbouring countries increased by two digits, pulling up the overall Asian economic growth. In the first half of 2003, China's imports from Northeast Asia, Southeast Asia and South Asia increased respectively by 48.5 per cent, 55.7 per cent and 81.9 per cent with a total volume of US$128.6 billion. More than 60 per cent of the total increased import volume of China, worth US$160 billion, was from the Asia-Pacific nations in 2003. It is estimated that by the year 2020, China's total volume of import and export will increase to 2 US$ trillion annually. In such a scenario, China will become a larger market for other Asian nations.

So far, there are about 30,000 Chinese companies conducting multinational business operations worldwide. Asia will be their first choice for doing direct investments.[6]

The 'ASEAN+1' and 'ASEAN+3' free trade zone plans reflect the deepening interdependence among the economies of East Asia. In 2003, internal trade volumes in East Asia were much higher than those with the US. Huge favourable balances were achieved by ASEAN, Japan and Korea while trading with China. The Sino-Japanese trade volume reached US$ 133.58 billion with an increase of 31.1 per cent from 2002 to 2003. Japan also became the largest trading partner of China. In 2003, 18 per cent of the increase in global trade volume was attributed to China's strong economic growth. The percentage further grew in 2006 as China's total foreign trade volume was estimated to increase by 23.8 per cent up to US$1.76 trillion.[7]

In October 2004, China increased the bank annual interest rates by 0.27 per cent. The slight increase has created 'shocks' for the world and the Asian regional economies, as commented by *Financial Times* on the following day. In the past, the US economy directly influenced the world economy and a slow-down of the US economy used to greatly impact and even constrain the Chinese economy. However, today, it is the other way round.

China's trade with another Asian giant, India, is progressing strongly. The bilateral trade has climbed from virtually nothing, a decade ago, to US$25 billion today.[8] Comparing with trade volumes between China-Japan and China-Korea, the Sino-Indian trade has much room for exploration in the new century since the two nations complement each other in many fields. Both China and India are positive toward. Asian economic unification.The cooperation and coordination between China and India is vital to the Asian economic unification process—these two fast growing nations largely comprise the 'fourth engine' in the world economy.

Some Chinese economists are proposing to gradually build a Great China Free Trade Zone (including Mainland China, Taiwan, Hong Kong and Macao). If realized, the free trade zone will have a GDP of US$1.5 trillion, fourth largest economic capacity in the world, overall trade volume of US$1 trillion, 8.3 per cent of the world total, and a total foreign exchange reserve of US$330.3 billion surpassing that of Japan to become the highest in the world.

The European unification process exemplified that the Germany-France axle propelled the regional unification process. The US is the natural leader in the region of NAFTA. In the Asian economic unification process, there is also a need for leadership by strong nations. Could a rising China play this role?

China has been re-positioning itself as an equal partner in regional and international cooperation substituting the erstwhile Cold War position as the leader of the third world. Under the new policy, China is trying to act as a promoter in the regional unification process, and not a leader, accepting the ASEAN as the centre of the regional cooperation structure. China has realized that pursuing equal partnership is the best way for it to gain the respect of other Asian nations. China's rise will also have an impact upon the geo-political power structure of the world. China has long pursued a policy that opposes hegemonies and favours a multi-polar world. As the only permanent member of the UN Security Council from Asia, and with growing economic capacity and stronger regional and global influence, China—coordinating with other Asian partners— will certainly be more active on the international political stage to protect Asian interests and to contribute to world peace and justice.

However, to be able to play a leading role in Asian economic unification, China still needs the following: a tangible force big enough to influence the regional economy; a larger economic scale; an adequately open market; a freely convertible currency; a sufficient amount of capital reserve to be used for overseas investment; and cultural and political civilizations that match up to the current international standards. Not having been endowed these, China's influence on Asia and the world is still limited. Therefore, the middle solution is that China stick to its existing policy of concentrating on domestic political and economic affairs and in the mean time promote regional social and economic cooperation in Asia through collective leadership instead of seeking sole leadership.

Learning from Europe, China should try to improve its relationship with the other two big Asian nations, that is, Japan and India with more tolerance and magnanimity. Japan is the second largest economic power in the world and the largest regional economic power in Asia with a GDP of US$5 trillion (five times that of China). India is also the largest economic power in South Asia and the second largest nation in Asia, economically growing almost as fast as China, in recent years. China and India include almost half of the world population and have the largest markets in the world. If these three nations could get rid of the historical resentments and unite as Germany and France did, the Asian economic unification process will achieve velocity and gravity.

The China Threat

A rising China inevitably makes its neighbours psychologically worried. Besides, China is regarded as a challenge to the traditional strategic position of the US in Asia. Some Asian nations also fear that China will rise to become an intimidating superpower and a challenging force to the international order.

Looking back at the long history of China, it has nearly no records of any military expansion. The only military expansion took place under the Yuan Dynasty (1206-59 AD), which was launched by the Mongolian heroes Genghis Khan, and his grandson, Kublai Khan (founder of the Yuan Dynasty). In fact, under the Ming Dynasty, Zheng He, the Chinese government delegate, had even travelled around seven times (1405-1433 AD), to Southeast Asia spreading Chinese culture and native products without any wars or colonialism.[10] The wars in 1950s between China and India along the border and between China and Vietnam in 1970s resulted mainly from ideological differences.

China's near-contemporary history, as a matter of fact, is full of sufferings from foreign invasions and humiliations. For a long time, China had been a semi-colony under the invasive occupation of imperialism. In fact, China will not opt for military expansion, having lived through the anguish caused by foreign invasions. For example, China did not use military might to liberate Taiwan though it possesses the capacity. If the threat should ever occur, it would be the normal outcome of market competition. While pursuing the process of national economic development, it is normal that there will be competition between China and other Asian nations over markets and natural resources. Conflicts and disputes may arise. The key point is how the concerned politicians use their intelligence and consciousness to transcend and repair the 'fault lines' and resolve the conflicts and disputes within the framework of WTO and international laws.

As early as 1954, China and India put forward a proposal known as the Five Principles of Peaceful Coexistence which are still of great significance to international cooperation among the Asian nations and regions. On 4 March 2004, China's premier Wen Jiabao stressed again in Beijing, 'China's rise should not be a threat to anyone. No nations will be sacrificed due to the rise. China does not and will never seek to be a superpower.'

It seems that China's growing economic capacity serves as the justification for the contention about the 'China Threat'. However, that is not the case. China is facing many internal and external problems, especially internal ones, such as the high cost of economic growth, the big disparity between the eastern and western regions, inefficiency of the state-owned enterprises, a large number of unemployed and laid-off workers, the delayed reform of the political system, environmental problems, energy shortage, etc. All of these put a limit to China's economic development.

Even if the Chinese GDP overtakes that of the US in mid-21st century, it would not qualify China as a world leader. For instance, Japan's GDP per capita was once higher than US, yet it did not mean that Japan was powerful enough to lead the world. Therefore, China's rise would have to rely not only on economic growth, but also on the support of the forces of modern civilization and culture complying with common international values so as to win the respect of other Asian nations. The new ideology of the 'Building a Harmonized Society'[11] put forward by the new generation of China's political leaders shows that China wishes to make progress on civilization and culture.

Obviously, China has its own interests in promoting and participating in Asian regional economic unification. FDI has played an important role in China's economic development. China's foreign trade dependence rate is increasing every year, reaching 47 per cent in 2003, it is predicted to become 65-70 per cent in the next five years. The Chinese economy has become an inseparable part of the world economy.

Ideological differences may cause disputes or conflicts among Asian nations. However, the nations, including China, seeking higher social and economic efficiency by participating in regional economic unification will have to conform to international norms and standards. The process of Asian economic unification will no doubt accelerate China's political reform and its move towards democracy. This will certainly help the nation to become a strong and solid pier of world peace instead of becoming a challenging force to the international order.

Conclusion

Asian economic unification is indeed taking shape. In the course of the process of unification, disputes and conflicts, with clashing economic interests, will occur amongst Asian nations. However, the unification may provide a dynamic platform for democratic exchange and peaceful negotiations within the framework of international laws for the common good. National interests can find a higher gratification and fulfillment in international coordination and cooperation and can increase synergetic efficiency of all Asian nations. The collective leadership of the Asian economic cooperation scheme and a policy of 'open regionalism' shall certainly help to reduce China's influence in the unification process.

The regional economic unification process in Asia as a part of economic globalization shall no doubt produce a pan-Asian economic community. Asians shall have their own unified currency in the future, perhaps in 50 years time or longer, as experienced by the Europeans.

Of course, China's role in Asian economic unification can never be neglected. Not only will it greatly influence the unification process, but will also impact the whole world. As a philosopher said, 'Only when you have changed yourself, can you change others'—the impact of a rising China on Asia and the world either positive or negative, shall finally lie in the outcomes of the country's internal reforms.

Endnotes

1 Rolly, Horst (1999) 'Concerning India and China, Huntington sees no way of removing the existing fault line between the two nations': 354.

2 Qiang, Hu Yue (2003) The (10+3) Meeting of Leaders of the ASEAN, China, Japan and Korea, 2, 30 September, 2003. *(www.xinhua.com).*

3 'ASEAN to Form Free Trade Zone with China, Japan and India', Tempointeraktif.com 5 September 2003.

4 Wei, Li (2003). *Road to Common Prosperity: Examination of an FTA between India and China*, March: 1.

5 Jintao, Hu (2003) 'China's Goal in the first 20 years of the Century': 1. June. (*www.sina.com.cn*)

6 Zhong, Sun Jian (2003) *Going out Strategy: China Economic Reform*, 23 November.

7 Xiaoqi, Liao (2007) *Healthy Economic Growth of China*: 1 *(www.chinanews.com)*

8 Zhong, Wang Guo (2004) *Complemented Trade of Sino-India in New Century:* 32.

9 Lin, Chi Fu (2002) *China Business Daily*, 'Idea to Build Up the Great China Free Trade Zone', 11 May.

10 Kaizhi, Zhang (2003) *Chinese History* (Volume of Dynasties of YUAN, MING, QING) : 30-39, March.

11 Zemin, Jiang (2001) On the 'Three Represents', Beijing Foreign Language Press 2001: 7. The 'Three Represents' imply that the Communist Party of China, as the ruling party

in China, should represent the advanced productivity, the advanced culture and interests of majority of Chinese people.

References

Jinwen, Li (2000) *China's Economy in the 21st Century*, Beijing : Foreign Language Press.

Maddison, Engus (1999) *The Long Term Prospect of China's Economy*, Beijing: Xinhua Publishing House.

Chuncheng, Lu and Yao Chacheng (eds) (1999) *Transcending the Economic Globalization*, Beijing Business Books Publishing House of China

Roy, Denny (1998) *China's Foreign Relations*, London: Macmillan Press Ltd.

Huntington, Samuel (1996) *The Clash of Civilizations and Remaking of the World Order*. New York: Simon and Schuster.

Bracken, Paul (2000) *Will China Be Number 1?*, Time Magzine, 22 May.

Cun Quian, (2003) *China's Emerge Makes Asia Change*, 11 December 11. http://www.newgx.com.cn,

Frank, Andre Gunder (1998) *Reoriented: Economic Globalization in Asian Age*, University of California Press. September.

Wei, Li (2004) *A Road to Common Prosperity: Examination of An FTA between India and China*, in Towards as Asian Economy Community-Vision of New Asia by Nagesh Kumar (ed.), New elhi: RIS and Singapore: ISEAS.

Rolly, Horst (1996) 'On Belonging Together and Being Different', in M. K. Raha (ed.) *Dimensions of Human Society and Culture*, New Delhi: Gyan Books.

8

India and the Asian Economic Integration

Mukul G. Asher and Rahul Sen[1]

Introduction

Since 1991, India formally adopted a new economic paradigm involving integration with the world economy in a market-consistent manner, and rebalancing of the state-market mix in favour of the latter. This was in response to the realization that the relatively inwardlooking growth model adopted since independence in 1947 had become inappropriate to deal with the end of the Cold war and with globalization[2] and associated technical changes. The proximate cause of the adoption was, however, the severe macroeconomic crisis, particularly concerning the balance of payments (Das, 2006).

The crisis was turned into an opportunity for restructuring, deregulating and liberalizing the economy. Around the same time, India initiated a 'Look East' Policy (LEP) to revitalize the civilizational and economic links with the rest of Asia, particularly with ASEAN,[3] China, Japan and South Korea.

The period since the adoption of the new economic paradigm and the LEP has witnessed substantial transformation of India's global relations, including those with the rest of Asia. This has primarily been due to the recognition of India's increasing capacities to address its developmental challenges, and the market potential of its US$1000 billion economy to provide substantial commercial opportunities.

India has grown at an annual rate of nearly 6 per cent per annum since 1980. Contrary to perceptions, it has been able to sustain high levels of growth without significantly increasing income inequality.[4] India has no parallel in managing relatively peaceful and democratic transfer of political and economic power among different social classes. It thus appears that our growth experience has been moderately inclusive, though much more efforts towards greater inclusiveness are required.

Compared to East Asia, India's growth strategy has relied relatively more on domestic markets, consumption rather than investments, decentralized, transformative entrepreneurial-based rather than state-led development,[5] and financial and capital market intermediation in allocation of savings[6] (Das, 2006; Huang, 2006; Morgan Stanley, 2006). India's de facto growth strategy is consistent with the bottom-up diagnostic approach to reforms advocated by Rodrik (2006).

As India begins to pursue policies leading to higher savings and investments,[7] and as the role of external sector increases,[8] differences in growth characteristics between India and East Asia may narrow.[9] India is also attempting to develop a robust diversified manufacturing base[10] (Bradsher, 2006); and to modernize its agricultural and plantation sectors.

The emphasis is thus on creating a more balanced and resilient economy, and increasing India's share in the world economy (Thirlwell, 2004). Some analysts, such as Poddar and Yi (2007) have revised India's potential growth rate upwards to about 8 per cent until 2020, significantly higher than that projected earlier. India's growth strategy and trajectory thus provide an avenue for global risk diversification for businesses and investors from around the world. In January 2007, Standard and Poor's raised India's external debt grade to investment grade, with stable outlook. India ranked 43rd on the Global Competitiveness Index (GCI) in 2006, moving up two places from the previous year. It scored well on indicators relating to innovation and sophistication of firm operations as well as in adoption of technologies from abroad. However, weaknesses remain in the large budget deficit (about 8 per cent of GDP), inadequate infrastructure investments, low level of efficiency in delivery of governance services, and a need for wider access to, and improvements in, quality of health and educational services. (GCI, 2006-07). Better management of the environment is also essential for sustaining India's high growth.

It is in the above context that this chapter examines India's rising role in Asia, and argues that India's integration with the rest of Asia is qualitatively and quantitatively far deeper than has been acknowledged in academic and

Table 8.1: Macroeconomic Indicators of Selected Asian Countries, 2004

Countries	GDP	GDP growth 2000-04	Population	Per capita GDP	PPP GNI	Agriculture (% of GDP)	Industry (% of GDP)	Services (% of GDP)	Inflation (%) 2000-04
	(US$ bn)	(%)	(mn)	(US$)	(US$ bn)				
World	36525.7	4.1	6365	5696	56289.0	N.A	N.A	N.A	N.A
India	691.2	6.9	1079.7	623	3369	21	27	52.0	5.3
ASEAN	777.1	N. A	474.4	1638	2244	N.A	N.A	N.A	N. A
Indonesia	257.6	5.1	217.6	1176	753.0	17	46	38	6.1
Malaysia	117.7	7.1	25.2	4646	243.0	10	48	42	1.4
Philippines	86.4	6.1	82.9	1042	406.0	5	32	54	6.0
Singapore	106.8	8.7	4.3	24898	115.0	0	35	65	1.7
Thailand	163.4	6.2	62.3	2493	505.0	10	44	46.0	3.3
Vietnam	45.2	7.8	82.1	552	222	22	40	38	7.8
Northeast Asia	6952.2	N. A	1472.4	4722	N.A	N.A	N.A	N.A	N. A
China	1649.3	10.1	1296.5	1486	7170.0	15	51	35	3.9
Japan	4623.3	2.5	127.8	35914	3838.0	1	30	68	n. a
Korea, Republic of	679.6	4.7	48.1	14136	982.0	3	35	62	3.6
Others									
Australia	631.2	1.8	20.1	31647	588.0	3	26	71	n. a

Source: Compiled from World Bank (2006), ADB (2006).

policy research, and by policy makers and the media. Moreover, this market-based integration will continue to become deeper and wider in the future.

The rest of the chapter is organized as follows. An overview of macroeconomic and external sectors of selected Asian countries is provided in the second section. The third section discusses trends in India's merchandise and services trade in recent years. India has not only been unilaterally liberalizing its external sector, but has also been a participant in the emerging worldwide phenomenon of engaging like and strategically important trading partners through preferential trading agreements (PTAs) and economic partnership agreements. India's experience with PTAs and their current status is briefly summarized in the fourth section. India has steadily been liberalizing its inward and outward investment flows, involving both FDI and portfolio investments in the financial and capital markets. India's foreign investment policies are discussed in the fifth section. The final section provides the concluding observations.

India's Growth Prospects in Asian Comparative Perspective

Asia is projected to grow at 4.9 per cent during the period 2006-20 as compared to 3.5 per cent for the world as a whole (Table 8.2). Within Asia, China, India and Vietnam are projected to grow at the most rapid pace (Table 8.2). It should be noted that overall, the growth rates projected by the Economic Intelligence Unit (EIU) are much lower than generally perceived. As an example, China is projected to grow at 6 per cent annually during the 2006-20 period as compared to 9 to 10 per cent growth which is routinely reported. India's GDP per head is expected to grow at an annual rate of 4-6 per cent during 2006-20.[11] This is exceeded by China (5.4 per cent) (see Table 8.2).

EIU's projections for contribution to global growth[12] for the period 2006-20 suggest that the largest contribution will be by China (26.7 per cent), followed by the United States (15.9 per cent) and India (12.2 per cent) (EIU 2006-07). These countries are also projected to occupy the first three positions in GDP in PPP terms in 2020. The share of China in world GDP is projected at 19.4 per cent, the US at 19.0 per cent, and India 8.8 per cent (EIU 2006-09). It should, however, be stressed that in spite of the above, both China and India in 2020 will continue to have relatively low per capita incomes.

Demographic Trends

There are three demographic trends which are evident globally. First, fertility rates are dropping nearly everywhere. Second, life expectancy is rising in many, though not all parts of the world. Third, developed countries are well advanced with respect to the above two trends as reflected in their declining share in world population. The non-developed countries are further behind, though variation among them is large (Asher and Nandy, 2006). The combined impact of these trends has led to the rapid ageing of the world's population.

Table 8.2: Real GDP Growth, Selected Asian Countries

(Annual average, per cent)

Countries	GDP			GDP/head		
	2006-10	2011-20	2006-20	2006-10	2011-20	2006-20
World	4.0	3.3	3.5	2.7	2.4	2.5
Asia	5.5	4.5	4.9	4.5	3.6	3.9
China	7.8	5.1	6.0	7.2	4.5	5.4
India	6.6	5.5	5.9	5.2	4.3	4.6
Indonesia	5.6	5.0	5.2	4.2	3.9	4.0
Malaysia	5.3	4.8	5.0	3.4	3.1	3.2
Philippines	5.2	4.7	4.9	3.4	3.1	3.2
Singapore	4.5	4.0	4.1	3.6	3.4	3.5
South Korea	4.0	3.9	4.0	3.6	3.6	3.6
Taiwan	4.5	3.4	3.8	4.2	3.0	3.4
Thailand	4.5	4.7	4.7	3.8	4.2	4.1
Vietnam	7.0	4.6	5.4	5.7	3.4	4.2

Source: Economist Intelligence Unit (2006)

Among the Asian countries, India is in a demographic gift phase, as reflected in rising working age population to total population ratio (Figure 8.1). This ratio has already begun to decline for China, Korea and Japan. India's ratio is projected to begin declining around 2030, and the decline will be gradual. Even in 2050, India will still have the highest share of working age to total population.

There are, therefore, significant demographic complementarities between India on the one hand and affluent, rapidly ageing Asian countries on the other (Asher and Nandy, 2006). These could be used to extend the economic space of the affluent countries through offshoring[13] and other means in a mutually beneficial manner without long-term physical movement of persons.[14]

Figure 8.1: Dynamics of Working Age Population in Selected Economies

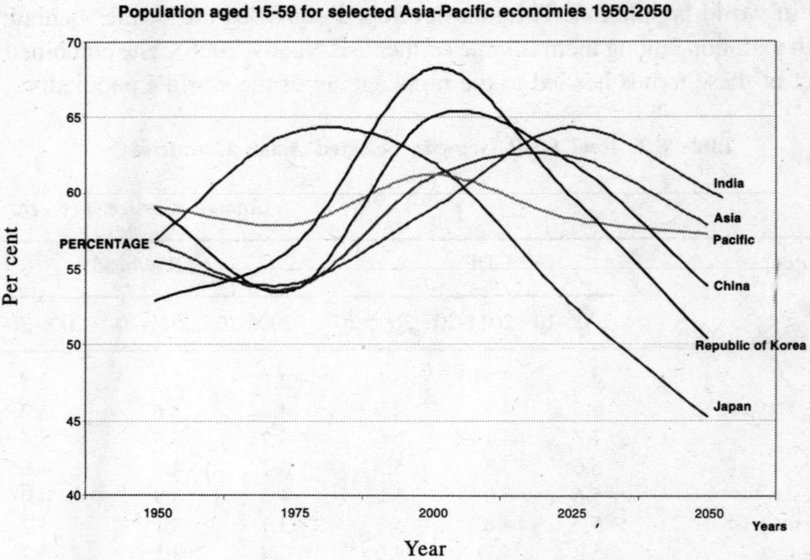

India's demographic advantage phase also implies that it will need to create a significant number of jobs or livelihood opportunities. Thus, between the period 2006-10 there will be 314 million additional new jobs which will need to be generated in the world, with India accounting for about a quarter of the total, China 14 per cent and Southeast Asia 11 per cent (Figure 8.2). India must, therefore, find a balance between creation of new jobs and livelihoods on the one hand and preserving existing jobs on the other, which favours the former. It must also improve the quality and employability of the output from its educational institutions; and reduce the ill-health and malnutrition.

External Sector Indicators

On the basis of the data on external sector indicators for selected Asian countries, the following observations may be made:

- The outward orientation of ASEAN countries as reflected in the trade to GDP ratio for 2004 of 162.0 is far higher than that for Northeast Asia (44.6). ASEAN's ratio is nearly three times the world average of 63.1. India's ratio at 36.7 is the second lowest among the sample countries, the lowest being Japan at 27.
- India's low ratio is largely due to the low level of merchandise trade. In services, India ranked fourth among the sample countries in 2005

(see Table 8.3). India thus needs to develop capacities to increase its merchandise trade substantially. Even then the gap between India on the one hand and China, Japan and Korea on the other is unlikely to narrow substantially.

- India's total remittance inflows were US$ 21.7 billion (3.1 per cent of GDP) in 2004 (The World Bank, 2006). The size of the remittance flows indicates the contribution of Indian workers in the region's economic activities. India has come to rely on these flows to help finance its substantial trade deficit. This represents a significant vulnerability for managing India's trade and current account deficits.
- India's total flows in 2005-06 were US$20.3 billion, comprising FDI of US$7.8 billion, and portfolio flows of US$12.5 billion, much smaller compared to those in ASEAN or Northeast Asian countries.

Figure 8.2: Growth in Global Working-Age Population (15-64)

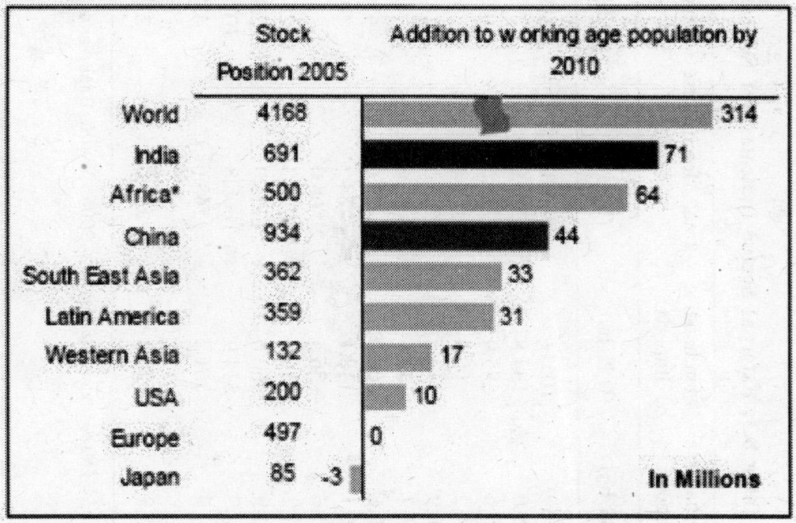

Note: Africa include a Group of 56 countries.
Source: UN, Morgan Stanley Research.

Trends in India's Merchandise Trade and Service Transactions

Merchandise Trade

While India's merchandise trade has grown rapidly in the past two decades, it has been accompanied by a change in direction towards Asia. It may be observed

Table 8.3: External Sector Indicators of Selected Asian Countries, 2005

Countries	Merchandise Exports	Merchandise Imports	Total Merchandise Trade	Service Exports	Service Imports	Services Trade	Trade/GDP	Net FDI Inflows
	(US$ bn)	(US$ bn)	(US$ bn)	(US$ bn)	(US$ bn)	(US$ bn)	(%)	(US$ mn)
World	10159	10511	20670	2415	2315	4730	N.A	632600.
India	95.0	134.8	229.8	56.0	52.2	108.2	8.8	5335
ASEAN	639.6	585.9	1225.5	107.7	120.3	228.0	N.A	25707
Indonesia	86.2	69.4	155.6	5.1	17.1	22.2	20.9	1023
Malaysia	140.9	114.6	255.5	18.9	21.5	40.4	107.6	4624
Philippines	41.2	47.4	88.6	4.4	5.7	10.1	24.1	469
Singapore	229.6	200.0	429.6	45.1	43.9	89.0	398.3	16032
Thailand	110.1	118.1	228.2	20.4	27.4	47.8	50.2	1949
Vietnam	31.6	36.4	68.0	3.8	4.7	8.5	30.1	1610
Northeast Asia	1637.2	1436.1	3073.3	225.7	273.3	499.0	N.A	70930
China	761.9	660.0	1421.9	73.9	83.1	157.0	18.4	54936
Japan	594.9	514.9	1009.8	107.9	132.5	240.4	31.7	7805
Korea, Republic of	284.4	261.2	545.6	43.9	57.7	101.6	61.2	8189
Others								
Australia	105.8	125.2	231.0	27.6	28.9	56.5	44.7	42469

Source: Compiled from *World Development Indicators 2006*, World Bank; and *International Trade Statistics, 2006*, WTO.

from Figure 8.3 that while the share of India's trade with developing Asia (mainly including China, Korea,[15] SAARC and ASEAN-4 countries) doubled from 12 per cent to 24 per cent over the period 1987-2004, that of the EU, one of India's major trading partners, declined from 30 per cent to 20 per cent over the same period. A comparatively lower decline is observed in India's trade with North America over the same period. It is to be noted that the share of developed Asia (including Australia and Japan), in India's trade witnessed a steady decline over this period.

Figure 8.4 provides detailed trends concerning India's merchandise trade by selected regions. India's merchandise trade with developing Asia has been growing rapidly. Since 2001-02, trade with developing Asia has been larger than that with the EU. India's total trade with developing Asia was estimated at US$45 billion in 2004-05. India's average growth of merchandise trade with developing Asia has been the highest compared to that with other major regions, viz. EU, North America and developed Asia. It is important to note that while India's average growth of merchandise trade developed Asia declined significantly during the period of Japanese economic recession, it has increased in recent years, growing at an average rate of 29 per cent during the 2003-05 period.[16]

Figures 8.5 and 8.6 present the trends in India's merchandise exports and imports to selected countries in Asia. It is observed that while India's merchandise exports to ASEAN-4 witnessed a significant break from the past trend, expanding from US$1.3 billion in 1998-9 to US$6.9 billion by 2004-05, its exports to China recorded an even further rapid increase from US$1 billion to US$ 4.6 billion over just a four-year time period from 2001-02 to 2004-05. This represents a break from trends during 1987-2000, when its total exports were less than US$1 billion.

ASEAN-4 has also been one of the most important contributors to India's merchandise imports from Asia—estimated at about US$8.1 billion in 2004-05—taking India's total merchandise trade with ASEAN-4 to US$15 billion.

Concomitantly, India's bilateral imports from China have also expanded from US$1.3 billion to US$6.7 billion between 2000 and 2004. India-China bilateral trade was US$11.3 billion in 2004-05, and is projected to be about US$25 billion by 2007.[17]

It may be noted that while India's exports to Australia and Japan have not been expanding significantly, these two countries have been playing a significant role as a source of imports. India's total imports from Australia nearly trebled in value from US$1.3 billion to US$ 3.6 billion during the period 2002-04.

Figure 8.3: Trends in India's Merchandise Trade by Region, 1987-2004

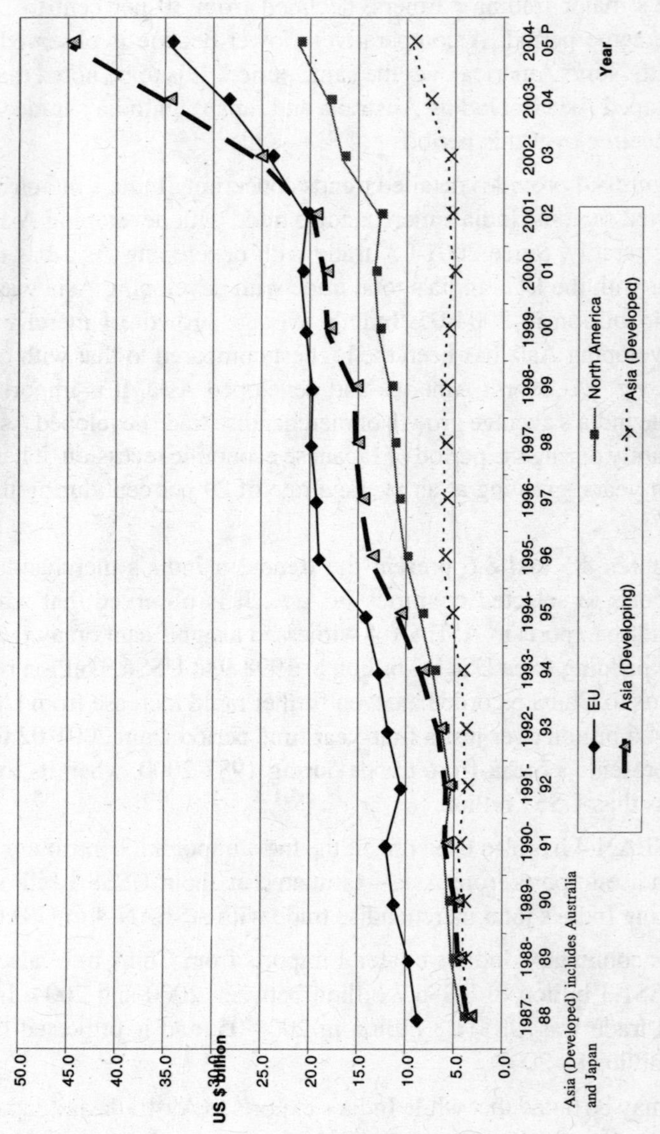

Source: RBI (2005).

Figure 8.4: Average Growth of India's Merchandise Trade by Region, 1988-2004

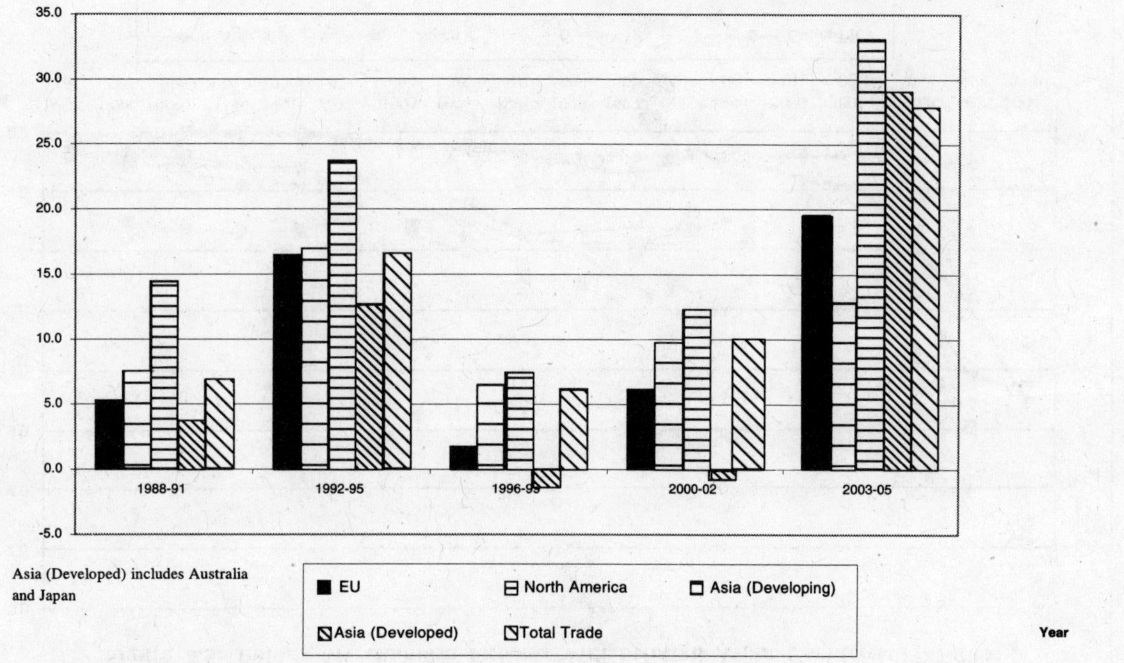

Source: RBI (2005).

Figure 8.5: India's Merchandise Exports with Selected Asian Countries 1987-2004

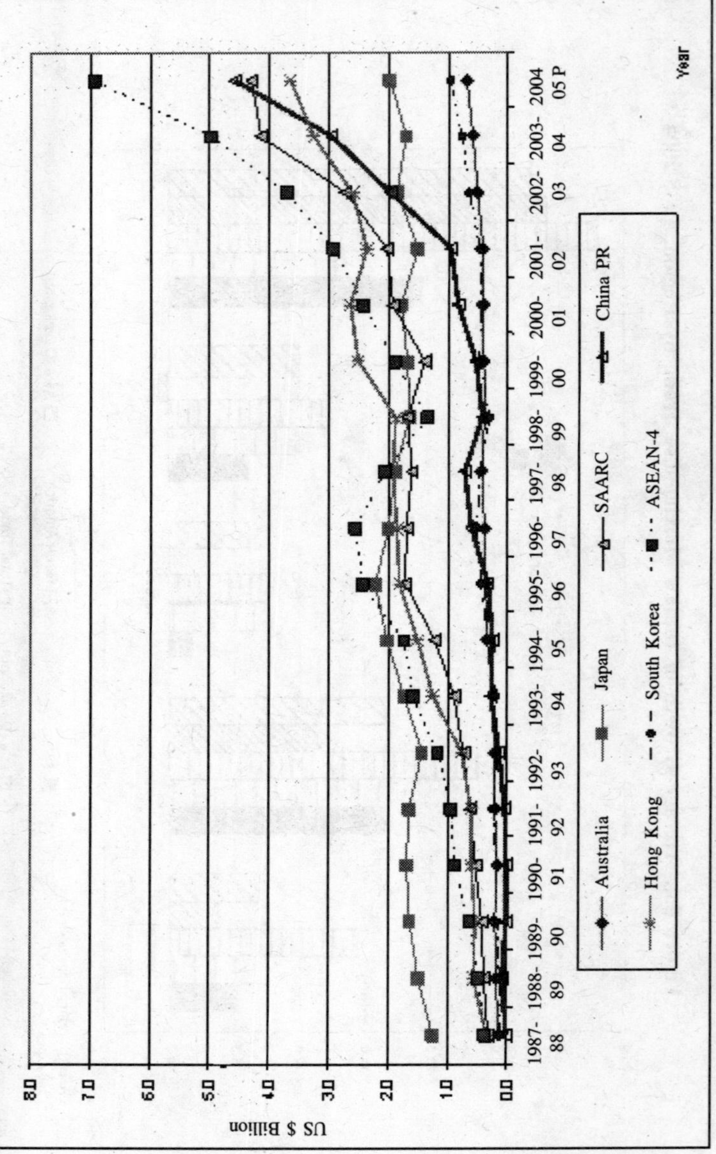

Source: RBI (2005).

Figure 8.6: India's Merchandise Imports from Selected Asian Economies: 1987-2004

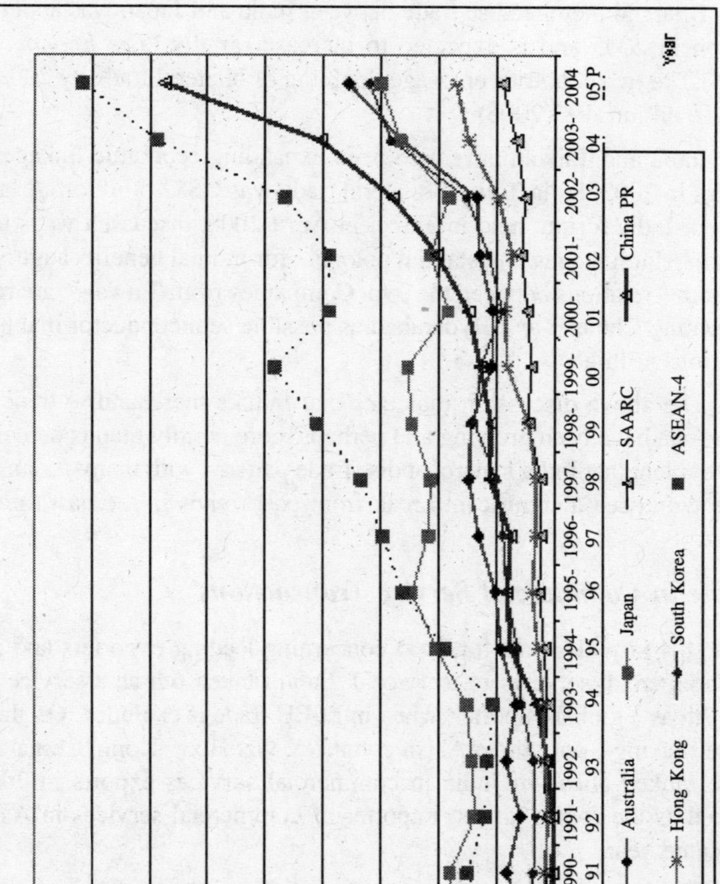

Source: RBI (2005).

India displaced Britain to become Australia's fourth biggest export market (Hartcher 2006) and it is among the largest purchasers of gold from Australia.

Bilateral merchandise trade between India and Japan was about US$ 6.8 billion in 2005 and is expected to increase rapidly (*The Economic Times*, 2006).The two countries envisage doubling of bilateral trade by 2009 to reach US$10 billion (RIS 2006).

India and Taiwan have also been expanding economic linkages (Asher, 2006). In 2005, India-Taiwan bilateral trade was US$2.5 billion. A large scale Taiwan-India forum, held in Taipei in April 2006, discussed ways to expand commercial linkages. Substantial potential for mutual benefits augurs well for expanded relations between the two. Companies from Taiwan[18] are reportedly evaluating Chennai and Hyderabad as possible semiconductor manufacturing locations in India.

The above discussion indicates that India's merchandise trade linkages with Asia have been growing and perhaps more rapidly than is perceived. It is also evident that India's merchandise trade patterns with many Asian countries have witnessed a significant break from past trends in the past three to four years.

Trade in Commercial Service Transactions

Table 8.4 provides data for 2005 concerning leading exporters and importers of commercial services in the world. India ranked 6th as a service exporter, and 7th as a global importer, when intra-EU trade is excluded. On the basis of these rankings, only three Asian countries, viz. Hong Kong, China and Japan were ranked ahead of India in commercial services exports in 2005. India ranked as the fourth largest importer of commercial services in Asia during the same year.

There are reasons to suggest that India's ranking will improve further in the coming years. First, travel and transport accounted for about 10 per cent each of total exports of services by India, while four-fifths were other commercial services, including IT services (WTO, 2005). The IT outsourcing industry amounted to US$31 billion in sales for the year ending 2006-07 where the IT services industry generated US$47.8 billion. A NASSCOM-McKinsey study has projected US$60 billion of IT exports by 2009-10, with total direct and indirect employment of 5 million persons.[19] Apart from these, India's potential in health care and education services trade is only beginning to be exploited.

Table 8.4: Leading Exporters and Importers in World Trade in Commercial Services (Excluding Intra–EU Trade), 2005

(Billion dollars and percentage)

Rank	Exporters	Value	Share in World (%)	Rank	Importers	Value	Share in World (%)
1	Extra-EU(25) Exports	480.3	27.1	1	Extra – EU (25) imports	422.4	24.4
2	United States	354.0	14.7	2	United States	281.2	12.0
3	Japan	107.9	4.5	3	Japan	132.6	5.6
4	China	73.9	3.1	4	China	83.2	3.5
5	HK, China	62.2	2.6	5	Canada	64.2	2.7
6	India	56.1	2.3	6	Korea, Republic	57.7	2.5
7	Canada	52.2	2.2	7	India	52.2	2.2
8	Singapore	45.1	1.9	8	Singapore	44.0	1.9
10	Korea, Republic of	43.9	1.8	9	Russian Federation	38.5	1.6
12	Australia	27.7	1.1	10	HK, China	32.4	1.4
15	Taipei, Chinese	25.6	1.1	11	Taipei, Chinese	31.4	1.3
16	Thailand	20.5	0.8	12	Australia	28.9	1.2
17	Malaysia	19.0	0.8	13	Thailand	27.5	1.2
				16	Indonesia	23.2	1.0
				18	Malaysia	21.6	0.9
	Total of above				Total of above		
	World (excluding intra EU (25)	1775.0	100.0		World (excluding intra-EU)	1730.0	100.0

Source: WTO (2006).

Traditionally, international organizations and individual countries have focused on merchandise trade statistics. The services trade transactions, however, are a significant proportion of total world trade. Thus, in 2005, the ratio of total merchandise trade to total GDP for the world was 23.3 per cent, while the corresponding ratio for services was 5.5 per cent. The total world trade in service transactions was US$ billion 4730 billion (23 per cent of the merchandise trade of US$20670 billion) (WTO, 2005). On a value-added rather than gross flow basis, the share of service transactions is likely to be even higher as production fragmentation is much more advanced in merchandise than in services.

Analysing the data on share of services trade to total trade in goods and services for major economies globally over 1995-2005, Asher and Sen (2007) observe that while this share is in the range of 15-25 per cent for most economies in the world and in Asia, it increased from about 20 per cent to 32 per cent over the past decade in the case of India. This is not to suggest that India can or should rely on the services sector as the primary engine of growth. Indeed, India is already placing emphasis on the manufacturing sector. There is also increasing realization that greater focus on agriculture, and on linkages between agriculture, manufacturing and services sectors is essential to sustain India's high growth.

Figure 8.7 compares India's ranking in people, infrastructure and taxes with selected offshoring locations. India's advantage is evident in all three areas, though the margin varies. Philippines and China are, however, close competitors. There are also indications that talent shortages may limit the growth of offshoring, which would adversely impact India, China and other countries. However, India can, in part, bridge the skill shortage as foreign professionals including non-resident Indians (NRIs) increasingly find India an attractive location to work (Yee, 2007). India's limited physical infrastructure and lower investments in health and education strongly suggest that there is no room for complacency by Indian policy makers, Indian industry and indeed individuals seeking better prospects.

Chanda and Krishnan (2006) focus on how Indian companies are engaging in increasing cross-border collaborations such as joint ventures and training arrangements between Indian and other Asian IT services firm. Motivations of Indian companies vary from the desire to be close to their MNC customers (for example, China, Singapore), to expand human talent pool (for example China, Philippines, and Vietnam), and to more effectively tap certain markets (such as, Japan and Korea). It is also worth noting that manpower for IT industries in many countries is being provided by the Indian diaspora. Some

Indian IT companies are taking a more sophisticated approach by expanding into high-cost markets abroad to provide greater value to customers in these markets (*Financial Times* 2007).

Figure 8.7: Relative Costs in India and Other Selected Offshore Locations in Asia

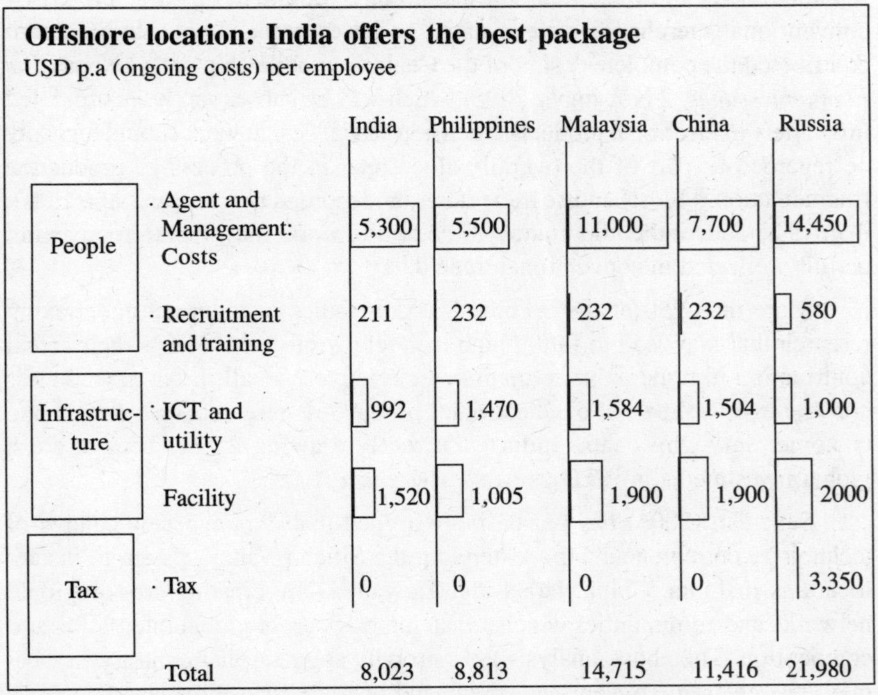

Source: Deutsche Bank Research (25 October 2005), Chart 8, p.4.

US companies are estimated to have saved over US$ 25 billion in 2005 through outsourcing (Chanda and Krishnan 2006). The organizations in Asian countries, however, do not appear to have taken sufficient advantage of the opportunities to realize cost savings by partnering India in offshoring (Asher and Nandy, 2006). Countries such as Malaysia which desire to create IT industries have also not pursued policies which are sufficiently conducive for deeper engagement and cooperation with the Indian IT industry and manpower.[20]

Top 250 global technology firms are outsourcing part of their work to small specialist firms, some of which are located in India, China and Taiwan. As a result, the Asian region is being welded into the global technology supply chain (*The Economist*, 7 October 2006, pp.73-4). This in turn benefits firms outside Asia as well.

It is important to note that while East Asia's integration with the global economy is evident in the analysis of production networks in trade in manufactured goods, such integration of India with the global economy, which is undoubtedly more service-and technology- oriented, is not captured by conventional merchandise trade data. As an example, Intel's India centre contributed the complete design of the Centrino mobile chip called Napa (*The Economic Times,* 2 November 2006) which will be subsequently incorporated in a variety of electronic products. Such non-trivial design work should logically be regarded as part of the overall value chain in the process of production fragmentation.[21] Merchandise trade flows are recorded by gross amounts rather than value-added; the importance of the design work may, therefore, may not be fully reflected in conventional trade data.

More than 250 of the Fortune 500 companies in India are undertaking research that may lead to future high technology products. While their actual contribution in trade value terms may be relatively small, India nevertheless constitutes a vital part of the electronics production, research, distribution and customer servicing chain. India is currently drawing 25 per cent of fresh global investments in R&D centers (*www.ibef.org*).

Saxenian (2006) has persuasively argued that dynamic new centres of technology entrepreneurship—extending the Silicon Valley system to distant locations in India, China, Israel and Taiwan[22]—are creating cross-regional networks and communities which are an integral part of global integration and competition. The above analysis thus strongly suggests that contrary to what may emerge from conventional merchandise trade focused research, India's integration with the rest of Asia is far greater, deeper and of high quality.

There is therefore a strong case for broadening the scope of production network and fragmentation definitions, found in the current literature; and to mandate WTO to undertake research on developing a robust database on trade in services. The aim should be to make services trade data as accessible to researchers, businesses and policy makers as merchandise trade data. Indian authorities and industry should also accord high priority to developing bilateral service trade flow database, at least for the IT and ITES services.

Besides IT and ITES services, there are several other areas of commercial services trade where India's potential is yet to be fully realized. One such area is the health care services sector. It has the potential to benefit substantially from demographic complementarities between India on the one hand and affluent and rapidly ageing Asian countries such as Japan, Korea, Australia, New Zealand and Singapore on the other (Asher and Nandy, 2006).[23] Hong Kong and Taiwan are also affluent and rapidly ageing economies and may consider constructive cooperation with India. India's strengths in generic drugs have the potential to help manage health care costs in high-income Asia. This is exemplified in the recent licensing of a drug to a Taiwanese company. Use of technology such as telemedicine can also help in managing health costs. Countries such as Japan, Korea and Singapore can reap substantial benefits by partnering Indian firms in this area.

Indian educational institutions are beginning to establish a presence in the rest of Asia, for example, the Global Indian International School (GIIS) has established three campuses in Japan, two in Singapore and one each in Malaysia,Thailand and New Zealand. The GIIS is involved in providing primary and secondary education. While it caters primarily to the Indian diaspora,[24] also attracts students from other nationalities. Similarly, the Delhi Public School (DPS) is expanding its presence in Asia. It is already operating in Indonesia, Nepal, Singapore and Sri Lanka. Other less well- known but good quality Indian educational institutions are also setting up operations in Asia.

The Government of India's state of Bihar has taken up the initiative to revive ancient Nalanda University as an institution of higher learning and cultural exchange between India and the rest of Asia (Velloor, 2007). The project envisages enlisting support of several nations, most notably Japan. This project also has the potential to provide a useful forum for India and ASEAN to forge deeper understanding.

At the tertiary level, Melaka Manipal Medical College[25] represents a low-key, but constructive engagement between India and Malaysia in the field of education. India's engineering and management institutes are gradually establishing their presence in the rest of Asia. It is now common for the Indian management institutes to have a component in their post-graduate programmes involving study visits to other Asian countries.

India will nevertheless continue to be a significant source of students for education export sectors of countries such as Australia, Singapore, New Zealand, China and Malaysia.

India is placing increasing emphasis on greater air and sea connectivity, including direct links with major cities in Asia. India has liberalized and deregulated its aviation and maritime transport services sector, resulting in increased competition that augurs well for facilitating greater economic linkages between India and the rest of Asia.

India is setting up the Services Export Promotion Council (SEPC) to increase the share of services in India's total exports. In addition to the above services, exports by the construction industry will also be emphasized (*www.ibef.org*).

India's Approach to PTAs in Asia

Unsatisfactory progress in multilateral trade liberalization in recent years has been one of the factors which has led many Asia-Pacific economies towards negotiating regional and bilateral PTAs, with trading partners within and outside Asia, though some of the major FTAs such as EU and North American Free Trade Agreement (NAFTA) pre-date this (Sen 2006, Dent 2006 and Aggarwal and Urata, 2006). This trend of proliferation of Asian FTAs has also led India to expand bilateral trade and investment linkages through economic partnership and PTAs with a number of Asian countries.

The key motivations for entering into such deals have been both strategic and economic. India envisages PTAs as important foreign policy tools to forge new strategic alliances with the rest of Asia, and to contribute to regional security efforts.

The PTAs are also expected to strengthen India's market- based economic integration with its neighbours and geographically proximate regions, viz. SAARC,[26] ASEAN and East Asia. India also aims to increase cross-regional trade linkages with Latin American and Middle-eastern countries, as indicated by the initiatives to form similar agreements with the MERCOSUR, SACU, GCC, Egypt and Chile. With India planning to expand bilateral trade and investment linkages through economic patneship agreements and PTAs with a number of Asian countries, the pace of India's trade integration with the rest of Asia—not just in merchandise trade, but also in commercial services—is likely to increase in the near future.

India's growing web of PTAs with Asian countries indicates its willingness to engage the rest of Asia towards forming an Asian Economic Community that is inclusive in its approach. As most of India's PTAs which are in force, are undergoing further negotiations, there is a distinct possibility of their becoming more comprehensive in the future—inclusion of services and investments are likely to be added. In particular, India is discussing comprehensive bilateral agreements with Japan and Korea. An economic agreement with China is also under discussion. Effective implementation of these PTAs and managing to reduce transaction costs due to possible trade and investment diversion created by diverse ROOs is crucial for realizing economic efficiencies and welfare improvement. It is striking that from the 16 countries included in Japan's proposal for a Comprehensive Economic Partnership in East Asia (involving ASEAN, China, Japan, Korea, India, Australia and New Zealand), currently India does not have PTA discussions only with Australia and New Zealand. Our perception is that these two countries will find India quite receptive in engaging in such discussions and deepening economic linkages. This will require a change in the mindest of policy, business and academic think-tank communities of these two countries.

After the recent deadlock in WTO talks, it has already been indicated by Indian policy makers that bilateralism is likely to emerge as one of the key instruments of India's commercial trade strategy (Sen, 2006). We are beginning to undertake WTO-plus commitments on tariff reduction, which adds a new dimension to the trade policy. India offered to substantially reduce duties on ASEAN's imports of agricultural products for 94 per cent of ASEAN exports to India, by offering to reduce refined palm oil tariff from 90 per cent to 60 per cent; crude palm oil tariff from 80 per cent to 50 per cent; black tea tariff from 10 per cent to 50 per cent and that on pepper from 70 per cent to 50 per cent.

India's per capita income is about half that of ASEAN. Even though reduction in India's poverty rate has been about 1 percent per year in recent years, the number of absolute poor (US$1 per day) is still at an unacceptable level of 170 million persons (ILO 2007). Most of the poor are in the rural sector engaged in agriculture and, therefore, India has legitimate interests in protecting its large number of small farmers. It should, however, speed up reforms of the agricultural sector with the aim of competing with ASEAN.[27] Tea, pepper, and coffee from Vietnam and palm oil from Malaysia and Indonesia are perceived in India to be particularly sensitive products for the rural population. Indian businesses in manufacturing and services will not be able to reap full benefits of the ASEAN market (with or without the FTA) unless agricultural reforms are undertaken urgently.

Foreign Investment Flows

With economic reforms in 1991, both inward and outward investment policies in India have been gradually liberalized, increasing the receptiveness of the economy to foreign investment flows. India's foreign exchange reserves were US$225 billion at end July 2007. Indian market capitalization has more than trebled in value over more than a decade to reach US$1000 billion.[28]

As of December 2006, 1000 FIIs had invested US$46 billion in India's capital markets. Between 2000 and 2005, India received US$8.4 billion in private equity (Tucker and Leahy, 2006). A study by Bain and Company has projected that by 2010 India is likely to receive US$7 billion a year in private equity (Tucker and Leahy, 2006). India's FDI inward stock was estimated at US$51 billion in 2005, and is projected to be US$109 billion by 2010. FDI outward stock was US$11 billion in 2005, and is projected to be US$29 billion by 2010 (EIU 2006, p.114).

Current trends suggest that EIU's projections are achievable. India's net FDI inflow increased from US$ 5.5 billion in 2005-06 to US$15.7 billion in 2006-07. In the first half of 2007, the FDI inflow was US$11.4 billion, much of which was initial first mile investment, which is likely to generate significant additional investments in the future. India has also had a strong inflow of portfolio investments, with such flows exceeding the FDI in some years (see Figure 8.8).

India is increasingly becoming an attractive destination for global investors. According to AT Kearney 2005 Survey, India was ranked as second most favourable destination for global FDI after China. It is observed from Figure 8.9 that while China and India rank quite high in the FDI Confidence Index, some of the other Asian countries such as Japan, Singapore, Thailand and Korea are ranked below the global top 10 destinations. It is important to note that while India appears to be attracting much lower FDI inflows compared to that of China, the interest of foreign investors in India is relatively recent. FDI into China (and many other East Asian countries) is driven by capital-intensive manufacturing while in the case of India it is driven more towards skill and knowledge intensive areas involving service transactions in information and communication technology, financial services and in R&D.

Although India is yet to attract substantial FDI in heavy and light manufacturing, the success of India's automobiles and steel industry continues to improve investor perceptions.[29] Malaysia's Petronas has acquired a 10 per cent stake in Cairns India Limited. A Korean company, Pohang Iron and Steel, has recently invested $12 billion in building a steel plant in the eastern state of Orissa. Global automakers such as Volkswagen and BMW are planning to assemble cars in India for domestic consumption and export (Giridharadas, 2006). India produced nearly 8 million motor vehicles in 2005, of which 1.3 million were passenger cars. Auto industry sales are expected to increase from US$36 billion in 2005 to US$145 billion by 2016. Korean and Japanese auto producers have specially aggressive plans for India, but Indian companies are also gearing up for global competition (Yee, 2006b).

In August 2007, the Japanese Prime Minister visited India with a business delegation of over 200 members to lay the foundation for much deeper

Figure 8.8: Trends in India's Total Foreign Investment Flows: 1990-2004

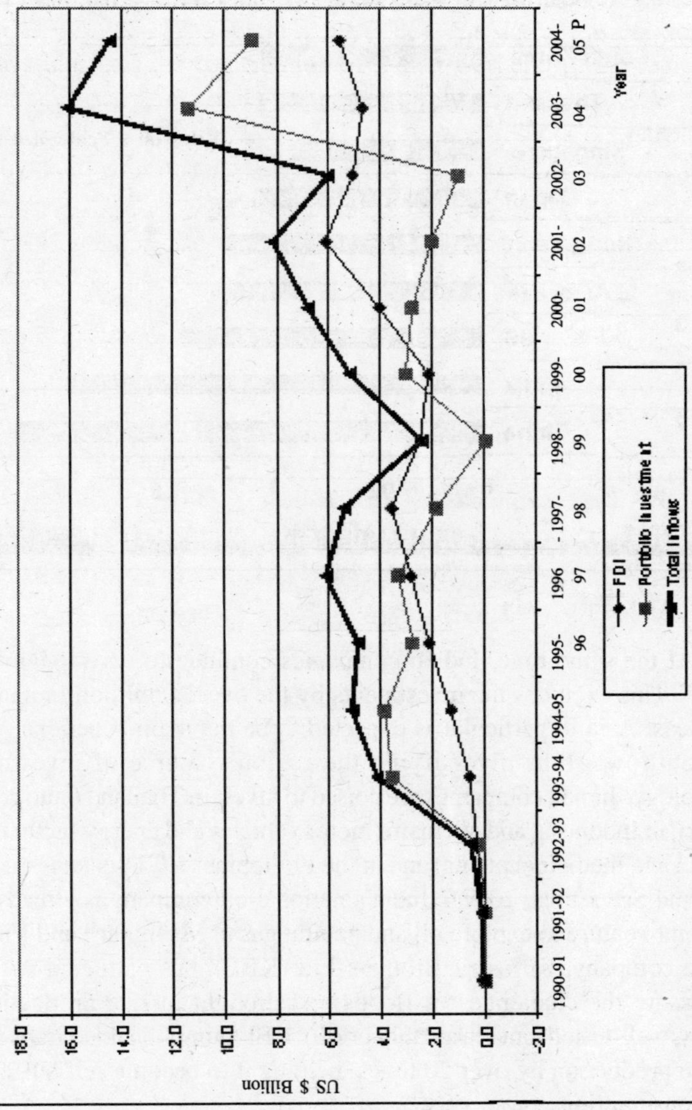

Source: RBI (2005).

engagement between the two countries. Japan is the dominant partner in the US$ 90 billion project to develop the Delhi-Mumbai industrial Corridor (DMIC). Japan appears determined to develop more even handed economic engagement with China and India.

Figure 8.9: Comparisons of FDI Confidence Index for Selected Asian Economies

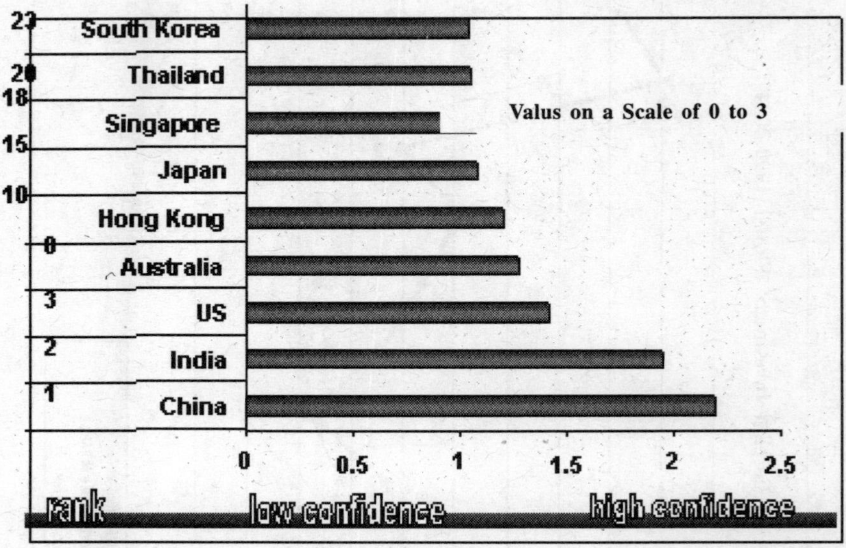

Source: AT Kearney (2006).

At the same time, Indian companies continue to invest significantly in Asia.[30] This excludes the investments by the over 20 million Indian diaspora. Southeast Asia in particular is expected to be the main beneficiary of India's FDI outflows, thus diversifying the region's source of investments and technology. Indian companies are poised to invest in Thailand (auto components sector), in Indonesia and Vietnam (motor vehicles and energy sector), Malaysia (herbal and medicinal plants) and in the Philippines (ICT sector), among others (Sen and Srivastava, 2007). India's national oil company is already involved in a joint venture to explore oil and natural gas in Myanmar[31] and Vietnam. An Indian company, Kirloskar Brothers Ltd (KBL), has partnered with Laos in addressing the challenges of floods and drought in rice production. High quality, well-tested, but reasonably priced KBL pumps enabled Laos to increase its rice production by over 20 times, helping it to become self-sufficient in its key consumption commodity.

Indian companies have also invested in manufacturing companies in South Korea. An Indian company, Burrup Fertilizers, is the first such company in secondary processing of gas in Western Australia, with an investment of Australian dollar 630 million (Srinivasan, 2006). India's Suzlon Energy commissioned its largest comprehensive global manufacturing facility in China in early 2007 (*Business Line*, 30 January 2007). The global ambition of Indian companies is also highlighted by India's Tata Steel acquisition the Anglo-Dutch steel company Corus for £5.75 billion, (US$11.3 billion). This will increase Tata's steel production capacity to nearly 25 million tons, ranking it among the top five steel companies in the world.[32]

The Vietnamese Prime Minister visited India in July 2007 with a large business delegation. This augurs well for establishing a robust economic partnership commensurate with India's close political relations with Vietnam. The two-way flow of investments between and India and rest of Asia is becoming an increasing reality. The IT companies from the Philippines and Vietnam's can also invest in India, the way their Malaysian and Singapore counterparts have done. Recently, a Malaysian-owned company based in Thailand won a competitive contract to modernize a zoo in Mumbai (*The Indian Express*, 27 December, 2006).

This suggests the increasing variety of economic linkages between India and ASEAN. More such market-based linkages can be expected to continue.

Concluding Remarks

The analysis in this chapter strongly suggests that India has been far more intricately integrated into the rest of Asia than has commonly perceived or acknowledged. This is particularly the case if overall value chain division is defined to include R&D, physical production, distribution, customer servicing and feedback. Over-concentration on gross merchandise trade flows in the conventional literature appears to have distorted the analysis of economic integration. This integration has been primarily market and private sector driven.

The increasingly critical role of services in international trade strongly suggests that greater intellectual and other resources should be devoted to developing as robust a database for services trade as is currently available for merchandise trade.

The role of Indian professionals and skilled and unskilled workers in contributing to Asia's economic growth and dynamism also appears to have been underemphasized. In several key Asian countries, including Japan, Malaysia and Singapore (and to a lesser extent in Australia), there has been a noticeable increase in the size of the Indian diaspora. If the experience of the Indian diaspora in the US is any guide, then an acceleration in economic linkages and increase in comfort levels between India and these countries may be expected. Increasing presence of the Indian media and entertainment firms and products globally, including in Asia and Pacific countries, is also contributing positively to comfort levels.

The analysis also suggests that while India and some of the other Asian countries are competitive in some areas, there are also considerable opportunities for cooperation. Computable general equilibrium (GCE) simulations by Kumar (this volume) suggest that India's inclusion in ASEAN plus Japan, China and South Korea grouping would generate additional welfare gains of US$48 billion. These results suggest welfare enhancing win-win gains from India's complementary strengths.

The East Asian Summit (EAS) in December 2005 in Kuala Lumpur involving ASEAN, India, China, Japan, Korea, Australia and New Zealand represented a credible approach towards increasing Asia's role in global affairs through deeper economic partnership and integration.[33] Japan's proposal for Comprehensive Economic Partnership in East Asia (CEPEA) involving the entities mentioned above (ASEAN+6), therefore, deserves support (Kitamura, 2006). The CEPEA will cover trade in goods and services, investment, trade facilitation and intellectual property. Japan has also proposed to set up an OECD-like forum for these countries. The proposal is at an early stage and much groundwork needs to be laid before concrete steps are taken towards realizing the vision.[34]

The dynamics of India's integration with the rest of Asia has been private sector led, with market forces playing a dominant role. Indian companies and India as a country, however, are competing with the state-led capitalism of most East Asian countries such as China, Singapore and Malaysia, where the demarcation line between the public and private sector is not sharp due to an intricate web of interconnections between these companies and political and government figures; and where state-direction of other societal institutions is the norm.

India has demonstrated its commitment to partnering the rest of Asia in playing a more meaningful role through its constructive economic cooperation security initiatives. India sincerely hopes that the rest of Asia will exhibit pragmatism in mutually enriching cooperation to shape the Asian economic community and enable Asia to play a large role in global affairs. The rest of Asia has an important stake in India's successful adjustment to globalization as this would contribute to Asia's stability and prosperity and provide global risk diversification.

Endnotes

1 The authors would like to thank Amarendu Nandy for excellent research assistance. The views expressed in this paper are personal. The usual caveat applies.

2 For the purpose of this paper, the globalization phenomenon may be defined as involving shrinkage of economic distances between nations, impacting the real economy and financial, capital and manpower flows. Three novel aspects of the current globalization are the scale and pace of integration, with merchandise exports now accounting for over 20 per cent of world GDP compared to 8 per cent in 1913, and 15 per cent in 1990; transformation of the international division of labour; and growth of trade in tasks within manufacturing and services (Wolf, 2006).

3 ASEAN, established in 1967, comprises ten Southeast Asian Countries, namely Brunei Darussalam, Cambodia, Indonesia, Laos, Malaysia, Myanmar, Philippines, Singapore, Thailand and Vietnam.

4 This is exemplified by the fact that India's Gini coefficient is 0.33 (based on expenditure) compared to that of 0.45 for China and 0.38 for the US in 2000 (World Bank 2006). India should focus on substantially raising the per capita income through inclusive and sustained high growth to reduce absolute poverty, rather than trying to directly address the inequalities. India needs to make much more progress towards inclusive growth, including addressing imbalances in quality of governance and in standards of living among its districts (Indiresan, 2006).

5 For the period 2001-05 the share of private sector in capital expenditure averaged 62%—the corresponding shares of public sector and MNCs were 32% and 5.7% respectively, (*Business Standard* 26 October 2006). In the 2006 list of Forbes magazine's Fabulous 50 publicly traded companies with revenue or market capitalization of at least US$ 5 billion in the Asia Pacific, 12 Indian companies were selected, nearly all of them being from the private sector (Orr and DeCarlo, 2006). Other countries whose companies made the list were Japan (10), S. Korea and Taiwan (6 each), China and Australia (5 companies each), Hong Kong (4) and Indonesia, Malaysia and the Philippines. (one company each).

6 As of October 2006, asset under management by the Indian mutual funds amounted to US$68 billion, and these are growing at a healthy pace. The NYSE and Goldman Sachs have purchased 20 per cent equity in the National Stock Exchange of India (NSE) (*Business Line* 2007). The Bombay Stock Exchange (BSE), a listed company, is also reportedly seeking strategic partners who could collectively own 20 per cent of the equity.

7 India's savings and investments in 2006 are touching 34 per cent of GDP (*www.ibef.org*).

8 India's total international trade in goods and services is expected to be US$ 450 billion in 2006-07, more than 50 per cent of projected GDP (*Business Line*, 10 November 2006).

9 East Asia is also gradually incorporating some of the features of India's model, particularly encouraging entrepreneurship and competition into its growth strategy. Indications are that China is on the path towards less liberal and more nationalistic FDI regime. As Japan, Taiwan and South Korea would like to diversify their global investment risks, India represents an attractive opportunity. East Asia's 'embedded mercantilism' (Jayasuriya 2003), and state capitalism are, however, likely to change only very gradually unless a major economic or political crisis occurs in key countries. As India does not pursue mercantilist policies, and does not exhibit state capitalism characteristics, greater

engagement with it provides another opportunity for global risk diversification. Since India has also not been an aggressive and 'invading culture', this should provide comfort for other nations (Sabnavis, 2006).

[10] Thus, MNCs such as General Motors, Nokia and Motorola are preparing to build plants in western and southern India for manufacturing their products. Similarly, Posco of South Korea and Mittal Steel of the Netherlands have announced plans to build steel mills in eastern India. One of India's own private sector companies, Reliance, is also constructing one of the world's largest coal-fired power plants in Eastern India.

[11] Poddar and Yi (2007), however, project a much higher annual growth for this period for India at 8 per cent.

[12] Defined as increase in country's real GDP at constant 2005 PPP, as a share of increase in global GDP over the same period.

[13] Offshoring of tasks may be regarded as an equivalent to technological progress, which also produces winners and losers, but which leads to net welfare gains (Wolf, 2006).

[14] See Section 4.2 for elaboration.

[15] Korean business organization KOTRA (Korean Trade Centre) set up the Korean week in Mumbai to promote bilateral trade and investment between the two countries and increase trade from the existing US$6.7 billion to US$ 10 billion by 2010 (*Business Standard*, 22 November 2006).

[16] Japanese manufacturing companies, financial institutions and venture capitalists are exhibiting substantial interest in India. India and Japan's industry associations have signed a cooperation agreement to boost Japan's FDI in the electronics sector (Yee, 2006a). The focus will be on pharmaceuticals and manufacturing. This has been in part, a response to take advantage of India's markets in electronics, and in part a response to match aggressive investment strategies by Korean companies in India. One of the indications of Japan's growing economic linkages is the decision by Honda to make India's Honda operations report directly to Tokyo. (*Business Line* 2006), Nissan's decision to invest US$ 840 million in a car plant in India, with one-third of the projected 200,000 units for local consumption and the rest for exports, is another manifestation of growing bilateral ties (*Business Standard*, 1 January 2007).

[17] Bhattacharyay and De (2005), observe that economic cooperation between China and India can be sustained regardless of other ongoing multi-country cooperation initiatives. They argue in particular for increased economic cooperation between South-west China and the eastern states of India.

[18] A Taiwanese firm, Asustek, the world's largest maker of boards that connect the chips in personal computers, will partner with an Indian company to research and develop software next year (*Economic Daily News*, 21 November 2006).

[19] It is important to keep the employment share in perspective. India's labour force by 2009-10 is expected to be over 600 million, and, therefore, IT sector employment will be less than one percent. The employment generation strategies will, therefore, need to be considerably more broad-based. Team Lease (2006) provides an agenda for reforms in this area.

[20] This is indicated by the limited results from Malaysia's super corridor project in its capital. Malaysia has plans to initiate another IT-related project in the southern state of Johor Bahru. It thus has the opportunity to implement appropriate strategies to develop critical mass of IT sector enterprises. Malaysia's reported plans to set up an office of its

recently launched Johor development project, which seeks to encourage the IT sector in India, is a step in the right direction. However, more positive signals from Malaysia are needed.

21 India is aiming to be a centre for car design (Giriprakash 2006). To the extent that such work is translated into actual car production globally, it should be regarded as an integral part of the motor-vehicle production fragmentation.

22 The Indian Institute of Technology (Kharagpur) is in the process of signing an MOU with the National Chiao Tung University (NCTU) of Taiwan as part of a joint effort to facilitate exchange of research and train manpower in the area of chip design and fabrication (*Business Standard*, 24 November 2006)

23 Qantas has awarded a US$ 145 million contract to two Indian software companies. This is a recognition of the mutual economic benefits that have arisen as a result of the advantages of demographic complementarities between Australia and India (*Business Standard*, 10 November 2006).

24 Singapore and Malaysia do not permit their citizens to enroll in such international schools without case by case permission from the authorities. There is a strong case for liberalizing such restrictive practices, particularly as these two countries are projecting themselves as possible education hubs for the region. (*http://www.manipal.edu.my/melaka*).

25 Significant contribution of Indians is also evident in Malaysia's initiative in increasing domestically trained professionals in the health care sector through establishment of the Asian Institute of Medicine Science, and Technology (*www.aiast.edu.my*).

26 Benefits from SAFTA will be greater if Pakistan were to make a shift from a positive list of commodities to be traded with India (numbering around 1000 in 2006) to a negative list.

27 India must make urgent efforts to become more competitive in these areas through infusion of technology, knowledge, investments and modern land-use practices. The Commerce Ministry has indicated that the FTAs cannot wait until domestic reforms are complete, though specific areas such as the issue of inverted import duty structure due to FTAs which puts domestic industry at a competitive disadvantage will be addressed (*The Financial Express*, 10 November 2006).

28 India established three national multi-commodity exchanges in 2002-03, all of which are ranked among the twenty largest in the world as measured in terms of number of contracts traded (UNCTAD, 2006). These demutualized organizations have focused on establishing hi-tech, low-cost web-based trading. They are regulated by the Forward Markets Commission (FMC). As with Indian companies in general, these exchanges have been seeking international alliances and ventures. Some of the traded contracts have purely domestic focus, others such as precious metals, raw jute, and oilseeds, have the potential to take on international importance.

29 Even when Indian wages are adjusted for productivity differentials, India ranks as the most competitive in unit labour cost (19.7 per cent of the US costs) among the sample countries in a study by the Conference Board of the US (*Financial Times* 2006). India recently announced an Automotive Mission Plan for 2006-16 period. It envisages total sales in this sector increasing from US$35 billion in 2005 to US$145 billion in 2016; with exports increasing from US$ 4.1 billion to US$35 billion (*www.ibef.org*)

30 In September 2006 there were 220 inbound Merger and Acquisition (M&A) deals with a total value of US$8.6 billion while 112 outbound M&A deals were valued at US$7.2 billion. (*The Financial Times*, 2006)

[31] Through land custom station at Moreh in India's Manipur state, trade is estimated to be US$ 400 million in 2005 (*Business Line*, 2006). This is 200 times the officially registered trade of only US$2 million, leading to revenue loss and other distortions. The Indian Government is considering expanding trade infrastructure and other facilities at Moreh as also increasing the number of such trading areas along the 1600 km border with Myanmar. India is also keen to enhance banking and other facilities for bilateral trade. This is one of the methods by which India's neighbours can engage in win-win economic opportunities.

[32] See http://news.bbc.co.uk/2/hi/business/6315823.stm

[33] ASEAN + 3 (Japan, Korea, and China) approach preferred by some is sub-optimal as it leaves out key Asian economic entities such as India (Kumar, this volume).

[34] In the inaugural speech to the parliament, the Prime Minister of Japan Mr. Shinzo Abe emphasized the issue of compatibility of fundamental values which is often overlooked. To quote him 'I will further promote cooperation with the Association of Southeast Asian Nations (ASEAN), and as a democratic nation in Asia, I will engage in strategic dialogues at the leader's level with countries that share fundamental values such as Australia and India, with a view to widening the circle of free societies in Asia as well as in the world' (*http://www.kantei.go.jp/foreign/abespeech/2006/09/29speech_e.html*). Japan's Prime Minister has also proposed a quadrilateral dialogue among Japan, US, India and Australia (Datta Ray, 2006).

References

Aggarwal, K.V. and Urata, S. (2006) *Bilateral Trade Agreements in the Asia-Pacific: Origins, Evolution, and Implications*, New York: Routledge.

Association of South East Asian Nations (2005), *ASEAN Statistical Yearbook*, Manila, Philippines: ASEAN.

Asian Development Bank (ADB) (2006) *Key Indicators 2006*, Manila: ADB.

Asher, M.G. (2006), 'Case for a Robust India- Taiwan Economic Partnership', *Policy Briefs No.25*, New Delhi: Research and Information System (RIS).

Asher, M.G and R. Sen (2007) 'Towards Greater Economic Integration', *Asian Management Review*, 2(2): 21-28.

____________ (2006), 'BIMSTEC–Japan Economic Partnership: Opportunities and Challenges', CSIRD Discussion Paper No. 14, Kolkata: Centre for Studies on International Relations and Development (CSIRD).

____________ (2005), 'India-East Asia Integration: A Win-Win for Asia', *Economic and Political Weekly*, 60 (36), 3932-3941.

Asher, M.G. and A. Nandy (2006) Demographic Complementarities and Outsourcing: Implications and Challenges for India, Discussion Paper No.111, New Delhi: Research and Information Systems (RIS).

Becker, G.S. (2006) 'Missing Children', *Wall Street Journal*, 4 September: 15.

Bhide, A. and C. Schramm, (2007) 'Phelps's Prize', *Wall Street Journal*, January 30.

Bhattacharyay, B.N and P. De (2005) 'Promotion of Trade and Investments between China and India: Regional Challenges', Working Paper No.1508, Kolkata: CESIFO.

Bloom, D.E and D. Canning (2006) 'Booms, Busts and Echoes', *Finance and Development*, 43, (3).

Bradsher, K (2006) 'The Next Industrial Giant is ….India?' *New York Times*, 31 August.

Chanda, R and V. Krishnan (2006) 'India and Services Outsourcing in Asia: Trends, Prospects, and Implications' presented at the Workshop on 'Production Networks and Changing Trade and Investment Patterns: The Economic Emergence of China and India and Implications for Asia and Singapore', organized by Singapore Centre for Applied and Policy Economics (SCAPE), and National University of Singapore (NUS), 14-15 September

Confederation of Indian Industry (CII) (2006) *State of the Economy*, New Delhi: CII, September.

CII (2006), *Indian Industry Suggestions for Negotiating Free Trade Agreements*, New Delhi: CII, November.

Das G. (2006) 'The India model', *Foreign Affairs*, 85, (4), July/August.

Dent, C.M (2006), *New Free Trade Agreements in the Asia-Pacific*, London: Palgrave MacMillan.

De, P. (2006) 'Facilitating India's Overland Trade in the Eastern Neighborhood', *RIS Policy Brief No 29*, December.

Deutsche Bank Research (2006) *Outsourcing to India: Crouching Tiger set to Pounce*, India Special, Current Issues, Frankfurt, 25 October.

Datta Ray, S.K. (2006) 'Other end of the see-saw', *The Hindustan Times*, December 11.

Editorial (2006) 'Caution on ASEAN FTA', *Business Line*, 31 August, *http://www.thehindubusinessline.com/2006/08/31/stories/2006083100331000.htm*

(2006), 'Bangladesh: Too Busy to Trade', New York: *The Economist*: 38, 30 September.

(2007), 'NYSE, Goldman, Softbank acquire stake in NSE', *Business Line*, January 11.

Economist Intelligence Unit (EIU) (2006) World Investment Prospects to 2010: Boom or Backlash?, New York: *The Economist*, Columbia Program on International Investment.

Frankel, J. and D. Romer (1999) 'Does Trade Cause Growth?', *American Economic Review*, 89: 379-399.

Giridharadas, A. (2006) 'Global automakers join rush to produce in India', *International Herald Tribune*, September. http:*//www.iht.com/articles/2006/09/11/business/auto.php*

Giriprakash, K. (2006) 'Global car designs eying India', *Business Line*, 11 November.

Hartcher, P. (2006) 'India's passage to power', *Sydney Morning Herald*, 25 September.

Huang Y. (2006) 'The Microeconomic rise of India', *Far Eastern Economic Review*, 169, (2) March.

India Brand Equity Foundation (IBEF) *www.ibef.org*

Indiresan, P.V. (2006) 'Inclusive without being altruistic', *Business Line*, 13 November .

Interview with Masahiro Takedagawa (President and CEO, Honda Siel Cars India Ltd) with N. Ramakrishnan (2006), *Business Line*, 22 September.

International Labour Organization (ILO) (2007) *Global Economic Trends*, Geneva: ILO.

International Monetary Fund (IMF) (2006a) *International Trade Statistics*, Washington, DC: IMF.

IMF (2006b), *World Economic Outlook Database*, Washington, DC: IMF.

Jalan, B. (2005), *The Future of India: Politics, Economics and Governance*, USA: Penguin Viking.

Jayasuriya, K. (2003), 'Embedded mercantilism and open regionalism: the crisis of a regional political project', *Third World Quarterly Journal of Emerging Areas*, 24 (2), April.

Johnson, J. (2007) 'India opens western-style supermarkets', *Financial Times*, 30 January.

Johnson, J (2006), 'Engaging India: Hotels and Financial Reform', *Financial Times*, 26 October.

Kalam, A.P.J Abul and Y. S. Rajan (1998) *India 2020: A Vision for the New Millennium*, New Delhi: Penguin Books.

Karnani, A. (2006) 'Mirage at the bottom of the pyramid', *Business Standard*, September.

Kitamura, T. (2006), 'Japan's New Deal for Asia', *Far Eastern Economic Review*, 169 (7) 41-44.

Kumar, N. (2005) Towards a broader Asian Community: Agenda for the East Asia Summit, Discussion Pape*r 100*, New Delhi: Research and Information System (RIS)

Leahy, J (2006) 'India comes a long way in short time', *Financial Times*, 4 October.

Leeuwen, H. V. (2006) 'Qantas Airways plans to outsource 400 technology jobs to India', 30 September. *http://www.bloomberg.com/apps/news?pid= 20601091&sid= aEtVgXGy8aBc&refer=india*

Marsh, P. (2007) 'A New Twist to India IT outsourcing', *Financial Times*, 31 January.

Morgan, Stanley (2006) 'India and China: New Tigers of Asia', Part 2, Special Economic Analysis.

Mukherji, I.N. (2004), 'South Asian Free Trade Area and Indo-Pakistan Trade', *The Pakistan Development Review*, 43 (4): .943-958

Nageswaran, A.V. (2006) 'Investing in India and China', paper presented at the Harvard Project for Asian and International Relations (HPAIR), August.

National Association of Software and Service Companies (NASSCOM), *Strategic Review 2006*: The IT Industry in India, New Delhi: NASSCOM, February.

Orr, D. and S. DeCarlo (2006) 'The Fab 50', *Forbes*: 34-54, 2 October.

Padmanabhan, M. (2006) 'Ministry proposes full border trade with Myanmar at Moreh', *Business Line*, 6 October.

Poddar, T. and E Yi, (2007), India's Rising Growth Potential, Goldman Sachs Global Economics Paper No. 152.

Prahalad, C.K. (2005), The Fortune at the Bottom of the Pyramid: Eradicating Poverty through Profits, Pennsylvania: Wharton School Publishing.

Rajan, R. (2003), 'The Nexus between Trade Liberalization and Poverty in Asia' in Economic Globalization and Asia: Essays on Finance, Trade and Taxation, Singapore: World Scientific: 111-124.

RBI (2005), Handbook of Statistics of the Indian Economy, RBI: Mumbai.

Reddy, R. (2006), 'Creating Rural Wealth using ICT and Wireless Technology: A Franchising Model using Micro-equity', presented at the 89th Annual Conference of the Indian Economic Association, organized by the Department of Economics, Kurukshetra University, Kurukshetra, Haryana, December 28.

RIS (2006) 'India-Brazil-South Africa (IBSA) Economic Cooperation: Towards a Comprehensive Economic Partnership', *Policy Brief No 26*, New Delhi: RIS, June.

Rodrik, D. (2006), 'Development Lessons for Asia from Non-Asian Countries', *Asian Development Review*, 23 (1): 1-15.

Sabnavis, M. (2006), "The Indian are Coming", *Business Standard*, 3 November.

Saxenian, A. (2006), The New Argonauts: Regional Advantage in a Global Economy Cambridge, MA: Harvard University Press, 2006.

Sen, A. (2006), 'Bilaterals are the building blocks to multilateral set-up', *The Economic Times*, 12 October.

Sen, R. and S. Srivastava (2007) 'ASEAN-India Common Economic Partnership: Exploring Complementarities', in H. Nesadurai and S. Djiwandono (eds.) *Southeast Asia in a Globalizing World: Managing Competitive and Social Challenges*, forthcoming.

Sen, R. (2006) 'New Regionalism in Asia: A Comparative Analysis of Emerging Regional and Bilateral Trade Agreements involving ASEAN, China and India', *Journal of World Trade*, 40 (4): 553-596.

Sharma, N.S. (2006), 'The Rising Sun warms up to India', *Economic Times*, 10 December.

Shirsat, B.G. (2006) 'Private firms spend 71 per cent of India Inc's capex', *Business Standard*, 26 October.

Srinivasan, R. (2006), 'The Indian Investment in Burrup', *Business Line*, November 16.

Taneja, N. (2006) 'India- Pakistan Trade', Working Paper No.182, New Delhi, ICRIER

Team Lease Services (2006), India Labour Report, Bangalore.

The World Bank (2007), Doing Business: How to Reform, the International Bank for Reconstruction and Development (IBRD), Washington, DC: The World Bank, www.doingbusiness.org

__________(2006), *World Development Indicators*, Washington, DC: The World Bank, *http://devdata.worldbank.org/wdi2006/contents/cover.htm*

Thirlwell, M. P. (2004), 'The road to reform', in *India: The Next Economic Giant Australia:* Lowe Institute for International Policy.

Tucker, S. and J. Leahy (2006) 'India deals to hit $7 billion by 2010, says study', *Financial Times*, 14 September.

__________ (2006) 'On the march: how corporate India is finding the confidence to go global', *Financial Times*, 4 October.

United Nations (2006) *Overview of the World's Commodity Exchanges*, United Nations Conference on Trade and Development, Geneva: UN.

UN (2002), *World Population Aging 1950-2050*, Sales No. E. 02. XIII. 3, Department of Economic and Social Affairs, Population Division, New York: United Nations Publications.

Velloor, R. (2007) 'India's Ancient Place Learning Rises Again', *The Straits Times (Singapore)*, 1 January.

Wadhva, C. D. (2006) 'Management of Rising Power by China and India in the 21st Century: Scope for Strategic Partnership', *Vikalpa*, July-September 31 (3): 1-12.

World Bank (2006) *World Development Report* (2006), Washington, DC. The World Bank.

World Economic Forum (WEF) (2006), *Global Competitiveness Report 2006-2007*, Geneva: WEF.

World Trade Organization (WTO) (2006) *International Trade Statistics 2006*, Geneva: WTO.

Wolf, M. (2006), 'Share gains with Globalizations losers', *Financial Times*, September 5.

Woo, Y. P. (2005) 'A review of the APEC membership debate and prospects for India's Admission after 2007', URL : *http://www.asiapacificresearch.ca/caprn/cisp_project/2005/papers/woo_back.pdf*

Yee, A. (2006a) 'Japan and India sign electronics goods treaty', *Financial Times*, 7 September.

________ (2006b) 'Ambitious plan requires change of gear', *Financial Times*, September 28. *http://www.ft.com/cms/s/767f92b4-4e3d-11db-bcbc-0000779e2340.html*

________ (2006c) 'Microfinance: A Serious Business, not Charity', *Financial Times*, 15 November.

Yee, A. (2007) 'Engaging India: The Returning Diaspora', *Financial Times*, 25 January.

Part III
Trade and Investment

9

Forging an Integrated Asia-Pacific Region

Tiziana Bonapace and Mia Mikic

Introduction

When the drafters of GATT 1947 inked Article XXIV, it is unlikely that they could have forseen that half a century later, regional trading agreements (RTAs) would come to dominate trading relations among countries. The surge in RTAs since the establishment of the WTO in 1995 is perplexing, so much so that it has led to a vast literature replete with explanations, which include: a growing trade orientation in global production, expanding WTO membership (from 123 in 1995 to 148 in 2005) and the imperative of forging trading relations with rapidly growing markets in developing countries.

At a theoretical level, the phenomenon can be explained, to a certain degree, by the domino effect and by competitive regionalism. The domino effect (Baldwin, 1993) refers to the desire of countries to avoid marginalization as more and more countries become members of (multiple) RTAs. In other words, no one country wants to be left outside without being able to share in the benefits of belonging to the RTAs as the presumption of net gains is the one which made others join the RTAs in the first place. Competitive regionalism refers to countries seeking 'to secure their trade interests as well as establish spheres of influence that include but also go beyond trade policy' (Majluf 2004:1). Membership in the RTAs is sought to bolster own influence and, in general, cannot be done on a unilateral basis but is dependent on the remaining RTAs member(s)' acceptance of a new member.

No explanation, however, goes far enough in providing a sound clarification for this phenomenal explosion. Furthermore, just as there is no single reason that can explain regionalism, it is no less true that this reliance on RTAs will not disappear any time soon, and that they have become a permanent feature of the trading environment.

The focus should thus turn to ways in which RTAs can be combined with multilateral efforts of the WTO to make trade liberalization and economic integration beneficial to all, rather than seeking to decipher the reasons for this surge.

This chapter begins with a review of regionalism in the Asia-Pacific region, in which the existing RTAs are mapped with respect to their type and coverage. The second section offers a brief analysis of various configurations, focusing in particular on 'hubs and spokes'. The final part is a discussion on some of the possible mechanisms that could disperse the benefits enjoyed by parties in the RTAs to members of the multilateral system, so that the Economic and Social Commission for Asia and the Pacific, ESCAP, region evolves as a key building block of an enhanced global partnership for development.

Box: 9.1. Snapshot of regionalism—comparing trade agreements (in force and notified to the GATT/WTO) in the World and in the UNESCAP region, July 2007

Feature	World	UNESCAP
Number of RTAs notified	205	61
Number of RTAs in force but not notified	65*	29
FTA notified	124	53
CU notified	18	2
Partial scope agreements notified (PTA in ESCAP)	13	5
Economic integration agreement (FA in ESCAP)	48	1
Notified under enabling clause	21	10
Notified under GATT Article XXIV	136	31
Notified under GATS Article. V	48	20

Note: * based on 2005 data

Source: data for world downloaded from WTO website *http://www.wto.org/english/tratop_e/region_e/summary_e.xls* on 6 September 2007, and data for UNESCAP region from APTIAD *http://www.unescap.org/tid/aptiad*, 6 September 2007.

Regional Trade Integration in Asia and the Pacific: Adding Noodles to the Spaghetti Bowl?[1]

As indicated in Box 9.1, the UNESCAP region is the most prolific region in terms of new RTAs. In 1994, a year prior to the establishment of the WTO, there were less than 13 RTAs in this region, of which less than half were free trade agreements (FTAs) —AFTA, ANCERTA, Armenia-Russian Federation, EFTA-Turkey, Georgia-Russian Federation, Kyrgyz Republic-Russian Federation FTAs and the CIS. At last count, there were more than 140 bilateral trading agreements (BTAs) and RTAs at various stages of the negotiation process, involving UNESCAP members and associate members, of which 61 had been notified to the WTO (Box 9.1). More than half of them were signed in the past five years, while many more are under negotiation.[2]

Brief History of Regional Trade Integration in Asia and the Pacific

Asia is a region of trading nations. The history of international trade as an activity of economic importance stretches back to the times of the Silk Route, Venetian traders and Alexander the Macedonian. Trade made regents and communities powerful, and conversely the lack of trade led to their demise. This long experience with trade as an economic activity that enhanced well-being and influence, eventually led in the early 1970s to the adoption of economic policies that were centred on a liberal trading regime. Integration of the region into global markets and reliance on export-led growth accelerated. The pursuit of unilateral liberalization, with variations to accommodate industrial policies, emerged as a first-best policy and the world witnessed first the rise of Japan, followed by the 'Tigers of Asia' (Republic of Korea; Taiwan, Province of China; Singapore and Hong Kong, China), a decade or so later of the 'new exporters' (ASEAN-4 countries) and finally that of China and India. None of these economies at the time of their emergence were clearly involved in any RTA of significance.[3]

The first coordinated, widespread and trade-focused action on regional integration came with the Asia Pacific Economic Cooperation (APEC) in the late 1980s and during the 8th round of GATT negotiations (the Uruguay Round), when agricultural negotiations were deadlocked. By design, APEC was based on 'open regionalism' (extension of regionally agreed preferences to all the GATT/WTO members) and was meant to boost the objectives of multilateralism. With the conclusion of the Uruguay Round Agreements shortly afterwards, multilateralism and regionalism entered a golden period of mutually reinforcing liberalization in Asia and the Pacific. The allure of trade-spurred prosperity led other non-WTO developing and transition countries to continue to liberalize trade regimes while seeking WTO membership. Overall, however, the exploration of the regional route to liberalization remained tentative, bordering on the experimental, and generally restricted to partial scope agreements among developing countries of the region.

This changed dramatically by the end of the millennium. Regionalism in Asia and the Pacific took on an entirely 'new robe' and has not looked back since. The trigger appears to have been the 1997 financial crisis, which jolted countries of the region onto a path that was much more focused on Asian regional affinities and self-reliance. Shortly thereafter, the APEC process of liberalization stumbled and came to a virtual halt. APEC's largest trading nations, led by the US and Japan, when pushed to make liberalization commitments in sensitive sectors, decided that they would be willing to liberalize only within the context of the negotiated reciprocity of the WTO, and traditional preferential RTAs. Sensitive sectors notably, forestry and fisheries, were transferred to the WTO. At the same time, and perhaps even more importantly, once again Japan, but also the Republic of Korea, erstwhile stalwarts of multilateral liberalization, abandoned their earlier reticence with preferential trade agreements (PTAs) and in a major trade policy shift, turned their attention to regionalism. Regionalism, however, took on a new form insofar as it saw developed countries much more engaged than in the previous decades. It moved away from the earlier tentativeness of partial scope agreements and moved into much broader negative-list based negotiations, thus seeking compliance with WTO provisions contained in Article XXIV. Negotiations also covered a wider scope of issues, going beyond traditional tariff negotiations of FTAs. A key characteristic of this new age regionalism was that most of these negotiations took place and still are taking place, on a 'one-on-one' bilateral basis.

Current Status

These 'new age' BTAs and RTAs considerably in membership, style, design and effectiveness, in line with the diverse and heterogeneous nature of the political affinities and economic landscape of the ESCAP region. Many agreements are grounded in clear regional political alliances. Some appear to have common cultural affinities as a driving force, but most do not. Some have well-developed institutionalized rules of interaction while others have a more informal structure based on voluntary cooperation. Some are open to new members, while others have a moratorium on the same. The breadth of coverage varies as well (see a survey of agreements in the region on the UNESCAP website), with services covered in a few agreements while most do not cover services in any meaningful way. Agriculture may be wholly or partially excluded, while movement of factors of production, depth of tariff cuts, coverage of non-tariff measures and decision-making processes also vary widely. Likewise, the results achieved vary tremendously.

This surge in the number of various RTAs led to Asia and the Pacific region starting to assume the 'spaghetti bowl' look of the EU or (to a lesser extent) the Americas (Figure 9.1). The multiplicity of RTAs with their own liberalization paths, sets of rules of origin (ROO) and diverse approach to dispute settlement and other issues still outside the scope of the WTO (the so-called WTO plus issues) has led to a non-transparent trading environment, with no clear path of integration emerging from one trading nation to another. Instead of making trade easier and smoother, the multiple layers of agreed rules have increased the costs of compliance to traders. Consequently traders are known to often ignore the RTAs' preferences and rely on the multilateral most favoured nation (MFN) trading environment instead.[4]

The agreements depicted in Figure 9.2, are mostly negotiated under the format of free trade agreements while others are in the form of economic partnerships, with unclear distinctions as to what the differences are in effect. More often than not, these bilateral agreements raise doubts about the extent to which they are consistent with the GATT(1994) Article XXIV. While they do comply in terms of the liberalization timetable (typically up to 10 years as envisaged by the WTO),[5] the extent to which they meet other criteria is unclear. At the same time, WTO rules are also unclear, thus further adding to the fuzziness of the objectives of such agreements. For example, in terms of coverage of trade ('substantially all trade'), reciprocity (full reciprocity or symmetry) and intensity of liberalization (elimination of tariffs), these bilateral agreements appear to offer too little, but in the absence of quantifiable benchmarks at the WTO level, most such assertions remain untested.

Furthermore, when these RTAs have more than two partners, rarely do they agree on harmonized preferences for all partners. Instead the liberalization is driven by a number of possible bilateral agreements—without repetition—between the partners. Thus in the case of 3 partners, there are 3 bilateral preferential relationships (agreements), but in the case of 6 partners, there could potentially be 15 different bilateral deals.[6]

Emergence of 'Hub-and-Spoke' Structure in Asia and the Pacific

This criss-crossing web of preferential deals could evolve into a 'hub-and-spoke' structure of trading environment. A 'Hub-and-spoke' structure consists of one large market (hub) which enters into one-on-one (bilateral) trade agreements with a number of other countries (spokes). Spoke countries are

Figure 9.1: The Noodle Bowl

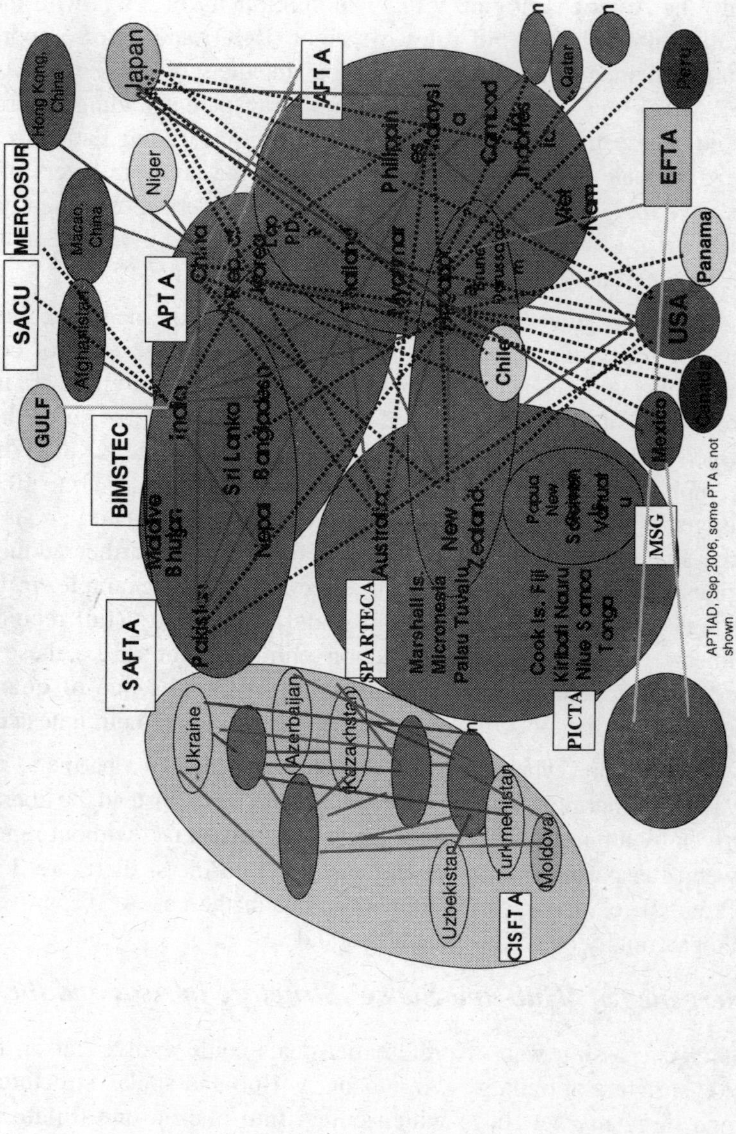

Figure 9.2: Bilateral Agreements among UNESCAP Members

*) This map includes bilateral FTAs and negotiations that involve at least one member county of ESCAP plus the US.

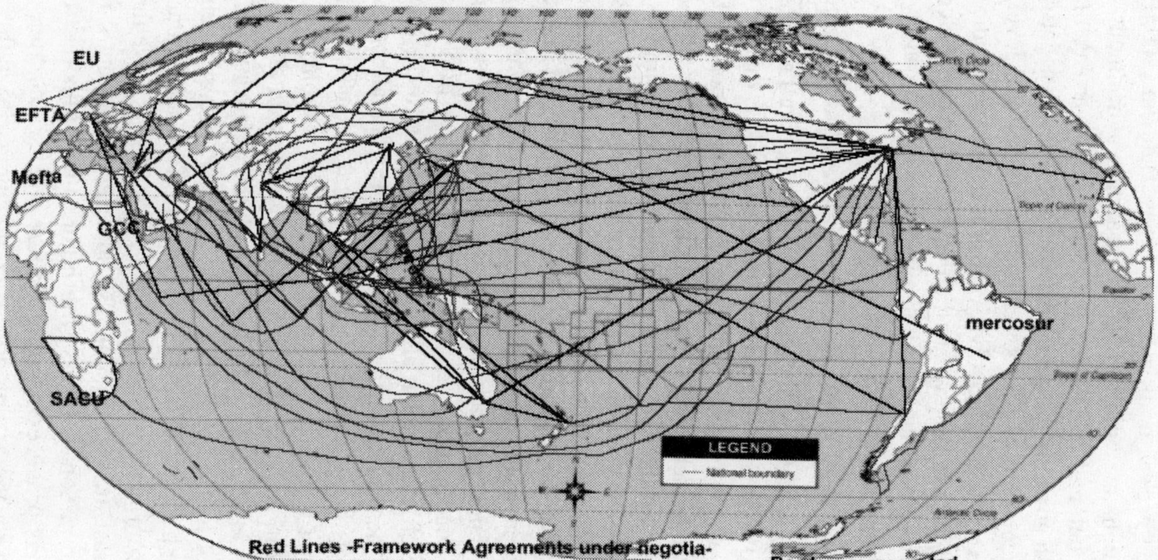

Red Lines -Framework Agreements under negotiations
Black lines - Existing Bilateral Agreements
Shapes - RTAs that negotiate as a block (borders in Asean not represented and Mefta is a US initiative

Borders represented are not authoritiative

typically smaller and have no market access agreements amongst each other. The spokes form a periphery and become marginalized, as the hub enjoys improved market access to all spoke countries. Baldwin (2003) emphasizes two levels of problems with this type of trading environment. First, at the economic level, hub-and-spokes with their criss-crossing arrangements increase the costs for both governments and private sectors through negative allocation, location and accumulation effects. Second, at the political level, a hub-and-spokes structure could introduce divisiveness as it gives economic and political leverage to the 'hub'. In Asia where there is more than one 'natural' hub, this could result in several competing hub-and-spoke systems, allowing for little cooperation among them.

a) Implications of liberalizing on a geographically discriminatory basis

Allocation, location and accumulation effects are standard static and dynamic effects expected upon the integration of national markets that previously were separated by various tariff and non-tariff barriers imposed at the border. Removal of these border barriers allows for more free flows of goods, services and/or factors of production (capital, labour and technology). These flows are not freed fully because of the remaining existence of barriers that are not directly trade related, even though they are increasingly the subject matter of discussions on trade liberalization, for example, adjustment of exchange rates, social labelling, environmental labelling, minimum native language content in radio and television programmes, minimum wages, various direct taxes, recognition of qualifications, etc. However, even freer flows that are partial allow for more efficient global allocation of resources if there were no other distortions but these trade barriers. The problem is that although globally the allocation effects bring welfare improvements, at the national level positive outcomes are not guaranteed. They depend on the interplay between the so-called trade creation, trade diversion, trade modification and, in some cases, trade deflection effects all of which arise with the reallocation of resources in the aftermath of trade liberalization. Trade creation occurs when an RTA, by removing trade barriers, also replaces high-cost domestic production by low-cost imports from other members of the RTA. This is a welfare increasing effect. In contrast, trade diversion, also switches supply but it replaces low-cost imports from non-members with high(er)-cost imports from members of RTA and thus produces negative welfare effects. The trade modification effect is based on the assumption of complementarity, rather than perfect substitutability of trade flows between countries in the agreement and third countries. So when preferential liberalization stimulates trade between partners it might positively affect trade with third countries if such trade mostly contains products which are complements to the intra-agreement based production and trade. Of course, this effect can also be negative depending on the actual degree of complementarity vs substitutability. The net effect is what an individual country harvests first from entering the RTA. Although there are some 'rules of thumb' for forming a net-trade creating RTA[7] (as opposed to a net-trade diverting one), they do not necessarily work in every case and it becomes all but impossible to predict if the RTA will be trade creating or trade diverting. The end result is complicated additionally by a potential impact on tariff revenues through the trade deflection effect, which arises in the case of free trade agreements but not in customs unions (CUs). A further layer of complications arises through dynamic effects—location and accumulation effects—which are set in motion as a result of the increase in size of the market.

b) What configuration is emerging in the Asia-Pacific region?

It would appear that the current criss-crossing of bilateral FTAs could evolve, into and organize itself, into a more systematic hub-and-spoke configuration. Both proactive and defensive trade strategies seem to be driving this process. On the one hand, the two or three major trading countries or trading blocs appear to be competing to establish trade hegemony in the region. At the same time, there are a number of smaller middle-income trading countries that are equally active in forging bilateral trade deals and also appear to be competing to establish dominance as a hub. This, however, may be more symptomatic of a defensive trade strategy, designed to avoid finding themselves at the spoke end of another major hub. A multi-layered constellation is thus emerging, made up of a dominant hub-and-spoke arrangement with substrata of other hub-and-spoke arrangements in which smaller economies may be trying to establish alternative hubs.

Taking this emerging scenario, the next question is whether under the current network of criss-crossing hub-and-spoke arrangements, the gravitational force of one large trading country will eventually prove to be too strong so that it emerges as the dominant hub. Under this scenario, alternative hubs dissolve and become tied to the hub by a separate agreement, each tailored to the particular and separate interests involved between the hub and the spoke. Preferential treatment between the hub and spoke is not necessarily extended to other spokes in an MNF manner. This is the least liberalizing of the configurations, as each spoke is likely to have comparative advantages in a different set of sectors, with the result that liberalization is tailored to fit the particular needs of each individual spoke. It is bilateralism based on exclusivity rather than the inclusiveness of MFN, and represents a radical departure from WTO rules and principles. Its driving force is the political relationship between the hub and the spoke, rather than a multilaterally agreed body of norms, rules and principles that apply equally to all. Furthermore, import-competing industries in the hub country will insist on including wide-ranging safeguard clauses and stringent ROO. Vested interests may become firmly entrenched and more difficult to dislodge in future liberalization attempts; and the more spokes are added to the hub, the more diluted the benefits for each of the spokes. Finally, if a hub country conducts freer trade with spokes that, in turn, are not involved in reducing trade barriers among each other, outer-rim trade, which typically consists of South-South trade, is displaced and spokes turn into 'spikes' as the hub continues to suck trade and investments towards itself.

c) Centrifugal forces: much ado about nothing?

The option of developing countries collectively establishing themselves through ASEAN, as the alternative hub, stands out in particular. At the same time, more skeptical analysts question whether ASEAN has deepened integration sufficiently and whether it will ever evolve into an integrated union of countries with free flow of goods, services and other production factors across its border.

Of course, trade and FDI liberalization has continued in ASEAN since the Asian crisis and members are on track to create a regional FTA before 2015, five years ahead of the initial plan. Overall, however, reform appears to have been more gradual, shallower and less resolute than the pace-setter China, and the tigers of East Asia two decades ago. Little progress has been made on the ASEAN Investment Area (AIA) and the ASEAN Framework Agreement on Services (AFAS), thus resulting in a mismatch between the speed at which deeper (behind the border) and shallower (border) integration is progressing. Given the increasing interlinkage between FDI and trade (almost two-thirds of trade in services consist of capital flows), the two dimensions of liberalization should be in proceeding in tandem, if ASEAN is to emerge as an integrated area that is more attractive to foreign investors and that will reap the benefits of integrating between East and South Asia in global markets.

Notwithstanding this relative slowness, a large number of trading partners—the US, Australia, New Zealand, Japan, Republic of Korea, China, India, Mercosur and, more recently, the EU—are at various stages of concluding FTAs with ASEAN. Given the slow progress in economic integration within ASEAN, especially when compared to its trading partners, it would seem that ASEAN is at the centre of a centrifugal force: a stationary centre, that acts outwards and draws energy from a body moving towards the centre. This raises the question of whether the force will gather momentum and attract more and more countries to its centre. Can ASEAN summon up the energy to turn itself into a cohesive and integrated union of countries? Will the ASEAN Charter muster the political drive that will enable countries to forgo a part of their nationally sovereign policy-making for the greater common good? Can the ASEAN Charter unify countries by enabling them to overcome their internal differences?

Consolidating and Globalizing Regionalism in Asia and the Pacific

Theoretical and empirical evidence supports the claim that the outcome of globally maximized welfare achieved by multilateralism cannot be replicated by a complex network of BTAs and RTAs in lieu of the multilateral trading system. It is beyond the scope of this chapter to go into an in-depth analysis of these arguments. Suffice it to say that the sum of welfare-maximizing interests of a number of RTAs comes short of the collective interest of all.

Are there any avenues which would allow a transfer of self-interest of RTAs into a collective interest of all, thus replicating the outcome of multilateralism? In this confusing scenario, a timely conclusion of the Doha Round, with sufficient depth and scope, that erodes and universalizes perceived benefits in BTAs would be essential for bringing about some order. At the end of the day, the more WTO negotiations achieve significant reductions in trade barriers,—that are extended to all 148 members on a non-discriminatory basis—the weaker the rationale for pursuing alternative discriminatory, more preferential FTAs, be they regional or bilateral. As Panagariya says (2000: 328): 'Once external tariffs drop to zero, tariff preferences and the spaghetti bowl created by them will automatically disappear'. This, however, ignores the political and other non-economic objectives underlying bilateral relations among countries, and seems politically unrealistic.

The question thus returns to the regional level. How should the myriad bilateral, regional and cross-continental initiatives coalesce and provide a fast track to global free trade under the multilateral trading system?

Three possible options, through geographic, functional and institutional integration of RTAs, are explored.

Geographic Integration

Perhaps intuitively, the obvious way of coalescing and fast- tracking these initiatives would be for one RTA to fold into another geographically-larger RTA which, in turn, would fold into ever larger geographic spaces until global trade is fully encompassed. This idea was central to the design of APEC and its principle of open regionalism. For such a process to occur an inner dynamic is required. What conditions trigger this dynamic? Basically, two conditions would need to be met. The first one relates to the creation of added benefits from an increase in size of the RTA (the 'domino effect'). This means that each country joining as a new agreement would need to increase the incentives for other countries to join. In a static sense, an increase in the number of members would increase the likelihood of a net trade creation as there would be a higher chance that more efficient suppliers do indeed become part of the RTA, thus minimizing or eliminating the effects of trade diversion. In a more dynamic sense, adding a country to the RTA would create a larger market thus allowing for better utilization of economies of scale and providing incentives for firms to locate to that market, that is, for FDI to be redirected from other markets to this enlarged market. This is in line with the creation of positive network-externalities as an increased number of firms join the market, leading to additional incentives for more producers to join and thus further increasing the costs of those remaining outside. Evidence from the expansion of the EU market to 25 members suggests that this effect does occur—if a country is left out of the enlarged market, it loses firms. A second condition requires that existing members show willingness to allow unrestricted entry. There is no guarantee that this will, in fact, be achieved. One reason is the uncertainty over whether the volume of net benefits will increase with a larger number of partners. There will thus be a reluctance to share benefits. Perhaps more important is the role played by other political, historical, social and cultural considerations and the fear that deep seated and irreconcilable differences among countries may make harmonization of policies all but impossible.

At a more practical level, the ongoing expansion of political and economic integration in the EU offers a useful example of geographic consolidation. When 10 new members joined the EU on 1 May 2004, 65 WTO notified RTAs were abrogated. The 10 new members terminated BTAs between themselves and the EU, between themselves and third parties and among themselves.

Moving to the Asia–Pacific, an example of the type of geographic integration envisaged is shown in panel 'c' of Figure 9.3. In this case, the Bangkok Agreement, as the only trade agreement that currently links South and East Asia, with three of its members sharing common membership with BIMSTEC (panel 'a'), might eventually coalesce into an initiative that promotes a wider East, Southeast and South Asian FTA. A third circle encompassing

SAFTA could also be added, particularly since Bangladesh, India and Sri Lanka belong to all three RTAs (panel b). An agreement open to all countries of Asia-Pacific, for example, the Asia-Pacific Trade Agreement (APTA), as the Bangkok Agreement will soon come to be known, could thus serve as a useful vehicle for laying some of the groundwork of this framework. The Bangkok Agreement has the advantage of being a relatively evolved text, which is the product of a long history of negotiations. Furthermore, the Bangkok Agreement's members represent a widely diverse development spectrum (with Republic of Korea at one end and Bangladesh and Lao PDR at the other end) and thus encompass true and tried rules across a representative group of the development cross-section of the region. Furthermore, a number of developing countries have expressed interest in joining APTA, notably Mongolia, which is the only WTO member that is not yet a part of any RTA. Bhutan, Cambodia, Nepal and Pakistan are among some of the countries that are also considering joining the agreement. The first session of the Ministerial Council of APTA was hosted by China on 2 November 2005. It provided an important political impetus and the potential for this text to evolve further as a modal South-South Agreement should be further explored. This will be disucssed further in the next section.

In East Asia, the current axis of integration, is centred around the ASEAN + China + Japan + Republic of Korea process, with each of the +3 countries negotiating separately with ASEAN. More recently, India signed an FTA with ASEAN which could have a significant impact on the western expansion of ASEAN. Although at a preliminary stage, Australia and New Zealand have also indicated interest in joining this axis, thus bringing about a cross-continental expansion.

Yet another potential axis of geographical consolidation draws in the Central Asian region in the wider Asian and Pacific regional cooperation frameworks. Figure 9.4 shows the current configuration of the main RTAs in Central Asia and the Caucasus. Here again it is clear that overlap and disparate initiatives provide scope for consolidation, both within the sub-region, and also with other RTAs in the Asian and Pacific region at large. The Russian Federation is a member of many RTAs involving former Soviet republics, such as the Central Asian Cooperation Organization (CACO) and the Eurasian Economic Union (EEU). At the same time there is a weak link between the economies of the former Soviet Union and those of the rest of Asia.

Traditionally, Russia and its history have been intertwined with that of the rest of Europe, while for most of the 20th Century, ideology drove its economic relations towards like-minded countries of the Council for Mutual Economic Assistance (or Comecon as it was known). Relations with Asia

Figure 9.3: Consolidating RTAs: an Example of a Geography-based Consolidation

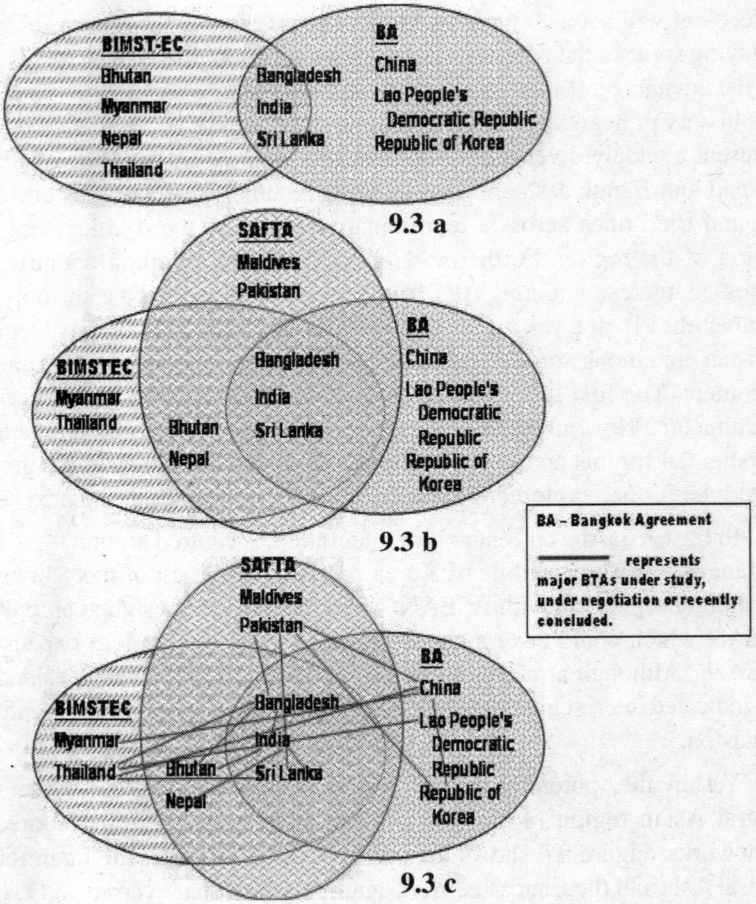

thus remained tentative at best. However, in the wake of the reform process, the Russian Federation has increasingly looked towards the East, while at the same time not ignoring its relations with the Western world. The linkages are evolving, driven in part by complementarities between supplies of natural resources in Central Asia and needs of energy-deficient, rapidly growing countries in East and South-east Asia. The Russian Federation is linked to Asia through groupings such as APEC and more recently, the Shanghai Cooperation Organization (SCO), which bring together the Russian Federation, China and selected Central Asian countries. SCO, however, has yet to formulate a RTA.

Figure 9.4: The need for Consolidation of RTAs in the CIS

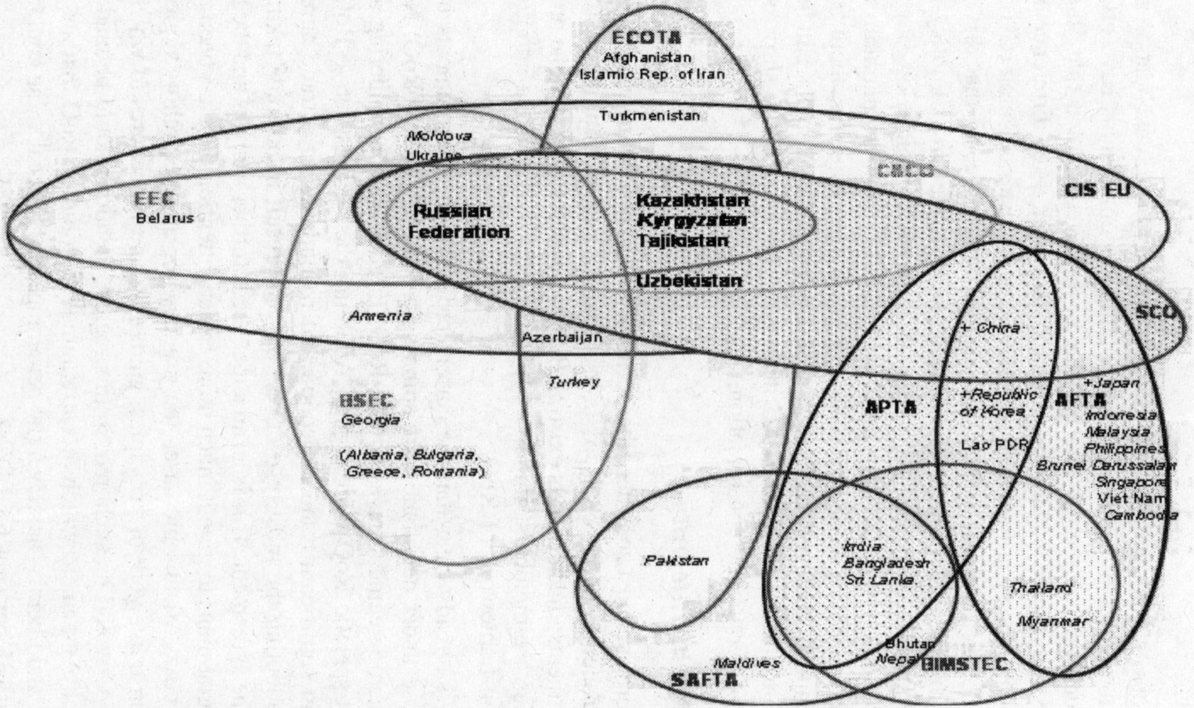

Note: WTO members are in italics.
Source: UNESCAP (2005).

Given the membership of China, India and the Republic of Korea in the Bangkok Agreement, an interesting option might be for Russia to join the Bangkok Agreement in a closer integration between Central Asian economies and other parts of Asia.

Notwithstanding these opportunities for geographic consolidation, realities linked to historical disputes and other political compulsions have often held back such developments. The EU has nevertheless shown that historical differences can give way to consolidation. However, a key difference between the EU and the Asia-Pacific is that the EU is a Customs Union (CU), with a common external trade policy, and an institutional set-up that drives a far greater degree of harmonization across a much broader area of policy-making than what exists in the ESCAP region. Geographic consolidation may thus be more feasible in a CU than in an FTA where members maintain a more independent policy stance vis-a-vis third countries. Thus far, there has been no example of such geographical consolidation having taken place in the Asia-Pacific region, besides the APEC initiative, which has yet to show concrete results of geographic consolidation.

Functional Integration

Therefore one must consider other forms of integration. Functional integration may proceed on the basis of consolidating and harmonizing differing commitments under various existing BTAs and RTAs of which one or various countries are members. Initially, efforts should focus on the adoption of a common framework of RoO.

It is already clear that the current proliferation of agreements in force, and those under negotiation are spinning a complex web of RoO. Not only does each agreement have its own RoO, in addition a bewildering array of product-specific RoO is emerging. Adopting the less restrictive RoO could result in significant trade deflection and redundancy of a trade agreement, while adopting the most restrictive RoO may result in no trade taking place under the agreement. This is an area that needs further analysis and the ESCAP Secretariat plans to give it much more critical attention than has been the case up till now. All this increases the urgency for an overarching region-wide common framework of principles, guidelines and procedures to which BTAs and RTAs would be anchored. In this regard, mention should be made of the Bangkok Agreement which recently agreed to common RoO that are simple, general and liberal—namely a flat percentage rate of local value content of 45 per cent (35 per cent for LDCs).

On the investment side, there are currently about 1800 bilateral investment treaties in place and, as evidenced by new-generation EPAs, trade and investment issues are increasingly treated in an integrated manner. The prospects for consolidation could go further to encompass closely related issues such as trade in services, competition policy and wider forms of economic cooperation such as financial and monetary cooperation. Eventually in the long term, these initiatives could serve as the building blocks for a common understanding on the international architecture that is needed to support and anchor these regional efforts.

Another interesting issue worthy of further study in the specific context of the ESCAP region is that of financial packages. Contrary to examples from other agreements around the world (for example, Euro-Mediterranean partnership, AGOA, CAFTA, etc.) trade liberalization and financial/aid packages, in all their varieties and forms, in the ESCAP region have remained separate entities. New age regionalism is, however, bringing with it a convergence between financial compensation packages and trade liberalization programmes. Newer agreements are devoting much greater attention to so-called flanking issues that encompass trade liberalization. Further, SAFTA under special and differential provisions to LDCs, foresees the establishment of a revenue compensation mechanism to assist in recovering revenue lost from SAFTA trade liberalization. The modalities on how this mechanism will work have not been agreed upon and, by current indications, there are doubts on whether this mechanism will ever come to fruition.

Nevertheless, the principle of compensating revenue loss from tariff reduction can be a facilitating factor in determining the success of an eventual FTA, if designed properly. One problem faced when setting up such a facility among a restricted group of developing countries is that many LDCs are grappling with poverty reducing challenges and fiscal constraints, and can ill-afford extensive compensatory packages.

This raises the question as to whether a regional financing facility that encompasses a wider set of countries should be set up, and whether linking such a facility to trade liberalization could be made to work at the regional level. A region-wide facility involving a much larger set of countries, both developed and developing would have clear advantages. The Asia-Pacific region, including its developed members, has built-up over US$3 trillion in foreign exchange reserves.[8] Region-wide mechanisms offer benefits such as scale economies in pooling resources, spread of risk, enhanced credibility and access to supplementary sources of financing, including private sources. Further, a regional facility is linked by geographical, cultural and historical factors that can provide a further stimulus for a cohesive approach to these issues.

How such compensatory mechanisms would work, as indicated in the SAFTA case, remains an open question. For example, should a common fund be set up? Who should fund it? Should only the more advanced countries provide financing? Should a portion of export income be used, and if yes, what percentage? On the import side, how should 'losers' be compensated? Should a proportion be calculated according to import volumes? What would trigger its use? Should it be used for revenue compensation as under SAFTA, or balance of payments shortfalls as under IMF/TIM, or only technical assistance to facilitate structural adjustment arising from trade liberalization? How should it be monitored? LDCs' face particular vulnerabilities. They do not have the resources to set up social safety nets, and worse, they do not have the resources to endure long-term structural unemployment. Should only LDCs have access to such compensatory financial resources? What about other developing countries? India and China despite their remarkable export and economic growth, after all, account for almost three quarters of the world's poorest people. Should sector-specific special credit schemes on a region-wide basis evolve that would allow some enterprises to invest in upgraded production for competing in an increasingly competitive global trading environment, the abolition of the Multi-Fibre Agreement being a case in point?

Institutional Changes and Integration

The simplest way of multilateralizing the benefits of regional agreements would be to speed up MFN-based liberalization negotiations under the umbrella of the WTO. This, however, is politically unrealistic as continued missed deadlines of the Doha Round can testify. Therefore, if multilateralism is to remain the centerpiece of international economic policy, alternative institutional strategies need to be put in place. This may require changes in rules, particularly by clarifying not only the RTAs but, more fundamentally, the type of membership.

One possibility is to allow the RTAs themselves to become negotiating parties. This of course would make more sense if all RTAs were CUs (similar to the EC) because a common external trade policy for all members requires a harmonization of national policies that enables secretariats of CU to negotiate more effectively with one voice on behalf of all members. This would reduce the number of negotiating parties and would hopefully simplify processes and shorten the timelines for reaching consensus.

There are only 11 CUs in the world today, of which only two involve members of ESCAP.[9] Some of the CUs appear to have more form on paper, than in actual operability. Nevertheless, as a start, one option would be for the WTO to extend the same recognition to these CUs as it does to the EC. In future, members of the CUs would not be separate negotiating parties even though they would retain their individual memberships in the WTO.

Yet, it is not certain if such type of institutional change at the global level would be relevant for all regional blocks. Regionalism in Asia-Pacific has followed its own path, characterized by a more flexible and fluid cooperation, than is the, case in other parts of the world. A focus on outward orientedness with the rest of the world is another key distinction. Regionalism was never intended to be inward-looking, in a fortress-like manner, nor are there indications that this is a likely trend. Pragmatism, based on market forces has prevailed over more institutionalized forms of cooperation. Nevertheless, given the current disorder and the increasing concerns that this is raising, questions have been asked as to whether a more structured approach—embedded in a supranational structure of governance—is necessary, with the EU model providing the most concrete example.

Countries are, however, still spread too far across the spectrum of political systems, and regulatory differences among them are also perhaps too wide for a European style institution-driven process of integration. Asia is perhaps better-off evolving its own process, starting with policy coordination focused on pragmatic forms of functional cooperation. In the absence of EU-style institutions, an intergovernmental organization with region-wide outreach such as UNESCAP in collaboration with development partners such as RIS, the ADB and sub-regional organizations is in an excellent position to promote a set of common and cohesive principles, practices and operational frameworks that set the foundations for regional economic integration. At the end of the day, vision should be tempered by realism and cost effectiveness.

Further Work

A key task, therefore, is to draw out the commonalities among agreements and promote their consolidation with a view to achieving a more rational process of Asia-Pacific-wide integration. In addition to the areas of work outlined above under geographic and functional integration, the secretariat has developed a 'one-stop' database which collates descriptive information on more than 140 RTAs/BTAs applicable to the ESCAP region. The database was expanded to include trade flows and the set of indicators to assess the implications of RTAs/BTAs on such flows.

In order to provide stakeholders (government, researchers and policy analysts) with a tool to monitor and analyse these initiatives, the UNESCAP secretariat has developed a database of these initiatives called APTIAD (available at *www.unescap.org/tid/aptiad*).This database has a 'one-stop' searchable function which contains: detailed descriptive and updatable information on the provisions of bilateral and regional agreements, and statistical data sets on trade flows, commodity composition and services trade by individual agreements.

The first phase in developing this database has been completed.[10] The current phase focuses on adding information related to the coverage of each agreement (contingent protection, standards, services and other areas) by each agreement; and developing analytical measures and indicators.

The further work to be carried out include the design of a modal trade agreement for developing countries, using existing agreements including APTA. The modal agreement is intended to provide government negotiators with a practical tool consisting of guidelines and principles in the negotiation of PTAs with developed and developing countries. The modal agreement will be developed through an analysis of the data sets and an in-depth study of the texts of agreements.

Conclusions

New patterns of regional cooperation are emerging driven by increased resources that have been made possible through spectacular growth in trade and investments. As countries continue to grow and become more integrated into regional and global trade flows the prospects for the region to emerge as a key building block of an enhanced global partnership for development look good. At the same time, the current process of regional and cross-continental fragmentation as evidenced by the largest proliferation of RTAs/BTAs in history is a cause for concern. Because these agreements contain inconsistent provisions, they are fragmenting the region's trade and investment integration process. Further, poor countries are effectively being excluded from this process, and are thus falling through the cracks.

Additional efforts are needed to prevent new divisions between the rich and poor, between aligned and non-aligned states, with trade being carved out along lines determined by political affinities—the so called coalition of the willing rather than economic efficiencies. At the regional level, deep-seated historical conflicts— the coalition of the unwilling—also appear to be preventing further integration of the region.

New economic opportunities should enable the region to rise above past political conflicts, as confidence in opening up to each other increases. This will require the mobilization of political leadership for an enhanced regional integration process. The interplay between bilateralism, regionalism and multilateralism needs to be managed so that the region can continue to consolidate its role as the key building block of an enhanced global partnership for development. Delivery on the Doha negotiations for a strengthened, open, rules-based, non-discriminatory, predictable and universal multilateral trading system is the centerpiece, supported by an integrated UNESCAP region featuring a regional framework for the consolidation of BTAs/RTAs into one region-wide and deeper WTO-consistent trade agreement.

Endnotes

1 This term, which describes a mixture of overlapping and intersecting preferential agreements with frequently inconsistent provisions, originally linked to the EU, is credited to Bhagwati (1992).

2 The terms PTA and RTA are used interchangeably in this paper. There are two CU notified from this region: Turkey-EU customs union effective from 1996 (notified in 19950), and EAEC in force since 1997 (notified in 1990) —both notified under GATT Article XXIV.

3 Although some of these countries were members of the Association of Southeast Asian Nations (ASEAN) established in 1967, at that time this bloc had no trade preferential arrangements. The founding document, the Bangkok Declaration, included announcements of active collaboration and mutual assistance in the field of economics, but it focused primarily on political and security issues.

4 This is particularly true in the case of the non-reciprocal GSP schemes making the 'utilization rate' of these schemes low.

5 Except that often when the agreement is between countries at different levels of development, there is an asymmetry in the timetable of liberalization, with the less developed partner being granted a longer transition period to implement the agreed liberalization commitments.

6 This assumes no repetition on bilateral combinations, implying that a deal between countries A and B is the same as between B and A. In practice, there could be two different set of rules (of origin) for an agreement theoretically double between countries A and B. Thus the combinations of agreements on rules of origin might and they become based on p(p-1) formula, where p is the number of countries. As emphasized in Crawford and Fiorentino (2005: 17-18) separate liberalization schedules are maintained as members prefer to maintain exclusions for sensitive products which are different across members, most often in agriculture products.

7 Based on empirical and theoretical literature, entry to RTAs is recommended which have many rather than few members; where the members have more developed economies than the new entrant; where lots of trade already existed before the formation of RTA; where the borders are shared; with countries that are engaged in multilateral liberalization, etc. These and other 'criteria' for a beneficial RTA are explored in World Bank (2000).

8 According to the International Financial Statistics Online by International Monetary Fund (September 2007), ESCAP members held SDR 2,384,238 million in foreign exchange reserves at the end of 2006.

[9] As mentioned earlier, Turkey-EU CU is effective from 1996, while EAEC is in force since 1997.

[10] The current version covers all the agreements reported to the WTO to this date in which at least one party is in the UNESCAP region. It also includes other agreements that have not been notified but for which there is official information readily available, and also those agreements under negotiation for which there has been at least a first formal negotiation round.

References

Baldwin, R.E. (2003) 'The Spoke Trap: Hub-and-Spoke Bilateralism in East Asia,' paper presented at Korea Institute for International Economic Policy (KIEP) seminar, KIEP 04-02.

________ (1993) 'A Domino Theory of Regionalism' NBER WP 4465, Cambridge.

Bhagwati, J. (2005) 'Reshaping the WTO' *Far Eastern Economic Review*, January/February issue.

________ (2002) *Free trade today*, Cambridge: MIT Press

________ (1992) 'Regionalism versus Multilateralism' *World Economy:* 535-55.

Bhagwati, J., P. Krishna and A. Panagariya (1999) *Trading Blocs, Alternative Approaches to Analyzing Preferential Trade Agreements*, Cambridge: MIT Press.

Bonapace, T. (2004) Regional Trade and Investment Architecture in Asia-Pacific: Emerging Trends and Imperatives, RIS Discussion paper No. 92/2005, New Delhi: RIS and reproduced in *Economic and Political Weekly,* 3 September 2005: 3941-3947.

Crawford, J.-A. and R.V. Fiorentino (2005) 'The Changing Landscape of Regional Trade Agreements' Discussion paper No. 8, Geneva: WTO.

Jajasekera, D. (2004) 'Intra-regional Trade Agreements in Asia', UNDP, Asia Pacific Regional Initiative on Trade, Economic Governance, and Human Development.

Krugman, P. (1991) 'Is Bilateralism Bad?' in E. Helpman and A. Razin(eds) *International Trade and Trade Policy*, Cambridge: MIT Press.

Kumar, N. (2004) 'A Broader Asian Community and a Possible Roadmap' presented at the conference on Asian Economic Integration: Vision of a New Asia, RIS, Tokyo, November 18-19 and reproduced in *Economic and Political Weekly*, 3 September 2005: 3926-3931.

Majluf, J.A. (2004) 'Swimming in the Spaghetti Bowl: Challenges for developing Countries Under 'New Regionalism' *Policy Issues in International Trade and Commodities Study Series*, No. 27, Geneva: UNCTAD.

Mikic, M. (2002) 'Preferential trading agreements: adding spices and noodles to a spaghetti bowl' *Cahiers de Commerce International,* Numero 3, Novembre, Universite Lumiere Lyon 2.

________ (1998) *International trade, theory and policy*, Basingstoke: Macmillan

Pal, P. (2005) 'Regional Trade Agreements in a Multilateral Trade Regime' *Foreign Trade Review*: 27-48.

Panagariya, A. (2000) 'Preferential Trade Liberalization: The Traditional Theory and New Developments,' *Journal of Economic literature,* XXXVIII (June): 287-331.

Sally, R. and R. Sen (2005) 'Whither Trade Policies in Southeast Asia? The Wider Asian and Global Context' *ASEAN Economic Bulletin*, April 22 (I): 92-115.

Schiff, M. and L.A. Winters (2003) *Regional Integration and Development*, Washington, DC: World Bank.

Thangavelu, S.M. and T.M. Heng (2005) 'Bilateral "WTO-Plus' Free Trade Agreements: The WTO Trade Policy Review of Singapore 2004" SCAPE Working Paper Series, Paper No. 2005/05.

Tsai, C. (2005) 'Regional Trading Arrangements and the Multilateral Trading System: Agriculture' OECD Trade Policy Working Paper No. 15, Paris: OECD.

UNESCAP (2005) 'Experiences with regionalism and Bilateralism in Asia and the Pacific with Focus on central Asia,' paper prepared for the International Conference on Strengthening Regional Cooperation for Managing Globalization, Moscow, 28-30 september.

World Bank (2005) Global Economic Prospects 2005, Washington, D.C.: World Bank.

_________ (2000) *Trade Blocs*, Washington, DC: World Bank available at *(http://www.worldbank.org/research/trade/pdf/trade%20blocs.pdf)*

WTO (2005) *World Trade Report*, Geneva: WTO.

10

Welfare Gains from Regional Economic Integration in Asia: ASEAN+3 or EAS

S.K. Mohanty and Sanjib Pohit

Introduction

Asia is emerging as a vibrant economic space in the new millennium, and it is gradually reviving its earlier position as a dominant global economic power as exhibited at the beginning of the nineteenth century.[1] In this new episode of Asia's resurgence in the twenty- first century, the integration of some of the East Asia countries has played an important role in inducing other Asian countries to engage in the high growth process. Consolidation of ASEAN countries in the 1990s, and their efforts in roping-in 'Plus' countries in regional economic integration, have triggered rapid economic growth in Asia during the last decade Lamberte (2005). A major step in this direction was a decision to launch the East Asian Summit (EAS) to deepen their level of integration.

Several studies (Kumar 2005) have observed that EAS could be the beginning of a process which would take the region towards the formation of an Asian Economic Community (AEC). These Summits have come at a time when Asia is expanding rapidly amidst new economic challenges. At the beginning of this decade, certain positive developments occurred in Asia that provided encouragment for the formation of AEC. After a prolonged phase, Japan has made a smart recovery from its recession (IMF, 2007). China and India have continued to maintain their high economic growth and such performances have been sustained over a long period of time (Rajan and Sen, 2005; Rahman and Andreu, 2006). As a result of the surging economic prosperity, the middle income group in ASEAN and Plus countries has been growing with high consumption propensity. This has been a major contributing factor for the fast expansion of the regional markets in Asia for production, investment, technology and skilled human power through integration of regional economies. Besides, regional economies have shown greater resilience to various forms of crisis including natural disasters such as earthquake, tsunami, and external shocks such as hike in petroleum prices, etc. The platform for wider Asian regional integration is near set for 'take off' and, therefore, a regional initiative like EAS is an important step in this direction.

The readiness of Plus countries is not different from that of ASEAN countries to join further integration process in AEC. Japan and Korea are already better placed in terms of their economic development than ASEAN and other Plus countries to complement the EAS process. India and China have achieved major strides in their economic development in recent decades. The emergence of these countries with their enormous import-dependence on neighbouring countries, has begun to transmit growth impulses to their partner countries, providing them the opportunity to also grow fast (Mohanty and Chaturvedi, 2006).[2] These large and fast growing countries have large synergies with ASEAN countries, and this would improve prospects of welfare effects mutually. Australia and New Zealand are developed countries that have complementarities with ASEAN in diversified sectors.

In the recent surge of Asia in terms of its robust economic performance, ASEAN has played a major role. During the last two decades, not only has trade among the ASEAN partner countries increased but even intra-regional trade of ASEAN+4 countries has increased substantially, which has contributed to surge of overall economic activities in Asia in terms of trade, investment and movement of skilled persons (Sinharoy 2004). Regional countries have revealed their strong preference for trade with close neighbours, and this has been an important factor in making Asian global trade 'Asia centric'. This trend would be even more profound with a deeper level of integration.

Unlike North America and Europe, Asia has not benefited substantially from the regional process due to lack of effective leadership in the long run. In the present situation, ASEAN commands effective leadership to take emerging Asian countries towards the right track. The 'Plus' countries have rallied around the 'Core ASEAN' countries to optimize synergies existing between them. In the absence of ASEAN in command, the possibility of economic integration in Asia with the mutual cooperation between 'Only plus Countries' or/and other Asian countries, is perhaps very low. Since, ASEAN is at the driver's seat, it has to think about the appropriate group of countries (ASEAN+3 or EAS) which are to carryout another liberalisation initiatives under the AEC, taking into account which group of countries is likely to generate the maximum welfare gain to ASEAN (Pitsuwan 2007).

Two issues need attention in order to take a view on the future membership architecture of AEC. These two pressing issues are: (a) what is the ideal size of AEC, and (b) what should be the coverage of economic liberalization to make AEC an effective regional trading arrangement.

Membership: It is apparent that the organisational architecture of AEC is closely linked to the economic interests of ASEAN. To what extent the large economic interest of ASEAN can be better served— whether with a small group of 'Plus countries', or with a larger group of 'Summit level' countries— is a critical issue which must be looked at by ASEAN keeping in view the absolute economic gains from the alternative arrangements. Ideally speaking, if ASEAN gets maximum advantages by forming close economic cooperation with ASEAN+6 than with ASEAN+3 (APT), then ASEAN should give a positive indication to ASEAN+6 to be the basis for forming AEC. The right to resolve the membership issue in AEC rests with the ASEAN and the regional caucus is yet to decide on this issue.

In the literature, two divergent views are discussed regarding the membership structure of AEC. Some of the Plus countries have taken the lead in arguing out the shape of the future AEC. While China has argued in favour of ASEAN+3 as natural partners for forming the AEC, Japan favours ASEAN+6 as the ideal group for the proposed AEC (Kawai and Wignaraja, 2007 and Kumar, 2006). The genesis of the Chinese proposal was that 'Plus Three' countries worked very closely during the period of the 'Asian financial crisis'; and they jointly mooted several initiatives to overcome the same AEC. Since they have worked together closely from the days of the economic crisis, they (APT) should exclusively form the core of the EAS. The position of Japan is that ASEAN+3 countries in 2004 decided to form the AEC with ASEAN+6, and this decision may be implemented when AEC is eventually formed (Kawai and Wignaraja, 2007 and Kumar, 2006). There is another view on the architecture of the AEC. Some others feel that if AEC is to start with a smaller group, then it should be with 'Plus' countries rather than including other 'new members' like Australia and New Zealand (Smith, 1998). In that case AEC may be formed with ASEAN+4 than with ASEAN+3. This may be treated as a revised Chinese proposal on AEC. The alternative responses to the question of membership of AEC, ASEAN+3, ASEAN+4 or ASEAN+6, are an area for further empirical examination.

Trade Liberalization: The trade liberalization issues would remain complex when EAS resolves its membership issue, and then proceeds to adopt a scheme of economic reforms which would enhance its regional welfare gains. In order to optimize the benefits and gains from regional initiatives to the individual partner countries, attempts need to be made to forge a broader regional framework, which will provide a seamless market and facilitate harnessing synergies more effectively. In the milieu of the large financial gains for the region, implications of wider and deeper regional integration are empirically examined by several studies, and the results are indicative of the need for a broader regional integration (Kumar 2005).[3]

The member countries may start with a Free Trade Area (FTA) with reduction of trade protection in the form of tariff and non-tariff barriers. It is often argued that economic liberalization may not be effective with an FTA because several FTAs are operational in the region and overall global tariff and non-tariff barriers are being lowered under multilateral trade negotiations. Therefore, in recent regional/bilateral trade arrangements, wider issues are included, for example, trade in services. Such agreements not only cover trade in services in specific sectors but also the mode of delivery of services. Many studies emphasize the fact that the largest interest of developing countries in services negotiation could be in the movement of natural persons, that is mode 4 (Mohanty, Pohit and Sinha Roy, 2004). Therefore, GATS issues need to be covered in the proposed trading arrangement. Some of the investment issues need to be incorporated in the regional integration arrangements (RIAs). In various RTAs, investment is prominently covered (Globerman and Shapiro, 1999). According to the existing laws in many countries, investment is restricted to flow within the political boundaries. In case mobility of investment is allowed freely within the AEC; welfare gain for the region can be enhanced through allocative efficiency of capital. In fact, allocative efficiency will enhance the productivity of the regional production process (Schiff and Winters, 2003), and the region is likely to be placed on a higher growth trajectory. Therefore deep trade integration in the AEC may be envisaged with comprehensive liberalization in several areas including trade investment and liberalization of trade in services.

This chapter makes an attempt to examine the optimal package of regional economic liberalisation which would maximize the benefit of ASEAN countries from further economic liberalization initiative. This would addresses two issues: (a) which ideal group of countries would benefit ASEAN the most from the three alternatives of country-combinations, that is, ASEAN+3, ASEAN+4 or ASEAN+6, (b) which comprehensive economic liberalization scheme (FTA,

FTA+ investment or FTA+investment+trade in services) would be appropriate for EAS countries to optimize the welfare of ASEAN countries. The simulation exercise is undertaken using a monopolistic version of Computable General Equilibrium (CGE) and assuming a seamless East Asian community without taking into account the existing bilateral/sub-regional/regional arrangements. In this chapter nine alternative simulations are considered, taking different combinations of country-groupings and depth of trade liberalization. The focus of the paper is to identify which country combination to provide maximum economic welfare to ASEAN countries in a comprehensive economic liberalization framework.

The Model

It is apparent from the recent spate of activities that AEC is to be reconstituted keeping ASEAN at the driver's seat. ASEAN is in full command to decide on the architectural design of the new caucus, based on its own economic interest from the regional grouping. The Applied General Equilibrium (AGE) model in this chapter is designed to accommodate alternative membership criteria as also various schemes of economic liberalization taking trade, investment and trade in services into consideration. As far as trade liberalization is concerned, the identified sectors are considered to be large to be put in a general equilibrium model, therefore certain key factors[4] in each of these sectors are considered for liberalization.

A monopolistic[5] version of the multi-regional AGE model is used in the present simulation analysis to estimate welfare implications of the AEC, which can take shape based on its present 'Summit level partners' and also to pursue some scheme of economic liberalisation from various alternative schemes available in the literature, taking into account world economic activity in 26 different aggregated sectors and 15 aggregated regions/countries and rest of the world.[6] The model estimation is primarily based on GTAP database, version 6, but it is supplemented by additional data from other sources.[7] Based on the country disaggregations available in GTAP 6, 11 out of the 16 country/regional groups are considered for the AEC country-grouping in the model. Similarly, global and regional/country economic actives are categorized into 5 agricultural sectors, 17 manufacturing sectors and 4 services sectors in each economy represented in the model.

This model accords special attention to three principal factors of production, namely, unskilled labour, skilled labour and capital. Among these factors, unskilled labour is considered perfectly mobile across sectors within a country and not across the AEC. This assumption is common for all scenarios in the model. However, it is assumed that factors such as skilled labour and investment are perfectly mobile across AEC, depending upon the model specifications in different scenarios.[8]

Based on the above factors and alternative country groupings of the AEC, this exercise resulted in nine alternative scenarios. The core issue is which alternative country grouping of AEC is likely to generate optimal welfare gains for the ASEAN countries. The choices of country-groupings are ASEAN+3, ASEAN+4 and ASEAN+6. Optimization of economic welfare from liberalization by these groups of countries would identify the group most suitable for the formation of the AEC.

For effective regional arrangement, deeper integration is required in EAS. For this consideration we have gradually intensified the depth of integration in the proposed region in various scenarios. To begin with, the first scenario could be liberalization of tariff, followed by liberalization of tariff and investment together and the last scenario covers simultaneous liberalization of trade, investment and movement of natural persons.

Table 10.1: Alternative Scenarios for EAS from Simulation Analysis

	ASEAN+3	ASEAN+4	ASEAN+6
FTA	I	II	III
FTA+ Investment	IV	V	IV
FTA+ Investment+Services	VII	VIII	IX

Note: These scenarios are simulated using monopolistic CGE models.
Source: Authors.

In this chapter, nine alternative scenarios are conceptualized (see Table 10.1). We focus on the sequence in which the three alternative groups of countries are expected to perform—from shallow to deeper level of integration. Even in each simulation, variations in the performances of individual countries are examined along with the extent to which regional countries are coping with a deeper level of economic liberalization. (In the subsequent discussions on scenario analysis, the numbering pattern of simulations as presented in Table 10.1 will be followed.)

Towards an Optimal Size of EAS and Depth of Trade Liberalization: Simulation Results

The experiences of some of the successful RTAs across the world suggest that significant welfare gains to individual member countries occur due to substantial trade liberalization along with free cross border investment and movements of skilled labour.[9] With the fast increasing growth in the global demand for technology-intensive products (UNCTAD, 2004; Mohanty and Arockiasamy, 2007) and rapidly growing capital intensive production process of such products, free movement of investment within the region combined with industrial technology is bound to rise (Kumar, 2004). Many countries in East Asia have acquired competitiveness in desired lines of production and are becoming production power houses for Asia and also for the rest of the world (Wilson et al 2005). In recent years, several Asian countries have strengthened their skilled manpower through massive investment in human development; and management of human resources is considered to be a key area of potential gains for these economies. Moreover, in the WTO negotiations, developing countries hope to achieve their long-term interest of free movement of skilled labour, with the phrase 'movement of natural persons' under GATS mode 4. In the regional context, free movement of skilled labour has immense potential for the development of the region as it allows temporary engagement of skilled labour for the facilitation of specialized assignments prevents permanent migration (Mohanty, Pohit and Sinha Roy, 2004).

In the context of the East Asian Caucus, welfare gains arising from complete trade liberalization along with free cross-border investment and movements of skilled labour within the region are examined. Regional countries are better placed to benefit more by adopting an overarching FTA among East Asian countries, instead of engaging themselves in bilateral FTAs and sectoral cooperation. The implications of deepening of regional integration among the AEC countries in different schemes of regional cooperation, is empirically examined. Since the structure of the AEC at present is in a fluid state, we confine the scope of our discussion to welfare gains for the AEC which is yet to take the shape of formal country-grouping and to the adoption of a scheme of economic liberalization from among many alternatives.

Alternative Schemes of AEC and Regional Welfare Gains

Very often the regional process is not preferred to a multilateral process on the ground that the former is trade diverting in nature, which would increase regional welfare at the cost of global welfare. Hence, to make the process of AEC more meaningful, it should be trade creating in nature rather than trade diverting. The trade liberalization policies, following the formation of AEC, would result in reallocation of productive factors across sectors owing to an increase in demand for tradable sectors within the region. In the process, allocative efficiency of the existing factor endowments would be altered, and so also relative real prices of different factors. The scale of production and the level of production would also undergo significant changes in different regional economies. On the whole, the implications of such restructuring are reflected in the estimation of welfare gains, which are physically quantifiable.

With the formation of an FTA under AEC, the regional welfare gains could be within a range of US$40 billion to US$176.1 billion, depending upon the composition of membership and the depth of economic liberalization between member countries as shown in Table 10.2. The results indicate that the proposed FTA is likely to enhance the welfare of both region and individual member countries. The AEC would be trade creating in nature where both the AEC and the global economy are likely to benefit in terms of positive welfare gains. The magnitude of absolute gains in regional welfare will also enhance global welfare. Depending upon the membership structure of AEC and the level of trade liberalization, the additional global welfare could range between US$6.7 billion to US$740.1 billion in a year. All the major regions of the world would benefit from the trade liberalization in AEC when its sequence of liberalization is more comprehensive (it covers all issues including trade, investment and trade in services among the regional partners).

It is shown in Table 10.2 that ASEAN and 'Plus 3' countries would have limited welfare gain when AEC takes the shape of APT, and their overall regional gain increases when they move from a shallow to a deeper level of integration. Most of the countries in the regional caucus show a similar experience.

When India is included in the regional caucus, it makes significant difference to the whole region and also to individual countries in terms of welfare gain. For example, the absolute level of welfare rises between 30.5 per cent to more than 34 per cent in various schemes of trade liberalization when India joins ASEAN+3 in AEC as compared to a situation when ASEAN+3 alone forms AEC. If APT forms AEC and the group resorts to comprehensive liberalization covering trade, investment and skilled labour movement, the additional welfare gain for the region could be to the tune of US$87.3 billion per annum, but on adding India to the group, regional welfare is likely to be enhanced to US$113.6 billion per annum. The gains could be even higher if ASEAN+6 form the core of AEC. The region is likely to benefit more when investment and skilled labour are allowed to move freely within the AEC. The magnitude of absolute increase in welfare gains under the comprehensive trading arrangement would be US$ 176.1 billion per annum.

Table 10.2: Absolute Change in Welfare Gains from the East Asian Economic Integration

(million US$)

Country	Scenario:I	Scenario:II	Scenario:III	Scenario:IV	Scenario:V	Scenario:VI	Scenario:VII	Scenario:VIII	Scenario:IX
	FTA			FTA and Investment			FTA, Investment and Trade in Services		
	ASEAN+3	ASEAN+4	ASEAN+6	ASEAN+3	ASEAN+4	ASEAN+6	ASEAN+3	ASEAN+4	ASEAN+6
Indonesia	2091	2434	2670	903	995	2320	13009	15806	22300
Malaysia	1942	2270	2435	1897	2992	3243	1692	1956	2670
Philippines	597	733	809	806	981	1076	1179	1383	2005
Singapore	1060	1281	1300	1180	1457	1483	698	755	1164
Thailand	2554	2981	3272	3202	3806	4236	1958	2520	3765
Japan	22090	24786	27804	56639	66118	70451	40236	61313	91029
Korea, South	4857	5749	6271	8382	9971	10716	6503	7650	10976
China	7402	9362	10832	380	4683	8571	11561	17193	30128
India	-122	2680	2947	124	5352	5803	3428	5026	6462
Australia	-222	-225	3683	-308	-221	6534	1477	5369	5926
New Zealand	-21	-3	893	5	52	1582	224	655	1667
South Asia	-256	-185	-242	-310	-396	-559	634	2295	3336
NAFTA	-7330	-7375	-10122	-15881	-17261	-26502	20910	98944	151839
EEA	-9988	-9486	-11875	-12845	-11591	-17810	17516	84667	125641
Oceania	-16	-18	-22	-14	-16	-23	46	138	230
Rest of the World	-17287	-17064	-22260	-29051	-29264	-44894	39106	186044	281046

Notes: Additional increase in welfare in terms of GDP for each country in the event of regional integration.
Source: Authors' computations.

Liberalization among AEC countries may lead to different levels of welfare gain for individual countries depending upon the maturity of economies, composition of trade, level of openness, trade potential, etc. As the size of member countries differs significantly, the welfare effect of a country/region is viewed in relation to its GDP. Table 10.3 provides the estimates of the potential welfare effect with respect to GDP for each country and also for the region. The overall responses of member countries indicate that the level of gain increases as one moves towards deeper level of integration, though there are some exceptions. Within the ASEAN, countries such as Indonesia and the Philippines, which are performing well to catch up with other, more advanced countries of the region, are likely to gain more from the most comprehensive economic cooperation than others. China has been articulating the structure of AEC as APT to start with, but the results show that China's economic interest in AEC lies in comprehensive economic cooperation with a wider group of countries, that is, with ASEAN+4 or ASEAN+6. India may be comfortable with either investment liberalization along with trade or comprehensive economic cooperation.

There are concerns about the implications of the formation of EAS on regions which fall outside the AEC. For ASEAN and Plus countries, NAFTA and European Economic Area (EEA) are extremely critical economic units for trade and investment. Several studies have displyed concern about the negative fall-out of the EAS on those regions outside AEC. In order to avoid such a situation, some studies argue that an APEC type of RTA may be pursued based on the principle of 'open regionalism' (Ethier, 2000; Soh, 2004). In this chapter, we analyse the issue in order to mitigate the concerns of the adverse effects of AEC on those regions/groupings. The negative impact of the AEC on regions like NAFTA and EEA is of different magnitude in some simulation scenarios in the AGE model because those country groupings are not engaged in this regional arrangement. NAFTA and EEA are engaged in negotiations with ASEAN and Plus countries on a bilateral basis. When those cases are examined separately, the positive effects generated in the bilateral engagements may possibly be over compensated which they are losing under the shallow form of regional integration in AEC. The results show that NAFTA and EEA are likely to benefit positively when there is a deeper level of regional integration in AEC, covering investment and free movement of 'natural persons' along with trade liberalization. These results may hold good irrespective of nature of size of membership architecture of the AEC. It is interesting to note that the percentage change in welfare gain may be significantly large for NAFTA and EEA, when the membership structure of AEC is large and there is deep regional integration.

Table 10.3: Percentage Change in Welfare from the East Asian Integration

(in percent)

	Scenario:I	Scenario:II	Scenario:III	Scenario:IV	Scenario:V	Scenario:VI	Scenario:VII	Scenario:VIII	Scenario:IX
	FTA			FTA and Investment			FTA Investment & Trade in Services		
Country	ASEAN+3	ASEAN+4	ASEAN+6	ASEAN+3	ASEAN+4	ASEAN+6	ASEAN+3	ASEAN+4	ASEAN+6
Indonesia	-0.4	0.5	0.6	-0.2	0.2	0.5	2.7	3.3	4.7
Malaysia	2.3	2.7	2.9	2.1	3.3	3.6	2.0	2.3	3.1
Philippines	0.8	1.0	1.1	1.1	1.3	1.5	1.7	2.0	2.8
Singapore	1.3	1.6	1.6	1.4	1.8	1.8	0.9	1.0	1.5
Thailand	2.3	2.6	2.9	2.7	3.2	3.6	1.7	2.2	3.3
Japan	0.5	0.6	0.7	1.3	1.5	1.6	1.0	1.5	2.2
Korea, South	1.2	1.4	1.5	1.9	2.3	2.5	1.6	1.9	2.7
China	0.6	0.7	0.8	0.0	0.3	0.6	0.9	1.3	2.3
India	-0.1	1.9	2.0	0.1	3.5	3.8	2.4	3.5	4.5
Australia	-0.1	-0.1	1.0	-0.1	-0.1	1.8	0.4	1.5	1.7
New Zealand	0.0	0.0	1.8	0.0	0.1	3.0	0.5	1.3	3.3
South Asia	-0.1	-0.1	-0.1	-0.1	-0.2	-0.2	0.3	1.0	1.5
NAFTA	-0.1	-0.1	-0.1	-0.1	-0.1	-0.2	0.2	0.9	1.3
EEA	-0.1	-0.1	-0.1	-0.2	-0.1	-0.2	0.2	1.0	1.5
Oceania	-0.1	-0.1	-0.2	-0.1	-0.1	-0.2	0.3	1.0	1.7
Rest of World	-0.1	-0.1	-0.1	-0.1	-0.1	-0.2	0.2	0.9	1.4

Note: Additional increase in welfare as a percentage of GDP of individual countries in the event of FTA and CEC in the region.
Source: Authors' computrations.

Implications of Deeper Integration on Different Schemes of AEC

The existing literature presents the fact that deep integration is more advantageous than shallow integration (El-Agreaa, 1999). When member countries are placed at different levels of economic development, the effect of different levels of integration may be diverse (Frankel, 1997). From nine alternative simulations, it is observed that the effects of regional integration with ASEAN+6 are better than the with ASEAN+3 because of the size of welfare effects accruing to the AEC region. The larger the size of the AEC, the larger would be the quantum of gains from the regional caucus as shown in Figure 10.1. Between ASEAN+3 and ASEAN+4, the gain from integration jumps up significantly from simple FTA to FTA combined with investment liberalization, while liberalisation with 'free movement of natural persons' adds little to overall welfare of AEC.

Figure 10.1: Effects of Deeper Integration on AEC

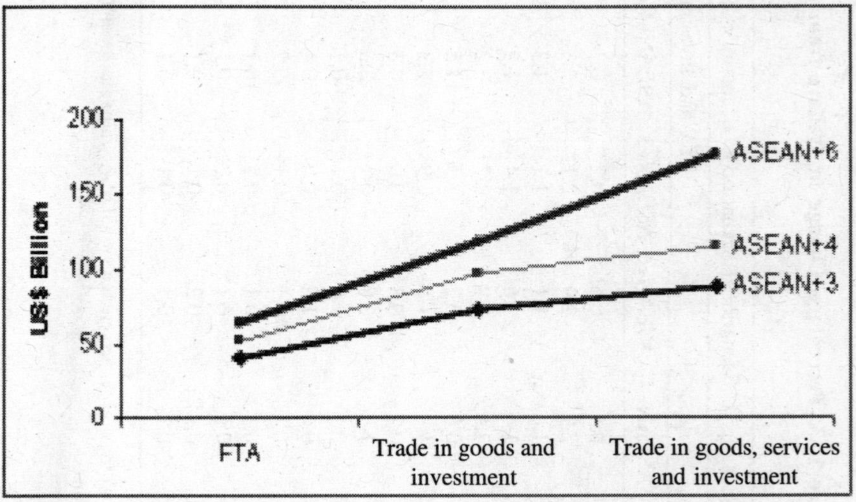

Source: Based on simulation results.

A comparison between ASEAN+3 and ASEAN+6 is striking in terms of gains from regional integration under different liberalization schemes. Regional engagement in only tariff reduction may have differential effects on the two alternative country-groupings. When the two country-groupings engage in a deeper level of regional integration, that is, FTA along with investment, the rate of increase in welfare gains would be much higher in ASEAN+6 than in ASEAN+3. If both the groups again engage in further trade liberalization, the divergence in welfare gains would increase sharply between the two groups. While the rate of incremental welfare gain is likely to decline in case of ASEAN+3 (under comprehensive economic cooperation or CEC), it may rise steadily in case of ASEAN+6 (under CEC scenario). This suggests that AEC is likely to benefit more if its membership base is relatively larger. The results support the Japanese suggestion that AEC should comprise of ASEAN+6 rather than ASEAN+3. The second observation is that there should be a deeper level of integration rather than a shallow level in order to maximize regional welfare effects.

The Gain for ASEAN Countries in Different Groupings

As discussed earlier, ASEAN is on the driver's seat in AEC and its economic interests should be accorded priority while deciding on the membership issue in AEC. The membership composition should be such that ASEAN as a group gains the maximum welfare from the formation of new regional caucus. For this reason, we have regrouped welfare gain in each of the nine alternative scenarios separately and each scenario, we have estimated percentage welfare gains with respect to the group's GDP for the four groups separately, namely, ASEAN, ASEAN+3, ASEAN+4 and ASEAN+6.

Figure 10.2: Gains for the ASEAN in Various Schemes of RTA

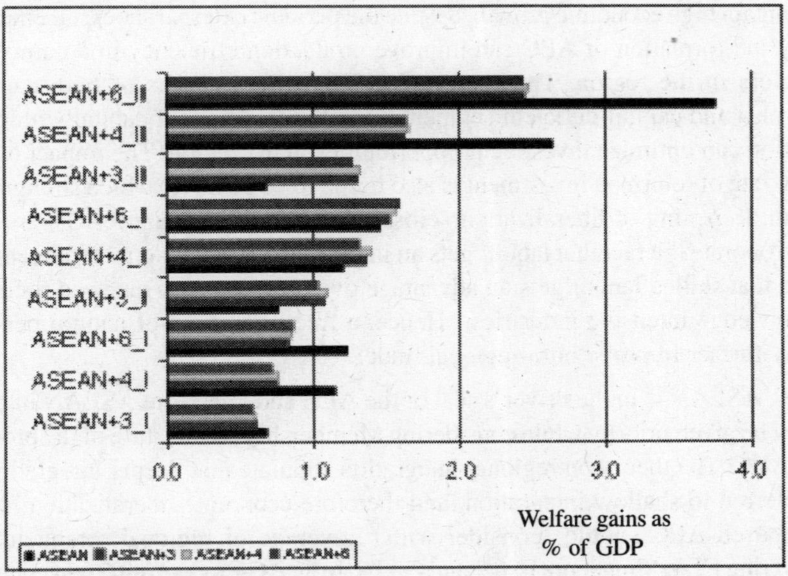

Source: Based on simulation results.
Note: ASEAN+3_I denotes ASEAN+3 in FTA, ASEAN+3_II in FTA and investment and ASEAN+3_III in FTA, investment and services

The results show that ASEAN with any group of countries (that is, ASEAN+4 and ASEAN+6) is likely to gain if it is engaged in a deeper level of integration. With ASEAN+3, ASEAN group of countries is not likely to gain much, irrespective of the level of economic integration. As the size of the AEC increases, the prospects of ASEAN getting welfare gains increases. ASEAN is likely to gain more with ASEAN+6. The results support the Japanese argument that AEC should be ASEAN+6 to optimize regional welfare.

Conclusions

The experience of Asia with regionalism is very recent, but its achievements from the regional process have been unique and commendable. The trade pattern of the ASEAN-Plus countries is steadily tilting in favour of developing countries, and is also becoming more 'Asia centric'. With a strong trade bias towards neighbouring countries, surge in intra-regional trade has been the hallmark of this region. Intra-regional trade in the ASEAN+6 region comprises both resource-based and technology-intensive products, and the divergent export basket provides ample opportunities to its member countries, which are at different levels of economic development.

The Asian countries have learnt to depend on the regional process to maintain high economic growth, despite the periodic external shocks. It emerges that the formation of AEC can improve production efficiency in a number of sectors in the region. The proposed AEC region consists of both capital-surplus and capital-deficient segments, and the free flow of capital within the region can optimize investment opportunities in the region. The impact on the real rate of return on investment is also found to be positive, which strengthens with deepening of liberalization across sectors in AEC countries. The results corroborate the fact that labour gets an impetus from the regional arrangement, and that skilled labour gets an advantage over others due to renewed focus on knowledge intensive industries. Hence, a free movement of natural persons may further improve intra-regional trade.

ASEAN is in the driver's seat of the AEC and, therefore ASEAN interest may be given priority while considering Membership architecture of the process of AEC. The theory on regional integration stipulate that deeper integration is preferred to shallow integration, and therefore economic liberalization in the proposed AEC should consider wider coverage of regional arrangements covering FTA, 'Singapore issue' and GATS. In an AGE model, different country-groupings for EAS are combined with different levels of regional integration to identify the appropriate size of AEC and the suitable level of trade integration to optimize welfare gains of the AEC and the ASEAN as a group.

The empirical findings show that welfare gains from the formation of AEC may range between US$40 billion to US$176.1 billion per annum, depending upon the composition of membership and depth of economic liberalization in the proposed arrangement. The formation of the AEC would be global welfare enhancing rather than trade diverting which is a typical feature in many RTAs. Depending upon the structure of AEC, including membership and depth of liberalization, global welfare effects (including other regions of the world), are likely to be enhanced between US$6.7 billion to US$ 740.1 billion per annum.

India's inclusion in the AEC makes a significant difference to the whole region, and the region gains substantially in terms of additional economic welfare. When India joins the EAS, the absolute level of welfare of the caucus rises between 30.5 per cent to more than 34 per cent depending upon the level of liberalization. In case the AEC is formed with ASEAN+3, and liberalization takes place with comprehensive economic integration covering trade, investment and skilled labour movement, the additional gain for the region could be US$87.3 billion per annum. However, the regional gains go up substantially to US$113.6 billion in a year when India joins the caucus. Under the similar conditions, the entry of Australia and New Zealand in EAS may enhance incremental gains of the region to the extent of US$ 176.1 billion per annum.

Most of the regions of the world and AEC countries are likely to benefit from the trade liberalization in AEC when its liberalization is more comprehensive covering trade, 'Singapore issues' and GATS simultaneously and AEC covers all 'Plus' countries in it. If AEC comprises ASEAN+3, the group of ASEAN countries may not gain much irrespective of their level of economic integration. ASEAN is likely to gain more only when the EAS group is larger in size, particularly with ASEAN+6. The results support the Japanese argument that AEC should comprise ASEAN+6 to optimize regional welfare.

Endnotes

1. In a seminal work, Maddison (1998) found that Asia contributed 59.4 per cent of global income in 1820, and the continent is likely to regain its past global economic status by 2030 following the rapid growth of Asian countries. The early symptoms of such predictions are taking shape as many Asian countries have been maintaining sustained and high economic growth over a long period.
2. See, for example Mohanty and Chaturvedi (2006).
3. For details, see Kumar (2005).

[4] We have taken tariff liberalization to cover trade; investment representing 'Singapore Issues' and 'movement of natural persons' representing services.

[5] In the AGE model, we have taken three sectors, agriculture, manufacturing and services, where the manufacturing sector is assumed as having a monopolistic structure and other two sectors are operating under perfect competition.

[6] The present model is an updated version of an earlier model, which was used to analyse the implications of the formation of JACIK (Japan, ASEAN, china, India and South Korea) on individual countries and on the region as a whole (Mohanty, Pohit and Sinha Roy 2004).

[7] The database provided by the GTAP is not sufficient to solve an AGE model based on monopolistic competition. Therefore, other databases have been used to meet the requirements of the model, for example, *Handbook of Industrial Statistics*, UNIDO; World Development Indicator, UNDP; etc.

[8] In certain scenarios in this model, free movement of skilled labour and investment are not allowed.

[9] The experiences of NAFTA and EU indicate that the effects of deeper level of regional integration have been significant and enduring for the member countries of the RIAs.

References

Agarwala, Ramgopal (2005), 'Asia's Re-emergence: When Can Asia Reclaim Its Place in the World Economy' in Asian Development Bank (ed.) *Asian Economic Cooperation and Integration: Progress, Prospects and Challenges*, Mnila:ADB.

El-Agraa, Ali M. (1999), *Regional Integration: Experience, Theory and Measurement*, London.: Macmillan Press.

Ethier, W. (2000), 'The New Regionalism', in H.D. Dixon (ed.), *Controversies in Macroeconomics: Growth, Trade and Policy*, pp. 150-162, Massachusetts: Blackwell Publishers.

Frankel, Jeffrey (1997), Regional Trading Blocs in the World Economic System, Institute of International Economies, Washington, D.C.

IMF (2007), *World Economic Outlook*.

Globerman, S. and D. Shapire (1999), 'The impact of Government Policies on Foreign Direct Investment: The Canadian Experience', *Journal of International Business Studies*, 30 (3), 513-532.

Kawai, Masahire and Ganeshan Wignaraja (2007), 'ASEAN+3 on ASEAN+6: Which way forward?' Paper presented in the International Conference of CELAO, 21-23 June, Seoul, Korea.

Kumar, Nagesh (2006), Towards a Broader Asian Community: Agenda for the East Asia Summit, RIS Discussion Paper No. 100. New Delhi: RIS.

Kumar, Nagesh (2005), 'Regional Economic Cooperation in Asia: Relevance and a Possible Roadmap for a Broader Asian Economic Community', Theme Paper for 4th High Level Conference on Asian Economic Integration: Towards an Asian Economic Community, RIS and ISEAS, 18-19 November, New Delhi.

__________ (2004) (ed.) *Towards an Asian Economic Community: Vision of a New Asia*, New Delhi: RIS and Singapore: Institute of Southeast Asian Studies.

Lamberte, Marico B. (2005), 'An overview of Economic Cooperation and Integration in Asia', ADB (ed.) *Asian Economic Cooperation and Integration: Progress, Prospects and Challenges*, Asian Development Bank, Manila: 3-41.

Maddison, Angus (1998), *Chinese Economic Performance in the Long Run*, Paris:OECD.

Mohanty, S. K. (2007), 'Towards A New East Asian Economic Integration': Trends, Potentials and Challenges for an Emerging Pan-Continental RTA, *ORF Journal*, forthcoming.

Mohanty, S. K. and Robert Arockiasamy (2007), *Prospects for Making India's Manufacturing Sector Export Oriented*, Government of India:Ministry of Commerce and Industries.

Mohanty, S. K. and Sachin Chaturvedi (2006), 'Rising Tiger and Leaping Dragon: Emerging Global Dynamics, *IDS Bulletin*, January, 37 (1). 62-70, London.

Mohanty, S.K., Sanjeeb Pohit and Saikat Sinha Roy (2004) Implications of Economic Cooperation among JACIK. Countries: ACGE modelling approach', in Towards and Asian Economic Community: Vision of a New Asia, Nagesh Kumar (ed.), RIS and ISEAS, New Delhi and Singapore.

Pitsuwan, Suren (2007), Keynote Address, Workshop on 'Building A Better Asia', Nippon Foundation and its associates, 9-15 September, Beijing.

Rahman, Rita Dulci and Jose Miguel Andreu (2006), *China and India: Towards Global Economic Supremacy*?, Academic Foundation, New Delhi.

Rajan, Ramkishen S. and Rahul Sen (2005), 'The New Wave of Free Trade Agreement in Asia: With Particular Reference to ASEAN, People's Republic of China and India', ADB (ed.) *Asian Economic Cooperation and Integration: Progress, Prospects and Challenges. Asian Development Bank, Manila*: 123-160.

Schiff, Maurice and L. Alan Winters (2003), Regional Integration and Development, IBRD, World Bank, Washington DC.

Sinha Roy, Saikat (2004), 'Complementarities and Potentials of Intra-regional Transfer of Investments Technology and Skills in Asia, in Nagesh Kumar (ed.), *Towards an Asian Economic Community: Vision of a New Asia*, New Delhi: RIS and Singapore: Institute of Southeast Asian Studies.

Smith, Anthony L. (1998), 'The AFTA-CER Dialogue: A New Zealand Perspective on an Emerging Trade Area Linkage', *ASEAN Economic Journal*: 14(3), 238-252.

Soh, Byeong-Hae (2004), 'Towards A New Rgionalism in East Asia', Journal of Economic Integration, September: 19 (3), 499.

UNCTAD (2004), *Trade and Development Report 2004*, Geneva: United Nations Conference on Trade and Development.

Wilsan, Peten et al (2005), 'Assessing Singapores Export Competitiveness through Dynamic Shift-share Analysis,' *ASEAN Economic Bulletin*: 22(2), 160-185, August.

Acknowledgement

The authors express their sincere gratitude to Dr Nagesh Kumar for his constant support and critical insights towards completion of the study.

Part IV
Monetary and Financial Cooperation

11

Monetary and Financial Cooperation in Asia

Ramkishen S. Rajan

Introduction

There are a number of factors that have motivated monetary and financial regionalism and cooperation in Asia. The first was the body blow that the region received from the financial crisis of 1997-8 and the perceived inadequate response to it from extra-regional players. The second are the ongoing concerns about the continued under-representation of Asia in the International Monetary Fund (IMF) quota distribution and Asia's apparent lack of voice in international monetary affairs, along with the belief that Asia has ample resources for regional self-help.[1] The third have been external developments in regionalism, particularly the deepening and broadening of the European Union (EU). To be sure, while many economists have remained circumspect about the potential benefits of deeper monetary integration in Asia (do the microeconomic benefits outweigh the macroeconomic costs arising from loss of monetary policy sovereignty?), and there are signs of emerging tensions within the EU regarding the net benefits of a single currency. Nevertheless, there is no doubting the inspiration that many Asian policy makers have drawn from the deepening and broadening of European regionalism, especially in the monetary and financial areas. The fourth has been the growing de facto economic interdependence (so-called "market driven regionalism") as well as the regional nature of spillovers ('contagion').[2]

There are many gradations of monetary and financial regionalism, ranging from the weak form that involves regional policy dialogue and surveillance, on the one hand, to exchange rate and monetary coordination, on the other. This chapter concentrates narrowly on some "medium forms" of monetary and financial regionalism, broadly defined as the development of regional liquidity arrangements and regional financial markets. In other words, the focus here is on policy initiatives underway in Asia to enhance monetary and financial regionalism and the analytical bases for these initiatives.[3] In particular, this chapter takes stock of the recent developments in monetary and financial regionalism in Asia, paying specific attention to the Chiang-Mai initiative (CMI) in the second section , the Asian Bond Fund (ABF) initiative in the third section, and the Asian Currency Unit (ACU) in the fourth section. The fifth section concludes with a discussion of the steps forward for the region and India.

Monetary Regionalism in Asia: CMI

It has long been recognized that inadequate liquidity can threaten the stability of international financial regimes (Bird and Rajan, 2002 and Rajan, 2003). Illiquidity can create crises even when economic fundamentals are sound, or it can make a bad situation worse when the fundamentals are weak. Moreover, once it becomes a problem, illiquidity further undermines the confidence of international capital markets. Capital outflows increase, thereby reducing liquidity still further. The speed and intensity of economic adjustment following a crisis is largely dictated by the scarcity of liquidity; it is the extreme shortage of liquidity that called for rapid adjustment in East Asia in 1998.[4]

Having appreciated the importance of ensuring adequate liquidity as a safeguard against future financial crises, many Asian countries consciously attempted to build up reserves immediately after the crisis, partly as a precautionary motive (Kharas, Rajan and Vostroknutova, 2007). Nonetheless, reserve accumulation (so-called 'floating with a life-jacket') is costly on many fronts since the country effectively swaps high yielding domestic assets for lower yielding foreign ones.[5] In view of this, it is recognized that countries need to buttress their own reserve holdings with external liquidity arrangements. The need to provide adequate liquidity to help forestall a crisis in a distressed economy and prevent its spread to other countries took centre stage in the reform of the financial architecture immediately after the crisis.

The IMF's response was to create the Contingent Credit Line (CCL). 'The CCL was conceived as a precautionary line of defence to help protect countries pursuing strong policies in the event of a balance of payments need arising from the spread of financial crises (IMF, 2001). The idea here was to establish a precautionary line of credit for countries with "sound" policies that might be affected by contagion from a crisis and to finance this from outside the Fund's quota-based resources by new arrangements to borrow (NAB). The negotiation of conditionality with potential users of the CCL would, therefore, take place before the country needed to draw on liquidity from the Fund. However, no country negotiated a CCL. Consequently, the facility underwent a major review and partial overhaul and was eventually shut down. The CCL has not been replaced by another similar liquidity facility and the international financial architecture has made limited progress in the area of liquidity enhancement as a financial safeguard.

Against this background, and in recognition of the fact that financial stability has the characteristics of a regional public good, it is understandable that Asian countries have been eager to promote regional monetary cooperation. The CMI has taken centre stage in this regard. It is a network of swap arrangements which was agreed among Asian plus Three (APT) countries in May 2000.[6] It is important to keep in mind that the CMI was not envisaged as either a mechanism for inappropriate currency pegging in the region or a mechanism for managing a crisis after it erupts. Rather, it is primarily aimed at preventing a crisis from erupting in the first instance.

The CMI has two components: (a) ASEAN Swap Arrangement (ASA) which was expanded from 5 to 10 countries, and from US$ 200 million to US$1 billion and increased again to US$2 billion;[7] and (b) networks of bilateral swap arrangements (BSAs) among the three North Asian countries (Japan, China and Korea) and one of the three and one of the ASEAN countries (see Figure 11.1).[8] The expanded ASA is to be made available for two years and is renewable upon mutual agreement of the members. Each member is allowed to draw a maximum of twice its commitment from the facility for a period of up to six months with the possibility of a further extension of six more months at most. The basic characteristics of the BSAs are as follows. Twenty per cent of the liquidity can be drawn automatically without conditionality for 630 days (90 days, renewable 7 times). Interest paid is LIBOR +1.5 per cent for the first 180 days, rising by 50 basis points for each renewal to a maximum of LIBOR +3 per cent. Importantly, the swap-providing countries form their own individual opinions on the potential swap recipient. Drawing of more than 20 per cent regional liquidity requires the country to come under IMF conditionality.

The CMI is an important step in Asian monetary regionalism as it is the first time that regional countries have pre-committed resources as a means of regional financial safeguard. However, it clearly remains a work in progress. A number of important details remain to be worked out if the CMI is to become an effective liquidity enhancing measure. The first is the inadequate size especially of the liquid component. For instance, the current aggregate size of just over $80 billion (as of July 2007) among the 13 APT countries (Figure 11.1) pales in comparison to the crisis packages offered to Korea, Indonesia and Thailand in 1997-8 (Chang and Rajan, 2001). The second is the issue of coordination between potential creditor countries. For instance, is the bilateral arrangement subject to regional approval? How is borrowing/lending to be distributed? Both these questions lead to the key issue of how to regionalize (though more commonly referred to as 'multilateralize') the CMI, which is a series of bilateral and rather uncoordinated swaps. In fact, in the Joint Ministerial Statements/of the 8th and 9th APT Finance Ministers' Meetings in Istanbul and Hyderabad, respectively, there was an agreement to re-evaluate the process/possibility of multilateralizing the arrangements.[9] As part of this, there was an agreement to look into developing a collective decision-making procedure to activate the swaps. It was also recognized that there is a of the need to improve on and link surveillance more closely and effectively to the CMI. Other issues relating to the CMI include raising the non IMF-linked share (what type of independent conditionality with teeth?) and making transparent and automatic the condition for withdrawal.

Over time, consideration should be given to transforming the CMI into a regional reserve pooling mechanism (Rajan and Siregar, 2004 and Rajan, Siregar and Bird, 2005). A regional reserve pool could involve three tiers of liquidity. The first tier is owned reserves which offers the highest degree of liquidity and has zero conditionality but is costly. The second tier is sub-divided into a country's own reserves placed with regional pool and other members' reserves with the pool. The third tier is conventional IMF lending. With such a structure, the degree of liquidity could be inversely related to the degree of conditionality. Overall though, it warrants repeating that effective deepening of regional monetary integration will not take place until there is a considerable strengthening of the regional surveillance mechanism with well worked out surveillance and policy conditionalities. As noted by Dayantra-Banda and Whalley (2007: 44):

> The system at present is aimed at insurance rather than achieving wider monetary and financial development and the current system does not require a single regional monetary authority. If monetary cooperation in ASEAN+3 is to take on a wider form, a system of simultaneous monetary development involving a common exchange rate policy, a single monetary authority and deeper financial market development are necessary foundations. Seemingly, a single monetary authority is needed to ultimately complete the monetary integration process in the region, but many problems confront the emergence of that authority.

Figure 11.1:The Chiang-Mai Initiative: Progress to Date (as of July 2007)

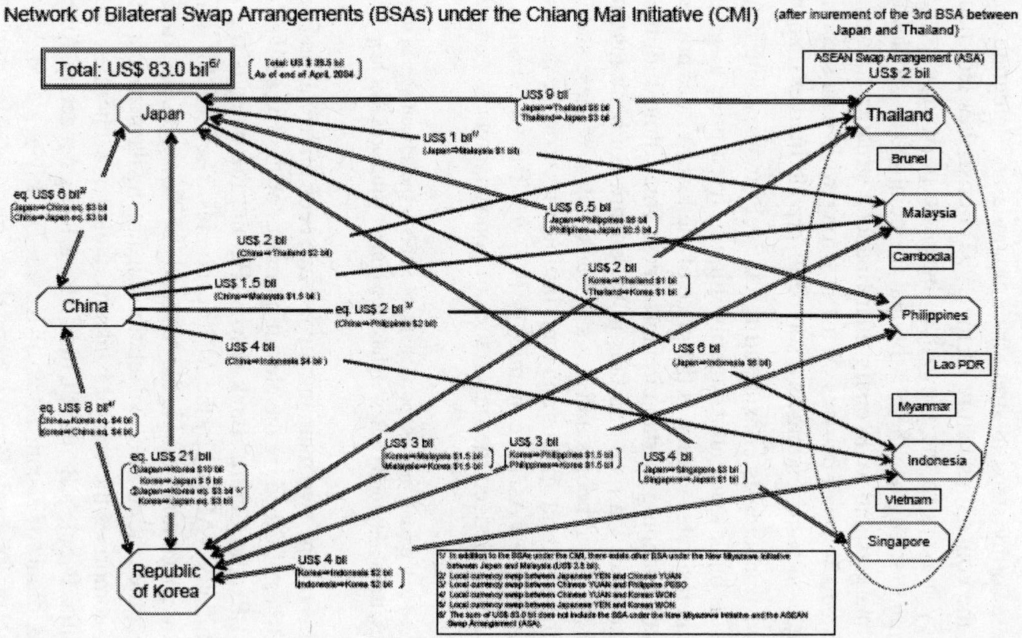

Source: Ministry of Finance, Japan (*website: http://www.mof.go.jp/english/if/CMI_0704.pdf*)

Financial Regionalism in Asia: ABF

The financial crisis of 1997-8 also made apparent the significant gaps and weaknesses in East Asia's financial sectors. While the regional economies are taking noteworthy steps to strengthen, upgrade and integrate their financial systems, the contagious nature of the 1997-8 crisis has led many observers and policy makers to the view that there are positive externalities from cooperating to strengthen their individual financial sectors, to develop regional financial markets and to diversify their financial structures, away from bank-based systems to bond markets. What is wrong with Asia's continued heavy dependence on bank lending as a source of private market financing?

Bond financing is considered a relatively more stable source of debt financing as bank loans are primarily illiquid, fixed-price assets in the sense that the interest rate—which is the price of the loan —does not vary much on the basis of changing market circumstances. Thus, almost all the adjustment has to take place via rises and falls in the quantity of bank lending, which in turn leads to sharp booms and busts in bank flows.[10] These sudden reversals in bank flows had calamitous and long-lasting effects on the domestic financial systems in the East Asian economies in 1997-98. The World Bank (2004: 157) has also acknowledged the importance of bond markets as compared to bank lending, noting;

> (c)ompared to the bank market, bond markets offers some advantages in terms of longer maturities, tradability, and back-weighted repayment structures that help support equity returns.[11]

In this regard, two main initiatives have been underway in East Asia. One is the ABF established by the eleven members of the Executives' Meeting of East Asia-Pacific Central Bank (EMEAP), and the other is the Asian Bond Market Initiative (ABMI) by the APT economies. The EMEAP is a cooperative organization of central banks in the Asia and Pacific region. Its primary objective 'is to strengthen the cooperative relationship among its members'. The EMEAP currently comprises the central banks from eleven economies: Reserve Bank of Australia, People's Bank of China, Hong Kong Monetary Authority, Bank Indonesia, Bank of Japan, Bank of Korea, Bank Negara Malaysia, Reserve Bank of New Zealand, Bangko Sentral ng Pilipinas, Monetary Authority of Singapore and Bank of Thailand" (see *http://www.emeap.org/*). The ABMI — which was endorsed at the ASEAN+3 Finance Ministers Meeting (AFMM) in Manila on August 2003—focuses primarily on developing efficient bond markets in Asia to enable the private and public sectors to raise and invest long-term capital. The activities of the ABMI are primarily concentrated on facilitating access to the market through a wider variety of issuers and enhancing market infrastructure to foster bond markets in Asia.[12]

The focus of the remainder of this section is specifically on the ABF which was established in on 2 June 2003. The first stage of the ABF essentially involved the regional governments voluntarily contributing about 1 per cent each of their reserves to a fund dedicated to purchasing regional sovereign and semi-sovereign bonds denominated in US dollars. The initial size of the ABF was about US$1 billion and the fund has been passively managed by the investment management unit of the Swiss-based BIS. The mandate is to invest in bonds in eight of the eleven member countries of EMEAP, the developed countries of Australia, New Zealand and Japan solely being lenders to the ABF. In a noteworthy next step, the ABF 2 (second stage of the ABF) was established in December 2004. The quantum of funds involved was doubled in magnitude (US$2 billion), and its mandate is to invest in selected domestic currency sovereign and quasi-sovereign bonds in the eight countries.

More specifically, the ABF 2 comprises two components (US$1 billion each): (a) a Pan-Asian Bond Index Fund (PAIF) and (b) a Fund of Bond Funds (FoBF). The PAIF is a single bond fund, while the FoBF is a two-layered structure with a parent fund investing in eight single market sub-funds (see Figure 11.2). The International Index Company (IIC), a joint venture between ABN Amro, JP Morgan and Morgan Stanley (iBoxx ABF), has created the benchmark indices for all nine funds. The funds will be passively managed to match the benchmark index. The seed money for single bond funds has been divided the basis of on pre-determined criteria and local fund managers have been appointed to manage the respective funds.

The specific criteria for market weights in each sub-fund (and distribution within PAIF) are based on: (a) the size of the local market; (b) the turnover ratio in that market; (c) the sovereign credit rating; and (d) a market openness factor. The market weights will be reviewed annually, with market openness being a particularly important factor in the allocation of weights (Ma and Remolona 2005). The parent fund is limited to investments by EMEAP member central banks only. While the initial phase of PAIF was confined to investments by EMEAP central banks only (US$1 billion), it was opened up to investments by other retail investors in Phase 2.

In broad terms, the objectives of the ABF are four-fold. First, to diversify debt financing from bank lending to bond financing by developing regional financial/capital markets by reducing supply side constraints and introducing low cost products, and by raising investor awareness and broadeing investor base on the demand side. Second, to encourage a convergence in financial and

Figure 11.2: Structure of Asian Bond Fund (ABF 2)

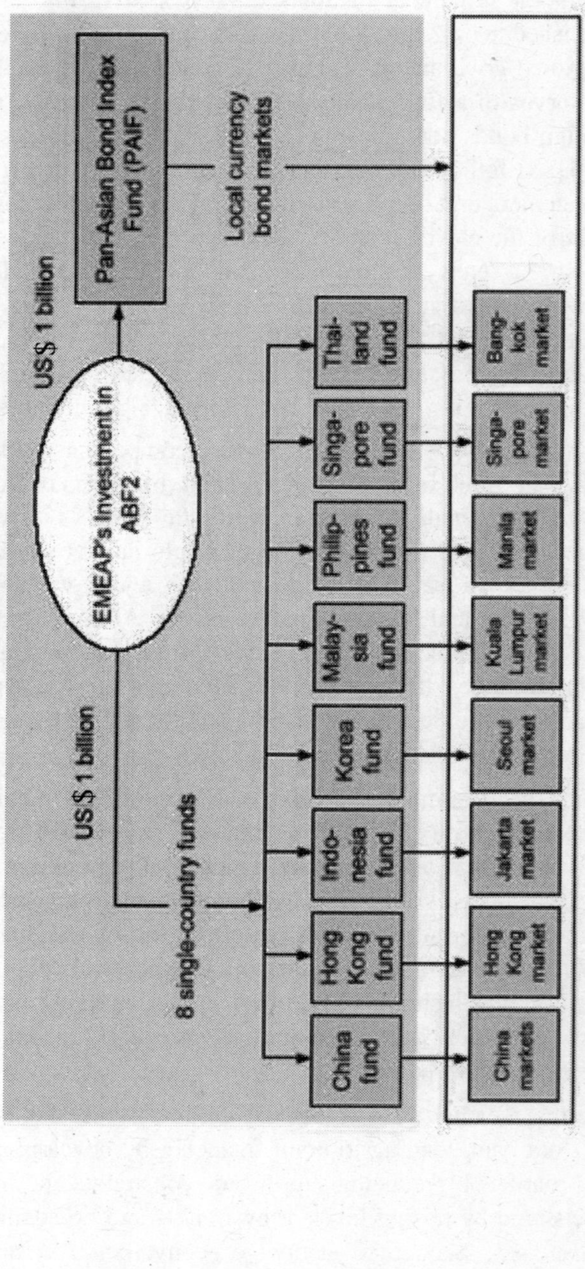

Source: Ma and Remolona (2005): p.86.

capital market policies and accelerate improvements in financial market infrastructures. Third, to recycle regional funds intra-regionally and also reduce the region's vulnerability to 'fickle' international investors. Fourth, to reduce the extent of currency and maturity mismatches (that is, 'double mismatches').The latter two objectives are discussed below in detail.

Asia as a whole holds the bulk of the world's savings. The excess of savings over investment along with quasi-managed exchange rates has given rise to large current account and overall balance of payments surpluses (McCauley, 2003 and Kharas, Rajan and Vostroknutova, 2007). Historically, the lack of sufficiently liquid financial instruments has led to much of Asia's savings being rechannelled outside the region, especially to the US. In relation to this, it is often noted that one of the reasons for the intensification of the regional financial crisis of 1997-8 was the fickleness of international investors, many of whom were extra-regional and who did not have much knowledge about regional economies or differences in economic fundamentals between the economies. There was significant 'panic herding' during that period as international creditors and investors chose to reduce exposures to all regional economies en masse once they were spooked by the crisis in Thailand and Indonesia, leading to a massive international bank run. Insofar as the ABF proposal promotes greater intra-regional financing, this might make the region somewhat less susceptible to extra-regional 'investor ignorance' which is said to have contributed to an indiscriminate and disorderly withdrawal of funds from regional markets in 1997-8.

Another source of vulnerability made apparent by the 1997-8 financial debacle was the large-scale accumulation of uncovered external debt. To the extent that a relatively larger proportion of a country's liabilities is denominated in foreign currency vis-à-vis its assets (so-called 'liability dollarization'), a currency devaluation could lead to sharp declines in the country's net worth, with calamitous effects on the financial and real sectors (so-called 'balance sheet' effects).[13] On the part of the developing Asia-Pacific economies, the ability to issue bonds in domestic currencies mitigates the concerns about currency mismatches (that is borrowing and interest payments in foreign currency but assets and revenue streams in local currency) which in turn could negatively impact the project's solvency in the event of a currency devaluation.[14] Thus, while the ABF 1 was solely focused on foreign currency bonds, the ABF 2 is notable in that it involves transacting solely in local currency bonds.

While the ABF is a welcome move for regional financial cooperation, it is important not to oversell the initiative. The first and foremost reason for this is the quantum of funding available. The current US$ 2 billion funding of ABF 2 is a drop in the bucket relative to the region's aggregate reserve holdings or infrastructural financing requirements. Second, if the supply of good quality sovereign and quasi-sovereign paper is limited (which appears to be the case), it could merely crowd out private bond purchases, hence leading to no new net financing.[15] This, in turn, implies the need to support 'public providers of infrastructure services in achieving commercial standards of creditworthiness to access capital markets on a sustainable basis over the long term' (World Bank, 2004).

Asian Currency Unit

While the ABF initiative is a modest steps in the right direction, a recent suggestion has been floated for an Asia Basket Currency (ABC) initiative. The basic idea is that while the ABF merely purchases and holds on to sovereign and quasi-sovereign bonds, the ABC Corporation would also create and issue basket currency bonds (weighted combination of regional currencies of the underlying national bonds) backed by regional sovereign bonds (Ito, 2003).[16] If successful, the ABC could provide a fillip for the eventual creation of an ACU.

The issue of ACU warrants some discussion, particularly in view of the recent initiative by the Asian Development Bank (ADB) to launch such a virtual unit of account. In a general sense, the ACU is a weighted average of regional currencies *a la* the European Currency Unit (ECU).[17] At the micro-level, the rationale for an ACU is to afford the opportunity for regional economic agents to invoice regional financial and trade transactions in the ACU, hence reducing the region's dependence on the US dollar and other external currencies. If successful, intra-regional intermediation of savings may be promoted, in the process possibly reducing the region's exposure to external shocks (as discussed previously). However, in reality, it is unlikely that the ACU will be used on a widespread basis for some time to come.

The experience of Europe is instructive in this regard. The initial creation of the ECU in 1974-5 did not lead to a widespread use of the unit. Even in the 1990s, until the actual creation of the euro, the vast majority of intra-European financial and trade transactions were not in ECUs but primarily in US dollars and other sovereign national European currencies. So it is not just the creation that is important; there has to be a coordinated agreement by regional bodies to start transacting in the new unit, failing which no one will want to take the first step.[18] The ACU has a better chance of success (in terms of becoming a significant regional vehicle currency) if a larger set of countries is included in the basket. Therefore, it is imperative that the ACU be broadened from the proposed APT countries to also include India, Australia and New Zealand (the other members of the East Asian Summit or EAS), all of which have significant financial market depth. (We take up the issue of membership again in the concluding section).

It has also been suggested that the ACU could be used as a means of enhancing 'internal' exchange rate stability if the regional central banks begin to stabilize their respective currencies to the regional unit (that is help, reduce the possibility of regional competitive devaluations). The notion of stabilization vis-à-vis an internal basket *a la* Europe's Exchange Rate Mechanism (ERM) is distinct from stabilization vis-à-vis an external unit which would require that the ACU, in turn, be pegged in some way to external currencies such as the US dollar or Euro, or some weighted average thereof. Of course, internal stability does not require the latter and, in fact, may exacerbate external currency stability. This may happen if regional countries substitute the use of external currencies for the ACU, hence being less concerned about fluctuations of their currencies relative to the external currencies. Conversely, effective external stability requires internal stability in the sense that if regional central banks do not explicitly or implicitly manage their currencies to the ACU, it is irrelevant whether the ACU per se is managed against the external currencies, as the proposed ACU will remain purely a theoretical construct. Indeed, the stated aim of the ADB at this stage is for the ACU to serve mainly as a means of benchmarking the extent of currency movements/deviations. As the ADB president, Haruhiko Kuroda, noted:

> The ACU…could be used to monitor the stability of participating currencies and would tangibly demonstrate the need for greater exchange rate coordination. What Asia needs here is basically an exchange rate that is flexible toward the rest of the world but relatively stable within the region (Kuroda 2005: p.5).

Focussing on the notion of stabilization vis-à-vis an internal basket (that is, regional currencies benchmarking movements to the ACU), while the potential microeconomic benefits noted above do not require internal stabilization, the latter could promote the more widespread use of the ACU. This is because the regional central banks will automatically begin to use the ACU more extensively as a reserve and possibly even as an intervention currency, thus providing an additional inducement for private agents to intensify the use of the unit in invoicing and transactions.

Needless to say, the long-term viability of internal stabilization in an era of open capital markets requires: an enhancement of regional surveillance, a degree of policy coordination, and an augmentation of regional liquidity arrangements. Nonetheless, given the divergence in economic and institutional structures in the region and absence of macroeconomic policy coordination and mechanisms for automatic intraregional fiscal transfers, any attempt at formal exchange rate coordination—let alone a full-fledged monetary union—is far too risky and premature and will likely be a failure, setting back prospects for other forms of economic integration.

Concluding Thoughts and Implications for India

Ever since the currency crisis of 1997-8 the APT economies have taken a number of steps to enhance regional policy dialogue and surveillance and information gathering (for example, the ASEAN+3 Economic Review and Policy Dialogue Process) as well as other measures to enhance regional cooperation. This chapter has taken stock of the two major initiatives underway in Asia to deepen monetary and financial regionalism, viz. CMI and the ABF. Beyond 'sound' macro policies, the new-style capital account crises have in turn made apparent the need to: (a) ensure availability of sufficient liquidity in the event of a bust; (b) diversify sources of funding/channels of intermediation to minimize intensity of busts; and (c) minimize balance sheet mismatches (both maturity as well as currency mismatches).[19] The aim of the CMI is to contribute to the first issue (that is, supplement existing sources of liquidity), while the ABF is meant to deal with the latter two.

With regard to the CMI, apart from issues relating to multilateralizing of the CMI, raising the non IMF-linked share and making transparent and automatic the condition for withdrawal, there is a need for further augmentation of the CMI in terms of expanding its size. Over time, consideration should be given to transforming the CMI into a regional reserve pooling mechanism with various tiers of liquidity, such that the degree of liquidity could be inversely related to the degree of conditionality. It warrants repeating, however, that effective deepening of regional monetary integration will not occur unless there is a considerable strengthening of the regional surveillance mechanism with well worked out surveillance and policy conditionality. Assuming this happens, Moon, Rhee and Yoon (2007: 20) have suggested the creation of an Asian Exchange Stabilization Fund (AESF). As they argue:

> Though initially insufficient and bilateral, the swap arrangement has continued to be strengthened, and it was agreed upon to develop the swap into a multilateral arrangement in a recent ADB meeting at Hyderabad, India on May 2006...The objective of the AESF

is more comprehensive in that it includes exchange rate stability in addition to liquidity support. In fact, the case of the EMS suggests that three pillars be combined into one institution: ECU, Provision of liquidity, and ERM. Thus, in Asia, once the (A)CU is created and once the provision of emergency liquidity can be strengthened through the CMI, then the next natural step will be to set up an appropriate exchange rate system. This could be carried out with the establishment of the AESF.

While this may be a plausible long-term goal, in the near-term, Asian countries need to persist with attempts to develop well-functioning financial markets and institutions. In particular, countries need to deepen and upgrade national and regional government and corporate bond markets as a means of reducing the region's heavy reliance on banks. Greater attention needs to be paid to lowering transactions costs in regional financial markets. In this respect, it is important to note that active discussions have been underway in the region about the possible creation of regional financial infrastructure (clearing and settlement systems, credit agency, etc.) as well as harmonization of withholding tax policies and capital account policies.[20] These issues are clearly not headline-grabbing in comparison to discussions on exchange rate coordination or a monetary union, for instance.[21] Nonetheless, the focus on upgrading and harmonizing market infrastructures and regulatory frameworks is critical if Asia hopes to successfully promote greater financial and monetary integration to make the region more resilient to local and external shocks.

While India is gradually integrating with its East Asian neighbours on a de facto and de jure basis in terms of trade and investment (for instance, see Asher 2007), the same cannot be said in the case of macroeconomics and finance. India has hitherto been excluded from even the softest forms of regional monetary and financial cooperation such as policy dialogue and surveillance, let alone more substantive initiatives such as the CMI, ABF and ACU. India has also not been accepted as a member of EMEAP (which as noted, is the regional meeting of the region's central bankers).[22] Dayaratna-Banda and Whalley (2007: 41) discuss the membership issue:

Another issue is where India, Australia and New Zealand (the later two are in the Asia-Pacific grouping) stand in this. ASEAN has already entered into a framework agreement with India on a comprehensive economic partnership. China has entered into arrangements with India, New Zealand and Australia, and Japan also has regional arrangements with these countries. Some initial negotiations for a free trade area between ASEAN, Australia, and New Zealand have also begun. These three countries have increasingly more open economies, and their links with East Asia are likely to expand over time. These economies have been increasingly integrating with East Asia. Including them in East Asian regional forums and arrangements expands the set of developed and fast growing economies with well-functioning economic and financial systems and markets...The possibility of ASEAN+6 monetary cooperation can thus not be ruled out.[23]

Cynics in India might argue that the East Asian monetary and financial initiatives have, thus far, not yielded any tangible results and there is no urgency for India to be a part of them.This viewpoint is clearly debatable. For instance, the regional dialogue appears to have had positive impact on the regional economies—the ASEAN+3 countries have been conducting Economic Review and Policy Dialogue (ERPD) at the Ministers' level annually and at the Deputies' level twice a year to discuss economic and financial developments in the region—and there has been better quality research on various dimensions of the region's macroeconomic and financial policies and procedures.[24]

In addition, one could counter that as India continues along the path of greater de facto capital and exchange account openness, and as India's macroeconomic business cycles become more correlated with regional and global markets, policy makers in the country will inevitably need to pay much more attention to the way in which the regional and international financial architecture is evolving. While India needs to remain an active participant in the ongoing debate on the reform of the IMF, it would be in its best interest to also ensure that it is accepted as a full-fledged member of regional financial initiatives so that it can help influence the manner in which these schemes evolve in the future. As a first concrete step, the Reserve Bank of India (RBI) should join the EMEAP, and that the Indian Ministry of Finance joins the ongoing ERPD in which finance and deputy finance ministers from the APT economies have been engaged in the last few years. These could be precursors to India's participation in deeper forms of regional monetary and financial initiatives in the future.

Endnotes

1 For instance, see Henning (2005). See Cooper and Truman (2007) and Mirakhor and Zaidi (2006) for recent discussions of IMF quota formulas and shares.

2 For a discussion of the definitions, types and channels of 'contagion', see Rajan (2003) and references cited within.

3 We do not examine the actual level of financial and monetary links that may already exist (these links may or may not have been facilitated by regional policy mechanisms). See Chapter 3 of this volume on de facto trade and financial integration in Asia. There is also a bourgeoning literature on the extent of business cycle synchronization in Asia and whether the Asian region qualifies as an optimum currency area (OCA) (for instance, see Moneta and Rüffer, 2006 and Watanabe and Ogura, 2006).

4 For instance, the East Asian process of "V-shaped" adjustment was not very different from the stylized patterns of previous currency crisis episodes in developing countries (Eichengreen and Rose 2001). However, the degree of initial contraction and subsequent recovery was far greater in East Asia, attributable to the severe liquidity crisis that was triggered by investors' panic (Rajan and Siregar, 2001).

[5] See Mohanty and Turner (2006) and Ouyang, Rajan and Willett (2007) for a discussion of the costs and liquidity dimensions of reserve accumulation in Asia.

[6] The ten ASEAN countries are Indonesia, Malaysia, Philippines, Singapore, Thailand and Brunei Darussalam, as well as the newer/transition members, viz. Cambodia, Laos, Myanmar, Vietnam, Timor-Leste (formerly East Timor).

[7] There are also a series of repurchase agreements (repos) that allow ASEAN members with collateral such as US Treasury bills to swap them for hard currency (usually US dollars) and then repurchase them at a later date.

[8] For details on the CMI and monetary regionalism in Asia more generally, see Park (2004).

[9] See 'The Joint Ministerial Statement of the 8th ASEAN+3 Finance Ministers' Meeting' (Istanbul, 4 May 2005) (*http://www.aseansec.org/17448.htm*). In May 2006, finance ministers tasked their deputies to further study the possibility of multilateralizing the CMI or to create a post-CMI framework.

[10] For instance, see Ito and Park, (eds.) (2004) and Eichengreen and Luengnaruemitchai (2007). For an overview of Asian bond markets, see Hamada, Jeon and Ryou (2004). Also see a BIS symposium on Asian bond markets *(http://www.bis.org/publ/bppdf/bispap30.htm)* as well as resources available on the portal created and maintained by the Asian Development Bank (ADB) *http://asianbondsonline.adb.org/*).

[11] According to one study, bank-based financial systems tend to be relatively more crisis-prone, and financial systems that are more bond financed-based tend to be associated with higher growth, whether or not there is a crisis (Arteta, 2005).

[12] Under the auspices of the ABMI, the APT has established a number of working groups to examine various aspects of capital markets, including creating securitized debt instruments and increasing the supply of local currency denominated, exploring possibilities of a regional settlement linkage and impediments to cross-border bond investment and issuance in the region, capacity building of local credit rating agencies in Asia and enhancing comparability and harmonization. More information on all these and other initiatives is available on *(http://asianbondsonline.adb.org/)*. Also see the review of ABMI working groups by Kawai (2007).

[13] The macroeconomic implications of these balance sheet effects have been explored by Rajan and Parulkar (2007), Rajan (2007) and Bird and Rajan (2006).

[14] It is important to ask the question as to why some countries are not able to borrow overseas in domestic currencies (so called "Original Sin" hypothesis *a la* Hausmann, Panizza and Stein (2001). Logically, if there is a significant risk premium imposed on a certain currency and if interest rates are "sufficiently" high, there will always be some potential borrowers. While this is true, the concern is that a potential solvency risk will merely be converted to a liquidity risk (to the extent that revenues in the event of a negative shock are not sufficiently high to meet the high interest payments). See Jeanne (2000).

[15] For a more detailed and forceful critique of such regional bond initiatives see Eichengreen (2004).

[16] In the 8th APT Finance Ministerial Meeting in Istanbul in May 2005, the joint statement made, reference to Asian currency basket bonds:

We will continue and expedite our efforts in undertaking a wide variety of studies and implementing various effective measures under the ABMI working groups….(W)e will introduce a roadmap that proposes gathering and sharing information in an integrated manner on bond market development and on our related efforts with the regular self-assessment conducted by member countries. The possible issuance of Asian currency-basket bonds could be explored under the auspices of the roadmap. We also agreed to embark on the study of Asian Bond Standards to explore the development of international bond markets in Asia through tailoring necessary infrastructure and setting the procedure entrusted by global issuers and investors.

See 'The Joint Ministerial Statement of the 8th ASEAN+3 Finance Ministers' Meeting', (Istanbul, 4 May 2005) (*http://www.aseansec.org/17448.htm*).

17 It is expected that the weights will be determined on the basis of regional country GDP and trade shares, with China, Japan and Korea expected to dominate the weighting scheme. For initial attempts at computing such a weighting scheme (which may not necessarily be the weights used by the ADB), see Ogawa and Shimuzu (2005) and Moon, Rhee and Yoon (2007). Also see Watanabe and Ogura (2006).

18 This inertial effect of existing currencies (that is advantage of incumbency) is based on the concept of "network externalities" or "lock in" effects, whereby there are limited incentives for economic agents to unilaterally take on a new currency (particularly for invoicing transactions). The network aspects of the internal currency status have been analysed theoretically by Matsuyama et al. (1993).

19 Some of these issues are elaborated upon by Ghosh (2006) who also discusses the role of the IMF in capital account crises.

20 Some of these financial infrastructural issues are being tackled by the ABMI.

21 For a recent critical discussion of exchange rate coordination issues in Asia, see Genberg (2006). This issue is also broached in Chapter 3 of this volume.

22 However, India is a member of the Bank for International Settlements (BIS).

23 India, Australia and New Zealand have joined the APT economies to be founding members of the EAS. The inaugural meeting was held in Kuala Lumpur, Malaysia in November 2005. See Kumar (2005) for a discussion of the EAS.

24 More specifically, the Japanese proposed the establishment of a Research Group at the Informal ASEAN+3 Finance and Central Bank Deputies' Meeting in November 2002, and agreed among ASEAN+3 in August 2003. The aim of the Research Group is 'to explore the ways to further strengthen financial cooperation and promote financial stability in the region by soliciting academic input from researchers and research institutes in ASEAN+3 countries.' (*http://www.mof.go.jp/jouhou/kokkin/ASEAN+3research.htm*).

References

Arteta, C.O. (2005) 'Does Bond Market Development Help Reduce the Cost of Crises? Evidence from Developing Countries,' mimeo (April).

Asher, M.G. (2007) India's Rising Role in Asia, Discussion Paper No.121, New Delhi: RIS.

Bird, G. and R.S. Rajan (2006). 'Does Devaluation Lead to Economic Recovery or Economic Contraction? Examining the Analytical Issues with Reference to Thailand,' *Journal of International Development*, 16: 141-56.

_________ (2002) 'The Evolving Asian Financial Architecture,' Essays in International Economics, 26 (February), Princeton University.

Chang, L.L. and R.S. Rajan (2001) 'The Economics and Politics of Monetary Regionalism in Asia,' *ASEAN Economic Bulletin*, 18: 103-18.

Cooper, R.N. and T. Truman (2007) 'The IMF Quota Formula: Linchpin of Fund Reform,' Policy Brief No.07-01, Peterson Institute, Washington DC.

Dayaratna-Banda, O.G. and J. Whalley (2007) 'Regional Monetary Arrangements in ASEAN+3 as Insurance through Reserve Accumulation and Swaps,' Working Paper No.22, The Centre for International Governance Innovation.

Eichengreen, B. (2004) 'Financial Development in Asia: The Way Forward,' mimeo (January).

Eichengreen, B. and P. Luengnaruemitchai (2007) 'Bond Markets as Conduits for Capital Flows: How Does Asia Compare?' in T. Ito and A. Rose (eds), *International Financial Issues in the Pacific Rim: Global Imbalances, Financial Liberalization, and Exchange Rate Policy*, NBER East Asia Seminar Volume 17, University of Chicago.

Eichengreen, B. and A. Rose (2001) 'To Defend or Not to Defend? That is the Question,' mimeo (February).

Genberg, H. (2006) 'Exchange-Rate Arrangements and Financial Integration in East Asia: On a Collision Course,' Working Paper No.41, Bank of Greece.

Ghosh, A. (2006) 'Capital Account Crises: Lessons from Crisis Prevention,' paper prepared for High-Level seminar on Crisis Prevention 10-11 July Singapore.

Hamada, K., S.C. Jeon and J.W. Ryou (2004) 'Asian Bonds Markets: Issues, Prospects and Tasks for Cooperation,' paper prepared for the "Korea and the World Economy III" Conference, 3-4 July.

Hausmann, R., U. Panizza and E. Stein (2001) 'Why do Countries Float the Way They Float?', *Journal of Development Economics*, 66: .387-414

Henning, R. (2005). 'Systemic Contextualism and Financial Regionalism: The Case of East Asia,' mimeo (August).

IMF (2001) *Annual Report 2001*, Washington, DC: IMF (September).

Ito, T. (2003) 'The ABC of Asian Bonds,' paper presented at the Second PECC Finance Forum Conference, Hua Hin, Thailand, 8-9 July.

Ito, T. and Y.C. Park (eds.) (2004) *Developing Asian Bond Markets*, Canberra: Asia Pacific Press.

Jeanne, O. (2000) 'Foreign Currency Debt and the Global Financial Architecture,' *European Economic Review*, 44: .719-27.

Kawai, M. (2007) 'Asian Bond Market Development: Progress, Prospects and Challenges.' Keynote address at the High Yield Debt Summit Asia 2007, 16-17 May Singapore.

Kharas, H., R.S. Rajan and E. Vostroknutova (2007) 'Finance' in H. Kharas and I. Gill (eds.), *An East Asian Renaissance: Ideas for Competitive Growth*, World Bank: Washington, DC.

Kumar, N. (2005) Towards a Broader Asian Community: Agenda for the East Asia Summit, Discussion Paper No.100, New Delhi: RIS.

Kuroda, H. (2005) 'Towards a Borderless Asia: A Perspective on Asian Economic Integration' speech by ADB President at the Emerging Markets Forum, 10 December Oxford.

Ma, G. and E.M. Remolona (2005) 'Opening Markets Through a Regional Bond Fund: Lessons from ABF2' *BIS Quarterly Review*, June: .81-92.

McCauley, R.N. (2003) 'Capital flows in East Asia since the 1997 Crisis,' *BIS Quarterly Review*, June: 41-55.

Mirakhor, A. and I. Zaidi (2006) 'Rethinking the Governance of the International Monetary Fund,' IMF Working Paper No.WP/06/273, December.

Mohanty, M.S. and P. Turner (2006) 'Foreign Exchange Reserve Accumulation in Emerging Markets: What are the Domestic Implications?' *BIS Quarterly Review*, September : 39-52

Moneta, F. and R. Rüffer (2006) 'Business Cycle Synchronisation in East Asia,' Working Paper Series No.671, European Central Bank (ECB).

Matsuyama, K., N. Kiyotaki and A. Matsui (1993) 'Toward a Theory of International Currency,' *Review of Economic Studies*, 60: 283-307.

Moon, W., Y. Rhee and D. Yoon (2007) 'Regional Currency Unit in Asia: Property and Perspective' mimeo, Korea Institute for International Economic Policy.

Ogawa, E. and J. Shimizu (2005) 'A Deviation Measurement for Coordinated Exchange Rate Policies in East Asia' Discussion Paper No.05-E-017, REITI.

Ouyang, A., R.S. Rajan and T.D. Willett (2007) 'Managing the Monetary Consequences of Reserve Accumulation in Emerging Asia,' mimeo (June).

Park, Y.C. (2004) 'Beyond the Chiang Mai Initiative: Prospects for Regional Financial and Monetary Integration in East Asia,' paper prepared for meeting on G-24, September.

Rajan, R.S. (2007) 'Managing New Style Currency Crises: The Swan Diagram Revisited,' *Journal of International Development*, 19: 583-606.

________ (2003) 'Safeguarding Against Capital Account Crises: Unilateral, Regional and Multilateral Options for East Asia' in G. de Brouwer (ed.), *Financial Governance in East Asia*, London: Routledge: 239-63.

Rajan, R.S. and M. Parulkar (2007) 'Real Sector Shocks and Monetary Policy Responses in a Financially Vulnerable Emerging Economy' *Emerging Markets Trade and Finance*, forthcoming.

Rajan, R.S. and R. Siregar (2004) 'Centralized Reserve Pooling for the ASEAN Plus Three (APT) Countries' in *Monetary and Financial Cooperation in East Asia*, Palgrave-McMillan Press for the Asian Development Bank, 285-330.

________ (2001) 'Private Capital Flows in East Asia: Boom, Bust and Beyond' in G. de Brouwer (ed.), *Financial Markets and Policies in East Asia*, London: Routledge, 47-81.

Rajan, R.S., R. Siregar and G. Bird (2005) 'The Precautionary Demand for Reserve Holdings in Asia: Examining the Case for a Regional Reserve Pool' *Asia-Pacific Journal of Economics and Business*, 5:.21-39.

Watanabe, S. and M. Ogura (2006) 'How Far Apart Are Two ACUs from Each Other?: Asian Currency Unit and Asian Currency Union' Working Paper No.06-E-20, Bank of Japan.

World Bank (2004). *Global Development Finance*, Washington, DC: World Bank.

12

Reducing Global Imbalances and Accelerating Growth: Role of Regional Financial Cooperation in Asia

Ramgopal Agarwala and Prabir De

Introduction

The purpose of this chapter is to present the following six propositions.

- First, the current and prospective global imbalances pose a serious threat to the world economy, both developed and developing economies.
- Second, the conventional medicine along the line of structural reforms is quite inadequate to tackle the problem and can even lead to global recession if the emphasis is mainly on demand reduction in the US.
- Third, these measures need to be combined with a Keynesian approach focusing on global demand augmentation in addition to demand switching to correct the global imbalances without a global deflation.
- Fourth, there is a high level of latent demand for national and regional investments in Southern Asia (about 10 per cent of GDP).[1] Such additional investment in Asia could amount to US$1 trillion over the medium-term and that could make a significant contribution to

reducing global imbalances while accelerating GDP growth in the region by about 2 percentage points.

- Fifth, only a fraction of the current surpluses of Asia is needed to finance these investments and such a redirection in the use of Asian surpluses would increase the rate of return on these surpluses while contributing to additional growth and poverty reduction in the region.
- Lastly, such a programme of regional cooperation presents a win-win-win opportunity for Southern Asia, Northern Asia and the rest of the world, and the international community (in particular the US, Northern Asia and Southern Asia) should work together in a concerted manner to promote such cooperation.

Risks of Global Imbalances

The most popular and emerging view on what is driving the global imbalances is the substantial increase in the surplus of savings over investment, particularly in emerging Asia and, more recently, in the oil-exporting countries. A recent World Bank report (2005) points out sharply the risks faced by the world economy due to the high current account deficits of the US economy. It notes that:

- Over the last two decades, the US has been transformed from a significant net international investor, in the 1970s, to the world's largest debtor;
- At the end of 2004, developing countries held an unprecedented level of foreign exchange reserves at $1.6 trillion which were 'excessive' for many countries and carried serious risk of capital losses and growing quasi-fiscal carrying costs;
- Looking ahead, the possibility of 'disorderly' adjustments of external payment imbalances in the global economy could pose acute risks to emerging markets.

Similar sentiments have been expressed by a large number of official bodies as well as individual experts. For example, the European Central Bank in its latest *Financial Stability Review* (2005) argues that large and growing financial imbalances continue to pose medium-term risks for the stability of foreign exchange and other financial markets. It goes on to say that a disorderly correction of the large US current account deficit and surpluses in Asia remained possible, particularly as the imbalances could increase further.

The International Monetary Fund (IMF) in its *World Economic Outlook* (WEO) (2005b) also presents a disturbing picture on the consequences of high global imbalances for the world economy. According to the *WEO*, the rise in global imbalances is mainly due to following reasons.

First, global investment and savings rates across the world as a whole, have tended to fall since the early 1970s.

Second, while investment rates have converged in the advanced countries, at about 20 per cent of GDP, savings rates have not. Among the significantly advanced economies, savings remain the highest in Japan and the lowest in the US, with the EU in the middle. This, to some extent, explains why Japan has a current account surplus, the US has a huge deficit and the EU is roughly in balance.

Third, Asian countries both save and invest a much higher share of GDP than other emerging market economies and oil producers. However, China's savings and investment rates have exploded to extraordinarily high levels, with savings outstripping investment. In other East Asian economies, savings have remained steady, but investment has fallen sharply since the 1997-98 crisis.

Fourth, China's savings rate is now running at close to 50 percent of GDP. Government savings are close to 12 per cent of GDP, household savings at 16 per cent and company savings at 22 per cent.

The *WEO* projections based on the assumption of constant real exchange rates, suggest little improvements in global imbalances. The US current account deficit is projected to remain at about 6 per cent of GDP into the medium term and the net external position of the US would continue to deteriorate, reaching a record 50 per cent of GDP by 2010, matched by rising net creditor positions in the rest of the world. However, the *WEO* regards these global imbalances as unsustainable in the long run and argues that the issue is not *whether* but *how* they will adjust. In the 'benign baseline scenario', where non-US residents are willing to continue increasing their holdings of US assets for a considerable period without demanding a large risk premium, there is some slowdown in GDP growth in the US but the current account deficit remains at 3.5 per cent of GDP by 2010 and 3 per cent over the long term with US net foreign liabilities eventually stabilizing at about 70 percent of GDP, which is hardly a healthy figure of foreign indebtedness.[2]

In the second scenario, the WEO assumes a combination of a temporary rise in protectionist pressures, accompanied by a sudden decline in demand for US assets including an abandonment of pegs in emerging Asia. The consequence of these shocks is a sharp contraction in US economic activity, a large depreciation of the dollar and a sharp contraction in the US trade balance. Together with the increase in protectionism, this would lead to rising inflationary pressures, requiring a significant monetary tightening, and thus, amplifying the contractionary effects on GDP growth. This would also be accompanied by a slowdown in economic activity in emerging Asia and a sharp slowdown in growth in the Euro area and Japan. In addition, in this scenario, there are significant risks of financial market disruption with further negative implications for global stability and growth. Noriel Roubini Global Economics Blog provides an excellent overview of the opinions of eminent economists in the US on the subject.[3]

There are some who believe that the US is helping to absorb the surplus savings of the world and the situation can continue indefinitely along these lines. For example, Richard Cooper states in his *Financial Times* (31 October 2004) column: 'America's current account deficit is not only sustainable, it is perfectly logical given the world's hunger for investment returns and dollar reserves'.

However, there is a long list of eminent economists who hold the opposite view and who have warned of the high risks posed by the global imbalances, in particular the high current account deficits of the US. The list includes Rubin, Sinai and Orszag, Summers, Peterson, Roach, Gross, Bergsten, Rogoff and Obstfeld, Eichengreen, and Volcker. As an illustration, one can perhaps concentrate on statements of Larry Summers,'[4] former Secretary of Treasury of the US. He has argued eloquently how the large current account deficits of the US carry significant risks to the US as well as to the rest of the world. For the US, he emphasizes the risk of the incipient protectionist pressures that are generated by a large trade deficit, and that are connected with the current furore over outsourcing. Second, he notes that dependence on foreign governments for short-term financing creates vulnerabilities in both the economic and political realms. He uses the term "balance of financial terror" to refer to a situation where the US relies on the costs to others of not financing the US current account deficit as an assurance that financing will continue. For the rest of the world, an Summers notes that a great deal of money is being invested at what is almost certainly a very low rate of return. Also, for countries trying to avoid appreciation of their exchange rates, there is the loss of domestic monetary control. He notes that much of the speculative bubble in Japan during the late 1980s that had such a catastrophic long-run impact on the Japanese economy was driven by liquidity produced by a desire to avoid excessive Yen appreciation.

Inadequacies of the Conventional Medicine

Despite the seriousness of the problem, there is a dearth of credible proposals for curing the malady. There are standard recipes: revaluation of currencies in Asia, in particular the Chinese Yuan; reflationary policies in EU, and reduction of fiscal deficits in the US. For all three of these recipes, there are doubts as to the extent to which concrete actions may be taken and to which probable actions can help cure the global imbalances.

On revaluation of the Chinese Yuan, an ADB Economist Dr Cyn-Young Park in her paper on 'Coping with Global Imbalances and Asian Currencies' has shown that a projected 10 percent revaluation of the renminbi would only improve the US trade balance by US$3.6 billion, a mere 0.02 per cent change in the current account as a percentage of GDP. Even with a 20 per cent revaluation, the situation changes little, contributing only to a 0.05 per cent reduction in the current account deficit. Dr Park argues that despite China's significant trade surplus with the US, this would be the case because imports from the China account for a relatively small share of total US imports, and exports to the China constitute an even smaller share of total US exports. On a broader front, the Chinese authorities may well be concerned about the deflationary effects of revaluation along the lines suggested by Ron Mckunnon who has argued that exchange rate flexibility in China could lead to repetitive appreciations resulting in severe deflation throughout China's economy and a zero-interest liquidity trap—as in Japan, when forced into repeated appreciations of the Yen in the 1980s and up to the mid-1990s. Any likely change in the exchange rate regime in China cannot be expected to have a significant impact on the current account deficit of the US.

Nor is the EU ready to adopt reflationary measures in the near-term. In its recent announcement, the European Central Bank (ECB) held its key interest rate steady at 2 per cent at its regular monthly policy-setting meeting, refusing to bow to pressures to cut rates to inject life into the eurozone's stagnating economy. The ECB fears that interest rate cuts would cause inflation. Nor are the prospects of reducing fiscal deficits particularly bright. Again to quote Larry Summers: 'There is much that one can argue about in the forecasts and the models, but I'm aware of no credible argument that without some form of discontinuity, the US current account deficit will not increase from its current high level'.

Perhaps in recognition of the weaknesses of the conventional remedies, World Bank's *Global Development Finance Report* (GDF) (2005) is projecting only a marginal fall in the US current account deficit over the medium-term:

from 5.6 per cent in 2004 to 5.3 per cent in 2007. The *WEO* exercise also does not suggest a much better prospect of reducing global imbalances through conventional measures. As noted in the *WEO* report, the model used there assumes higher price elasticities of demand for both exports and imports than is normally seen in standard export and import equations. Even then, greater exchange rate flexibility in emerging Asia reduces current account deficit of the US by 2015 by less than 0.5 percent of GDP compared with the baseline scenario. Similarly, the incremental effects of 'competition-friendly policies' in Europe and Japan on US current account deficit are less than 0.3 percent of GDP by 2010. In the WEO analysis, the benefits of reforms in terms of reducing the US current account deficit, come mainly from fiscal consolidation in the US (about 2 percentage points of GDP by 2010) but that may not be a realistic prospect until and unless the US faces a harder external budget constraint. Moreover, if the emphasis is on reducing demand in the US without compensating increase in demand elsewhere, it could lead to recessionary pressures in the world economy. Altogether, the conventional medicines do not offer a bright prospect of effectively dealing with the problem of global imbalances. They may be ineffective at best and even counterproductive (in the sense of causing global deflation) at worst.

Need for a Keynesian Approach

In this context, there is clearly a need for some out-of-the-box thinking and one such line could be to bring in Keynesian economics. Perhaps the focus should be shifted from demand switching alone to demand augmentation. The point has been made forcefully by Larry Summers:

> 'Notice that exchange rate manipulation and adjustments, even if they could be controlled or willed by policy makers, do not address the global demand-supply imbalance created by an increase in US saving. They serve simply to redistribute it from one country to another. For example, the scenario advocated by many, in which increased US global saving is associated with a depreciation in the dollar, may offset the adverse demand impact in the US of increased saving by switching the demand for expenditure from foreign goods to American goods, but only at the cost of increasing the demand-supply imbalance abroad. A healthy global adjustment process requires a healthy US economy, which requires increased national saving which, in turn, requires measures that replace the demand that is lost from increased national saving. Indeed, even with the assumption of constant US national savings, the global economy today appears to be suffering more from the deflationary pressures associated with too little demand than the inflationary pressures associated with too much demand.'

It is worth remembering that it is this kind of Keynesian strategy that helped China to maintain growth in the post-1997 period. Depreciation in exchange rates in Thailand, Korea, Indonesia and Japan during 1997-98 imposed strong deflationary pressures on China. Starting in March 1998, China took strong 'Keynesian' measures to slow its internal deflation. Its 'New Deal' encompassed a huge expansion of government expenditure on infrastructure and mass residential housing. Not only was fiscal deficit allowed to increase from 0.7 per cent of GDP in 1997 to 2.8 per cent in 2000 and further to 2.5 per cent in 2001 but there was heavy borrowing from China's state-owned banks in the form of what was called 'policy loans'. This was accompanied by expansionary monetary policy which included a reduction in China's inter-bank rates from 9 per cent in 1996 to 2.7 per cent by the end of 2002. The People's Bank of China also eased the austerity policy, which had been adopted in 1993, by pressuring the state banks to extend credit to the construction industry, exporters, home purchasers and infrastructure projects as well as to the struggling state-owned enterprises. Altogether the Keynesian package perhaps pumped in close to a trillion dollar stimulus in the Chinese economy during the period 1998-2002. That helped to boost the Chinese economy while the rest of East Asia went through an economic slowdown.

It is the contention of this chapter that Southern Asia can learn from the experience of China and can pump in about a trillion dollars of additional investment over the medium-term which can increase its GDP growth rate by about 2 percentage points and make a significant contribution towards reducing global imbalances.

Latent Demand for Higher Investment in Southern Asia

In this context, the saving-investment perspective provided by the *WEO* is particularly useful in understanding the sources of the current malady and seeking its cure. The increased current account balances could be due to a combination of increased investment or diminished savings in the US and increased savings or diminished investments in the rest of the world, in particular Asia. *WEO* and the IMF *Regional Report on Asia and Pacific* (IMF 2005a,b) point out that during the last few years when the US current account deficit has increased, the country's investment rate has remained largely stable; it is the decline in savings rate, both public and private, that has led to the imbalances. In Asia, saving rates have remained roughly stable and it is the investment rate that has declined: the problem is not 'saving glut' but 'investment drought'. This suggests that the solution may be sought in increasing US savings on the one hand and increasing Asian investments on the other. The IMF report also points out the risks of continued dependence of Asia on exports, particularly to the US and calls for greater attention to domestic demand generation. It is this context that the chapter examines the opportunity of increasing investments in Southern Asia (defined as including South Asia, Southeast Asia and Central Asia) and their implications for increasing growth in this region as well as reducing global imbalances.

During the period 1980-2005, East Asian GDP grew by 7.8 per cent per year and that in South Asia by 5.68 percent (see Table 12.1). The difference was largely because of the difference in investment rate (34.62 per cent of GDP in East Asia and 22.47 percent in South Asia) and not because of the efficiency of investment as income rate of return on investment (IRRI)[5] in East Asia being slightly lower (at 22.53 per cent) than that in South Asia (25.29 per cent). This point is also evident for the two dominant economies of the region: China and India. During the period 1980-2005, GDP in China grew by 9.54 percent per year and that in India by 5.97 per cent per year. The striking difference between the two economies was in terms of investment rate (37.84 per cent of GDP in China vs 23.33 per cent in India). As far as efficiency of investment was concerned, India's performance was, in fact, somewhat better than China. A similar picture about the importance of investment emerges from the experience of Southeast Asia after the financial crisis of 1996-7. During the period 1996-2005, average GDP growth rate in Indonesia, Malaysia, Philippines and Thailand was 2-5 per cent per year and the investment rates declined dramatically in 2005: the investment rate as a percentage of GDP was 20.12 percent in Indonesia, 27.26 per cent in Malaysia, 18.07 percent in Pakistan, 19.93 per cent in the Philippines, 16.78 per cent in Kyrgyz Republic, 15.75 per cent in Tajikistan and 20.24 per cent in Uzbekistan (Table 12.1). Thus, there is clearly an 'investment drought' in Southern Asia.

Table 12.1: Investment Deficit in Asia

Period	Region / Country	GDP growth rate	Investment rate	IRRI*
		%	% of GDP	%
1980-2005	East Asia & Pacific	7.80	34.62	22.53
	China	9.54	37.84	25.21
	Korea, Rep.	6.55	31.58	20.75
	Indonesia	5.34	25.85	20.67
	Malaysia	6.24	29.99	20.81
	Philippines	2.96	21.55	13.74

Table 12.1 continued

Table 12.1 continued

Period	Region / Country	GDP growth rate	Investment rate	IRRI*
		%	% of GDP	%
	Thailand	5.98	31.24	19.14
	Vietnam	6.71	24.79	27.07
1980-1996	Korea, Rep.	7.77	32.45	23.94
	Indonesia	7.04	29.51	23.87
	Malaysia	7.36	32.27	22.81
	Philippines	2.35	22.65	10.37
	Thailand	7.83	34.28	22.85
1996-2005	Korea, Rep.	4.53	30.82	14.71
	Indonesia	2.68	20.12	13.33
	Malaysia	4.71	27.26	17.29
	Philippines	4.29	19.93	21.51
	Thailand	2.82	27.12	10.41
1980-2005	South Asia	5.68	22.47	25.29
	Bangladesh	4.36	19.13	22.78
	India	5.97	23.33	25.59
	Pakistan	5.27	18.07	29.17
	Sri Lanka	4.58	25.18	18.19
2000-2005	Central Asia	9.37	21.26	44.06
	Turkmenistan	18.07	28.17	64.13
	Kyrgyz Republic	3.98	16.78	23.69
	Uzbekistan	5.22	20.24	25.78
	Tajikistan	9.32	15.75	59.14
	Kazakhstan	10.27	25.37	40.46

Note: * Income rate of return on investment
Source: Calculated based on *WDI* CD ROM 2007

A high rate of investment is, of course, not a sufficient condition for rapid growth but it has been a necessary condition for higher growth in East Asia and elsewhere. Table 12.2 captures this in context of Southern Asia. Looking ahead, it seems plausible to argue that if Southern Asian countries are to grow at 7-8 per cent per year, the investment rate may have to increase to 30 per cent plus. It has been estimated by the World Bank[6] that for achieving the target growth rate of 8 per cent per annum, India needs to increase its investment rate to 30 per cent of GDP while its rate of investment in 2005 was only 27 per cent of GDP at current price and is much lower if taken in terms of constant prices. Similar increases in investment rates will be necessary in other countries in Southern Asia, if the growth rates are to increase to 7 per cent per year and above.

Table 12.2: Income and Investment in Southern Asia

Country	GDP US$ billion	Investment US$ billion	IR* %	GDP Growth %
	Average of 2001 to 2005			
Bangladesh	52.64	12.47	23.69	5.43
India	618.19	169.18	27.37	7.08
Pakistan	86.43	14.67	16.98	4.88
Sri Lanka	18.81	4.45	23.64	3.80
Kazakhstan	35.36	9.48	26.80	10.36
Kyrgyz Republic	1.94	0.31	15.86	3.68
Tajikistan	1.65	0.26	16.00	9.52
Turkmenistan	5.81	1.47	25.35	17.96
Uzbekistan	11.40	2.50	21.94	5.50
Indonesia	213.17	41.72	19.57	4.38
Malaysia	107.14	23.75	22.17	4.43
Philippines	84.06	15.05	17.90	4.61
Thailand	144.72	38.71	26.75	5.00
Vietnam	40.91	14.05	34.34	7.46
Southern Asia	1422.23	348.06	24.47	6.72

Notes: GDP is taken at current US$; investment, represented by gross capital formation (taken at current US$); GDP growth considers annual average growth rate of GDP (taken at current US$); All attributes are taken as average for the period 2001-05, *Investment rate

Source: Calculated based on WDI CD-ROM 2007.

Where can such increase in investment rate come from? Obviously, the principal source of the increase has to be private sector investment. The *WEO* emphasizes the need for continued structural reforms to increase private investment. However, it is interesting to note that the *WEO* also finds the evidence of relatively low internal rate of private sector, at least for companies that are represented on the equity markets. This naturally leads to a discussion on the investment climate (IC) for the private sector. World Bank reports on the subject for India and other Southern Asian countries have emphasized the importance of reforms in the following areas: regulatory reforms including reduction entry and exit barriers, addressing impediments to the smooth functioning of labour, land and product markets, and streamlining the regulation of business start-ups, bankruptcy procedures, industrial and trade routines, addressing physical infrastructure bottlenecks and weaknesses in financial and other business services. Clearly reforms need to be continued at a vigorous pace to improve IC significantly.

One factor that is particularly relevant for the present discussion is the inadequacy of infrastructure facilities. Most of the IC surveys find inadequate infrastructure facilities as a key constraint on private sector investment. IMF (2005) argues that infrastructure investments in India need to increase from about 5 per cent of GDP to about 7 per cent. The report on infrastructure by the Development Committee of the World Bank and the IMF also highlights the gap in infrastructure investments in South Asia, though it does not put a number on the additional investment needs. The high growth economies of Asia such as China and Korea consistently invested more than 10 per cent of their GDP in infrastructure during periods of high growth. In the light of that experience, infrastructure investment deficits in Southern Asian countries could well be about 5 percent of GDP.

There is ample evidence of substantial deficits in the infrastructure sector across Asia.[7] Table 12.3 compares the estimates of infrastructure investment needs, noted in some recent studies including that of RIS. It is clear that there is substantial need in infrastructure sector in Asia, which, in other words, also offers large investment opportunities. As shown in Table 12.3, the new investment needs, as estimated in three studies, are expected to vary between US$165-412 billion (about 6.2 to 7.3 per cent of GDP) per annum for the period 2007-11. Meeting expected demands for economic and population growth and achieving the above government targets will, therefore, require massive investments in the infrastructure sector. In addition to the national infrastructure investments in Asian countries, there are un-met needs of regional infrastructure investments. Improving regional connectivity in roads, railways, air transport, ports and shipping, telecommunication, gas and oil pipelines, etc. could well require investment of hundreds of billions of dollars.[8]

Table 12.3: Estimates of Annual Infrastructure Investment Needs in Asia

	ADB-JBIC-WB*	UNESCAP#	RIS@
Infrastructure investment (US$ billion)	165	328	412
Infrastructure investment percentage of GDP)	6.2	6.8	7.3

Notes: *. Includes East Asia excluding South and Central Asia for the period 2006-10. Includes East Asia and Pacific, and South Asia for the period 2006-10, Includes developing countries and LDCs in South, Southeast and East Asian countries for the period 2007 to 2011.

These broad estimates of infrastructure investment needs are supported by aggregative analysis of investment needs in the region based on regression equations linking GDP growth to infrastructure investment needs presented in RIS (2007), which indicates that developing Asia (including LDCs) will need to spend an estimated total of US$412 billion per annum between 2007 and 2012 (or about 7.3 per cent of the combined GDP of developing Asia and LDCs) in infrastructure sectors such as roads, railways, airways, ports and electricity (see Table 12.4). India alone has to spend an investment of about US$410 billion in six infrastructure sectors, namely, road, railways, ports, power, aviation and urban infrastructure during the period 2007 to 2012 as against the estimate of US$320 billion during 2007-11 by the Planning Commission (Government of India, 2006). This study alternatively also suggests that about 8 percent GDP growth would result in increased demand for infrastructure services which, in turn, would require investment amounting to about 7.3 percent of GDP.

Table 12.4: Infrastructure Investments Needs in Developing Asia, 2007-12

Country	Investment (2007-12)	
	Amount (US$ billion)	Share in GDP (%)
China	208.33	10.78
India	68.33	9.89
Indonesia	26.67	6.46
Malaysia	13.33	7.87
Philippines	8.33	7.85
Thailand	11.67	7.22
Vietnam	6.67	5.80
Asian LDCs	74.67	4.60
Total	412.06	7.30

Source: RIS (2007).

The economies in Southern Asia have grown by over 6 percent per annum during 2001-05 and together their GDP in 2005 was over US$1.4 trillion (Table 12.2). A 10 percentage point boost in investment rate (private and public) over the next five years in Southern Asia can pump in about US$1 trillion over the next five to seven years. Combined with the conventional measures on exchange rate adjustments, structural reforms in Japan and the EU and austerity in the US, they could substantially reduce global imbalances while meeting the problem of 'too little demand' mentioned by Larry Summers.

Many of these investments (such as gas pipelines) seem to be viable on commercial terms and should be suitable for partnership with private investors. For many other infrastructure investments also Public-Private-Partnership (PPP) is emerging as the preferred instrument, where the private sector gets its normal financial rates of return while the public sector partner provides concessional funding based on the long-term direct and indirect benefits to the economy. New instruments such as special purpose vehicle (SPV) set up recently by the Government of India to fund mega infrastructure projects may be relevant for other Asian countries as well (see the Box 12.1). Concerns have been expressed by the IMF that these investments may lead to excessive debt burden of the government in many of these countries. These concerns may be exaggerated. The benefits from infrastructure investment should not be seen in narrow terms of direct collection from provision of infrastructure services but should include the indirect benefits in terms of increased income of the country and enhanced value of land and other assets. If provision of better infrastructure helps to increase private investment and accelerated GDP growth, the increased revenues therefrom may over time help these economies to manage their debt burden better. In the Chinese case of boosting investment after the Asian financial crisis, government revenue-GDP ratio increased from 5.8 per cent in 1997 to 10.3 per scent in 2003 and there has been no unmanageable increase in Government debt or in inflationary pressures.

Box 12.1: Financing Infrastructure through Public-Private Partnership

The Government of India has decided to set up a special purpose vehicle (SPV) to fund mega infrastructure projects. Borrowing up to Rs 100 billion by the SPV—India Infrastructure Finance Company Ltd (IIFCL)—during the current fiscal would be guaranteed by the government.

The SPV would fund projects in the public and private sectors as well as in the PPP scheme. Fresh annual limits for government guarantee would be decided at the beginning of every fiscal. Besides raising long-term funds from domestic and overseas markets, the SPV would also borrow from multilateral lending agencies.

The SPV, which would be 100 per cent government-owned, would fund projects in sectors such as road, bridges, railways, seaports, airports, inland waterways, power, urban transport, water supply, gas pipeline, special economic zones, international convention centres, tourism projects and more.

Source: *The Hindu Business Line*, 4 November 2005.

Sources of Funds for Financing Additional Investments

What is the source of funds for such large investments? Fortunately, Asia is sitting on a mountain of foreign exchange reserves where the current and prospective rate of return is extremely small. And most of the Asian countries with large reserves are looking for better investment opportunities than those provided by US Treasuries. A proper mechanism needs to be devised so that Asians can invest their surplus savings in the assets represented by regional investments. If such investment opportunities reduce the flow of funds into US treasuries, they would create a harder external budget constraint and help the US reduce to its excessive spending at a gradual and measured pace.

There are several specific proposals afloat for financing these infrastructure investments. For example, Kim Hak-Su, Executive Secretary of UNESCAP agued that 'At this stage of transformation, Asia and the Pacific region requires an institution like the European Investment Bank (EIB)—an independent, government-owned Asian Investment Bank to promote regional capital markets', Such an Asian Investment bank (AIB) could provide infrastructure loans and collaborate with the banking community in raising as well as investing resources. It could work with the private sector by co-financing and guaranteeing private investment financing. Malaysia has proposed the setting up of an Asian Infrastructure Development Fund to finance projects in the region. In a similar vein, Datuk Seri Abdullah Ahmad Badawi, Prime Minister of Malaysia said Asian countries could use 'a fraction' of their massive foreign exchange reserves as capital for the fund, which would invest in basic economic infrastructure including super highways and super railways linking and binding the Asian community. The programmes for Asian bonds can also help fund these investments.

Win-Win Outcome for the Major Players in the World Economy

From the above discussion, it is clear that in many countries, particularly in Southern Asia, higher investment would be highly desirable. Desirable adjustment would then see higher investment in many parts of the developing world, higher savings in the developed region (particularly in US) and a smooth shift in the global pattern of deficits, all without a significant recession.

Therefore, to be confident of a benign adjustment, one needs changes in policies in several places at once. Among the most important elements of such policies are significant movements in higher savings in the US and higher spending, relative to GDP, in the rest of the world, but particularly in emerging Asia. Coupled with these, a Keynesian approach focusing on global demand augmentation is necessary to correct the global imbalances without a global deflation. The result would not only be more balanced global growth, but each region would also be better-off.

The Southern Asian economies will of course be the most obvious beneficiaries of such a regional cooperation programme. Their GDP growth rate may increase by about 2 percentage points with substantial contribution to reduction in poverty. The regional investments will improve connectivity to land-locked countries in the region as well as to the remote regions in several countries of the region such as the Northeastern region of India and Northwestern region of Pakistan. Since the incidence of poverty tends to be high in landlocked countries and in these remote regions, the benefits of growth in terms of poverty reduction may be more than proportionate. However, substantial benefits will also accrue to other major players in the world economy.

The current global imbalances pose a serious threat to the US economy. As argued by many eminent economists in the US, a disorderly correction of these imbalances could lead to a sudden deprecation of the dollar, sharp increase in interest rates, a crisis in housing and stock markets and a hard landing of the economy. A large boost in investments in Southern Asia will create additional demand for exports of goods and services from the US and help to reduce its current account deficits. A gently hardening external budget constraint will also help improve its saving rate gradually, without causing a disruption. Altogether, there will be improved prospects of soft landing of the US economy.

Northern Asian countries, in particular Japan, China and Korea, will benefit from increased demand for investment goods and services from Southern Asia and that will help in better utilization of capacity in the capital goods sector, especially the construction sector. With declining current account deficits in the US they will face reduced risk of protectionism in the US and pressures for accelerated exchange rate appreciation from the US. These economies have excessively large foreign exchange reserves which are earning very low rates of return. The investments in Southern Asia can offer much better rates of return than the current rates. Similarly, EU will face reduced risk of excessive appreciation of Euro and pressures for accelerating growth in the region.

In view of these win-win-win opportunities, the international development community (especially Southern Asian countries, Northern Asian countries and the US) should work together in promoting regional cooperation in Asia. Such cooperation should not be seen as reducing the importance of the US in the region but as helping the US to reduce its external deficits while boosting growth in Asia.

Endnotes

1 By Southern Asia, we inply a geographic region combining South, Southeast and Central Asia.

[2] It is worth noting that in the context of the World Bank Initiative on Highly Indebted Poor Countries, an External debt/GDP ratio of 70 per cent is regarded as too high.

[3] See *www.roubinglobal.com/archives/2005/05/global-imbalanc.htm*

[4] See Lawrence H. Summers, Third Annual Stavros S. Niarchos Lecture, Institute for International Economics, Washington, DC 23 March 2004.

[5] Defined as GDP growth rate divided by investment-income ratio, which is equivalent to increase in income per unit of investment adjusted by relative price of capital goods and gross domestic output.

[6] See World Bank (2004) *India: Investment Climate Assessment 2004*, November.

[7] Based on regression methods and by using secondary data, Fay and Yepes (2003) estimated infrastructure investments needs in Asia. Also see Yepes (2004) and Chatterton and Pureto (2005).

[8] For example, according to UNESCAP, upgrading of 26,000 km roads falling under the Asian Highway requires US$18 billion during 2005-08, out of which Southern Asia needs approximately US$9 billion (UNESCAP 2006).

References

ADB-JBIC-WB (2005) *Connecting East Asia: A Framework for Infrastructure*, Asian Development Bank, Japan Bank for International Cooperation, World Bank.

Chatterton, I. and O. S. Pureto (2005), *Estimation of Infrastructure Investment Need in the South Asia Region*, Washington, DC:World Bank.

European Central Bank (2005), *Financial Stability Review 2005*, Brussels.

Fay, M. and T. Yepes (2003) *Investing in Infrastructure: What is Needed from 2000 to 2010?*, Policy Research Working Paper 3102, Washington, DC: World Bank.

IMF (2005a), *Asia Pacific Regional Outlook*, September, Washington DC: International Monetary Fund.

IMF (2005b), *World Economic Outlook (WEO): Building Institutions*, September, Washington DC: International Monetary Fund.

RIS (2007), *Regional Cooperation for Infrastructure Development in Asia: Towards a Regional Mechanism for Public-Private Partnership*, New Delhi.

________ (2005), High Risks of Global Imbalances: Role of Infrastructure Investments in Asia, *Policy Brief 16*, New Delhi.

UNESCAP (2006), *Enhancing Regional Cooperation in Infrastructure Development Including that Related to Disaster Management*, Bangkok: UNESCAP.

________ (2005), Report of the Subregional EGM Meeting, 25-26 April 2005, Bangkok.

World Bank (2005), *Global Development Finance 2005: Mobilizing Finance and Managing Vulnerability*, Washington DC: World Bank.

Yepes, T. (2004) *Expenditure on Infrastructure in East Asia Region, 2006-2010*, Background Paper for EAP Flagship 2005, Washington, DC: World Bank.

Part V
Regional Cooperation for Energy Security

13

Asian Energy Outlook to 2020: Trends, Patterns and Imperatives of Regional Cooperation

Kokichi Ito, Li Zhidong, Ryoichi Komiyama

Introduction

In the wake of the Cold War, economies around the world have become increasingly globalized against the background of trends such as the transition to market economies and the spread of information technology (IT). The countries (and territories) of Asia have achieved an overall high rate of economic growth thanks to the fast-paced expansion of trade and foreign direct investment (FDI), close mutual economic ties and industrialization. In the process, they have transformed the region into the growth centre for the entire world economy. Due to its economic advances, the region has also become a market with tremendous impact on global energy supply and demand. The medium-to-long-term outlook for global energy supply and demand envisions continued strong economic growth in Asia and a rapid rise in its energy demand. If this is true, the promotion of efforts to assure energy supply and to demand stability and address energy and environmental problems, from a perspective embracing all of Asia and in cooperation with the other countries in the region, will be of crucial importance to Japan in its future deployment of international energy policy.

The objective of this research was to produce a quantified profile of the future configuration of energy supply and demand in the world as a whole and

Asia in particular to 2020, by applying econometric means. The free trade agreements (FTAs) and other strong ties of interdependence among the economies in the region are expected to develop even further and keep rates of economic growth at high levels. Focusing on this region, the research consisted of comprehensive investigation of its energy economics. Thus far, the Institute has executed programmes of research on various topics with a focus on the region of Asia. The preparation of this outlook drew upon the findings of these programmes. This was supplemented by an in-depth analysis of the situation in each country, based on extensive information-sharing with counterpart institutions in other Asian countries through long-standing network links with them, in order to bring the resulting portrait of the supply and demand closer to reality.

Socio-economic Outlook

With the continued drive provided by the Asian economy, the world economy is expected to exhibit moderate growth at an overall rate of 2.7 per cent over the forecast period (that is, the years 2000- 20).

By region, North America and the European members of the Organization for Economic Cooperation and Development (OECD) are anticipated to exhibit stable economic growth at respective annual average rates of 2.6 per cent and 2.0 per cent. In the non-OECD countries of Europe such as the former Soviet Union, economies are getting on the path of sustained growth following the dismemberment of the Soviet Union in the 1990s, and are forecast to attain a corresponding rate of 3.3 per cent as a whole. As for Asia (outside Japan), in spite of some uncertainty associated with the prospects for economic growth in developed countries in other regions, the forecast is continued strong growth at a rate of 5.4 per cent, owing to the presence of economies with enormous markets such as China, the Association of Southeast Asian Nations (ASEAN), and India, as well as the reinforcement of mutual interdependence in the region and swift technological progress.

With the support of its surging domestic demand, the Chinese economy in particular sustained high rates of growth throughout the 1990s, and has kept them in the range of 7-9 per cent with the start of the 2000s. It managed to record a growth of 7.3 per cent in 2001 in spite of deceleration of the US economy and slumping performance among Asian newly industrializing economies (NIEs) and the ASEAN countries. Furthermore, following its admission into the World Trade Organization (WTO) in 2002, China posted high rates of economic growth, at 8.0 per cent in that year and 9.1 per cent in

2003. Although it is saddled with an array of problems such as internal economic disparities, the need for reform of state enterprises, unemployment and bad debt, China should be able to achieve high-order growth at rates averaging 7.2 per cent over the long term, provided that it continues to practice proper macroeconomic management.The forecast for Japan is comparatively low growth at a rate of 1.3 per cent owing to factors such as economic maturation and the decline in the labour population accompanying population decrease and ageing.

On the population front, although birth rates are tending to move downward in developing countries as they make economic progress, the world population is forecast to continue exhibiting a basic tone of expansion and reach some 7.7 billion in 2020 as compared to about 6.2 billion in 2000. Among the developed countries, a sustained increase is projected in the US but the tempo should slow to a gradual level. The US share of the world population is, therefore, not expected to expand. Japan's population is forecast to go into gradual decline after peaking within the next few years. In Europe, too, the population is projected to peak out from 2010 to 2020. In Asia, on the other hand, it is anticipated to continue growing, albeit at lower rates. In 2020, it is estimated that the countries of China and India will have respective populations of 1.4 and 1.3 billion, and that Asia as a whole will account for 53 per cent of the world population increase.

The outlook for crude oil prices was prepared on the basis of the price estimates in documents such as the *Annual Energy Outlook* (AEO) released by the Department of Energy (EIA/DOE) in the US. It envisages a moderate rise over the long term as oil production costs increase, with the per-barrel price reaching 24 dollars in 2010 and 27 dollars in 2020 (at 2000 values; the nominal price figures are 29 and 40 dollars, respectively).

As for natural gas prices, the general view is that they are linked with crude oil prices. However, in this outlook, which took account of the views of the International Energy Agency (IEA) and other institutions, it was assumed that they would not rise as fast as crude oil prices, in light of the ample supply capacity supported by new projects and more flexible price determination methods. The historical trend shows that coal prices do not have a very strong correlation with crude oil prices, and the forecast levels, which were based on the IEA outlook and other data, incorporate only a gradual increase in production costs.

World Energy Demand Outlook

Primary Energy Consumption Outlook

World primary energy consumption is forecast to increase at an average annual rate of 2.1 per cent over the forecast period, much higher than the corresponding rate of 1.7 per cent for the preceding 20-year period (1980-2000). The volume in 2020 is expected to reach 13.6 billion oil-equivalent tons, a 1.5-fold increase from the 9.1 billion tons in 2000.

About 70 per cent of the increase in energy consumption over the forecast period would derive from the non-OECD countries (mainly developing ones). The non-OECD Asian countries should account for about two-thirds of the total, and China, for about 30 per cent.

Along with population increase and economic growth, the share of the world primary energy consumption occupied by non-OECD countries is expected to increase from 41 per cent in 2000 to 51 per cent in 2020. Conversely, the same occupied by OECD countries is forecast to shrink from 59 per cent to 49 per cent. The Asian share is forecast to rise from 27 per cent in 2000 to 34 per cent in 2020, and the Chinese share, from a corresponding 10 to 15 per cent. China is now the world's biggest energy consumer after the US, and it should near the US consumption level by 2020. As such, its presence in the global energy market should become even larger.

Outlook for Fossil Fuel Consumption

Fossil fuels (coal, oil and natural gas) are expected to contribute about 90 per cent of the increase in primary energy consumption over the years 2000-20 and should, therefore, continue to play a major role as energy sources. Consumption of oil is predicted to show the largest increase of all fossil fuels and account for 35 per cent of the increase in primary energy consumption, followed by natural gas at 30 per cent and coal at 26 per cent.

World oil consumption is forecast to rise from the order of 70 million barrels per day in 2000 to that of 102 million barrels per day in 2020—an increase rate of 1.9 per cent. By region, Asia should account for about 50 per cent of this increase. By sector, it is estimated that about 60 per cent will come from the transportation sector. The share occupied by oil in primary energy consumption is forecast to decline slightly, from 39 per cent in 2000 to 37 per cent in 2020, however, it would remain the single-largest energy source.

Table 13.1: Major Energy and Economic Indicators

	Asia			World		
			Average annual growth rate (AAGR) (%)			Average annual growth rate (AAGR)(%)
	2000	2020	2000-20	2000	2020	2000-20
GDP (billions of US dollars at 1995 value)	9361	17805	3.3	34251	58570	2.7
GDP (developing Asia*)	3673	10,432	5.4			
Population (millions)	3322	4095	1.1	6179	7710	1.1
Primary energy consumption (millions of tons of oil-equivalent, Mtoe)	2423	4570	3.2	9057	13593	2.1
Coal (Mtoe)	1049	1811	2.8	2325	389	2.0
	(43%)	(40%)		(26%)	(26%)	
Oil (Mtoe)	938	1720	3.1	3494	5072	1.9
	(39%)	(38%)		(39%)	(37%)	
Natural gas (Mtoe)	237	598	4.7	207	390	2.6
	(10%)	(13%)		(23%)	(26%)	
Final energy consumption (Mtoe)	111	2826	3.2	6103	8900	1.9
Transportation sector (Mtoe)	346	786	4.2	1781	2730	2.2
	(23%)	(28%)		(29%)	(31%)	

Table 13.1 continued

Table 13.1 continued

	Asia			World		
			Average annual growth rate (AAGR)(%)			Average annual growth rate (AAGR)(%)
	2000	2020	2000-20	2000	2020	2000-20
Power sector (Mtoe)	276 (18%)	619 (22%)	4.1	1088 (18%)	1935 (22%)	2.9
CO_2 emissions (millions of tons of carbon-equivalent; Mt-C)	1975	3,627	3.1	6507	9852	2.1
GDP per capita of population (US dollars at 1995 value/person)	2818	4348	2.2	5544	7596	1.6
Primary energy consumption per capita of population (toe/person)	0.73	1.12	2.1	1.47	1.76	0.9
Primary energy consumption per unit of GDP**	259	257	-0.04	264	232	-0.65
CO_2 emissions per unit of GDP***	211	204	-0.18	190	168	-0.61
CO_2 emissions per unit of primary energy consumption****	0.815	0.794	-0.13	0.718	0.725	0.04
Automobile ownership volume (millions vehicles)	140	336	4.5	757	1222	2.4
Automobile ownership volume per thousand population (vehicles per thousand population)	42	82	3.4	123	159	1.3

* Asia excluding Japan ** toe/millions of US dollar at 1995 value, *** t-C/millions of US dollar at 1995 value, **** t-C/toe

Note: Figures in parentheses indicate percentage shares of totals.

Table 13.2: World Primary Energy Consumption

Primary energy consumption	Millions of toe			Share (%)			AAGR (%)	
	1980	2000	2020	1980	2000	2020	1980-2000	2000-20
Total	6481	9057	13593	100	100	100	1.7	2.1
Coal	1782	2325	3489	27	26	26	1.3	2
Oil	3008	3494	5072	46	39	37	0.8	1.9
Natural gas	1239	2107	3490	19	23	26	2.7	2.6
Nuclear	186	676	781	2.9	7.5	5.7	6.6	0.7
Hydro	148	223	339	2.3	2.5	2.5	2.1	2.1
Geothermal	12	45	123	0.2	0.5	0.9	6.6	5.2
Other renewables	106	187	299	1.6	2.1	2.2	2.9	2.4

Consumption of natural gas, which was to 2341 billion cubic meters in 2000, is forecast to hit 3877 billion cubic meters in 2020, at an average annual increase rate of 2.6 per cent, the highest among the fossil fuels. Installation of combined-cycle power generation systems fuelled with natural gas is spreading steadily due to advances in utilization technology and considerations of environmental compatibility. About 60 per cent of the increase in natural gas consumption should come from fuel input into the power sector. Expanded utilization led by this sector is expected to drive an increase in the natural gas share of primary consumption, from 23 per cent in 2000 to 26 per cent in 2020.

In oil-equivalent terms, world coal consumption is forecast to rise from 2.325 billion tons in 2000 to 3.489 billion tons in 2020, for an average annual increase rate of 2.0 per cent. By region, Asia should account for about 70 per cent of this increase, and China for about 40 per cent. By sector, about 90 per cent should come from the power sector as the trend towards input as fuel for generation deepens. The share of coal in primary energy consumption should remain more or less unchanged at around 26 per cent over the years 2000-20.

Outlook for Other Fuel Consumption

In oil-equivalent terms, consumption of power generated by nuclear power plants is forecast to rise from 676 million tons in 2000 to 781 million tons in 2020, an average annual increase rate of 0.7 per cent. The nuclear share of primary energy consumption is expected to decline from 8 per cent in 2000 to 6 per cent in 2020 owing to the fast-paced expansion of natural gas utilization in the power sectors of developed countries in North America and Europe and their virtual lack of prospects for construction of additional nuclear power plants. The increase in the generated output of nuclear power plants should be confined almost exclusively to a few countries in Asia. In East Asia, nevertheless, nuclear power will continue to play a vital role in Japan, South Korea and Taiwan, which have few domestic energy resource reserves, and China, with its rapidly growing demand for electricity.

There are high hopes for the diffusion of renewable energy sources with little environmental burden, such as hydropower, geothermal energy and new energy. Their share in primary energy consumption is forecast to increase from 5 per cent in 2000 to 6 per cent in 2020. However, they are not going to rank on par with fossil resources as pillars of the base energy supply, due to their high supply cost and supply instability deriving from natural influences, such as the intermittent nature of photovoltaics and wind power.

Outlook for Final Energy Consumption

Consumption of electrical power, a sophisticated form of energy utilization, grew at a swift rate averaging 3.1 per cent annually over the years 1980-2000. Over the forecast period, it is expected to grow at a corresponding one of 2.9 per cent and undergo a 1.8-fold increase relative to 2000. By sector, the swiftest increase is anticipated in the residential and commercial sector at 3.2 per cent. By region, consumption is forecast to grow at a 2.0 per cent pace in the OECD countries as opposed to 4.1 per cent in Asia as income levels rise in the latter. The share of final energy consumption occupied by petroleum products was 49 per cent in 2000 and is anticipated to remain in that area. Such products should, therefore, continue to account for almost half of the total. Energy consumption in the transportation sector, which has a massive demand for petroleum products, is forecast to increase at an average annual rate of 2.2 per cent as a reflection of motorization in developing countries.

Outlook for the Power Generation Structure

In 2000, coal-fired power accounted for the single-largest share of the world generated output at 39 per cent. The remainder was taken up by natural-gas-fired power nuclear power, and hydropower. The outlook for the forecast period contains a shift to natural-gas-fired power along with the spread of new technology such as combined-cycle systems fuelled with natural gas and efforts to alleviate environmental load. The share of the total generated output occupied by natural-gas-fired power is forecast to jump from 17 per cent in 2000 to 27 per cent in 2020. That occupied by coal-fired power, which was 39 per cent in 2000, is anticipated to stay at that level even as of 2020. Coal-fired power should remain the single-largest power supply source. In China and India in particular, it is anticipated to be the key source for supply of the rapidly expanding demand for power. Meanwhile, the share occupied by oil-fired power is likely to continue with a basic trend of decline, especially in the developed countries. It is estimated that the of nuclear power will shrink from 17 per cent in 2000 to 11 per cent in 2020, because of the almost complete lack of additional plant construction in developed countries, which are also leaning towards the decommissioning of aging facilities without replacement.

Energy Supply-Demand Outlook in Asia

Outlook for Primary Energy Consumption

Primary energy consumption in Asia is forecast to grow at an average annual rate of 3.2 per cent and reach 4.6 billion oil-equivalent tons in 2020, for a 1.9-fold increase from the corresponding total of 2.4 billion tons in 2000. Stronger growth is anticipated in countries achieving fast-paced economic growth, such as China, India, Vietnam, Thailand, Malaysia and Indonesia. About 50 per cent of the consumption increase over the period in question should derive from expanded consumption in China, followed by India at about 20 per cent, Indonesia and South Korea at about 5 per cent each and Thailand, Malaysia and the Philippines at about 3 per cent each. Japan's share of the increase is expected to be about 2 per cent, or around the same level as that of Vietnam, which is anticipated to achieve rapid economic growth. The share of primary energy consumption in Asia occupied by China is forecast to expand from 38 per cent in 2000 to 45 per cent in 2020. The outlook also envisions a corresponding expansion from 13 to 15 per cent for India, 4 to 5 per cent for Indonesia and 2 to 3 per cent for Thailand. In contrast, the share of Japan is predicted to decline from 22 per cent in 2000 to 12 per cent in 2020 owing to factors such as economic maturation and population decrease, thereby ranking the country third in this connection, behind China and India.

Outlook for Fossil Fuel Consumption

In Asia, fossil fuels (coal, oil and natural gas) are expected to continue to occupy a vital place as sources of energy, and to account for about 90 per cent of the increase in primary energy consumption over the forecast period, in the world as a whole. Among the fossil fuels, oil is anticipated to have the largest share of the increase at 36 per cent, followed by coal at 35 per cent and natural gas at 17 per cent.

Consumption of oil, which was of the order of 19 million barrels per day in 2000, is anticipated to increase by an average annual rate of 3.1 per cent and hit 35 million barrels per day in 2020. By region, it is estimated that China will account for about 50 per cent of the increase, and India, about 20 per cent. By sector, about 60 per cent should derive from transportation, with the residential/commercial and industrial sectors accounting for about 20 per cent respectively. The oil share in primary energy consumption should stay at roughly the same level; it is expected to dip from 39 per cent in 2000 to 38 per cent in 2020.

Consumption of natural gas is forecast to undergo a 2.5-fold increase, from 263 billion cubic metres in 2000 to 664 billion cubic metres in 2020, with the highest rate of growth of all fossil fuels (an annual average of 4.7 per cent). It is estimated that about 50 per cent of the consumption increase will derive from input as fuel in the power sector, and about 20 per cent, from the expanded demand in the residential/commercial sector along with the spread

Table 13.3: World Final Energy Consumption

Primary energy consumption	Millions of toe			Share (%)			AAGR (%)	
	1980	2000	2020	1980	2000	2020	1980-2000	2000-20
Total	4684	6103	8900	100	100	100	1.3	1.9
Industry	1896	2154	2944	40	35	33	0.6	1.6
Transportation	1146	1781	2730	24	29	31	2.2	2.2
Residential/ Commercial	1466	1987	2974	31	33	33	1.5	2
Non-energy, etc.	176	180	251	3.8	3	2.8	0.1	1.7
Energy source								
Total	4684	6103	8900	100	100	100	1.3	1.9
Coal	699	524	618	15	8.6	6.9	-1.4	0.8
Oil	2347	2970	4379	50	49	49	1.2	2
Natural gas	832	1151	1578	18	19	18	1.6	1.6
Electricity	585	1088	1935	12	18	22	3.1	2.9
Heat	120	237	262	2.6	3.9	2.9	3.4	0.5
Renewables	100	133	128	2.1	2.2	1.4	1.4	-0.2

Table 13.4: World Power Generation

Electricity generation	(TWh)			Share (%)			AAGR(%)	
	1980	2000	2020	1980	2000	2020	1980-2000	2000-20
Total	8246	15375	27518	100	100	100	3.2	3.0
Coal	3139	6014	10842	38	39	39	3.3	3.0
Oil	1655	1225	1689	20	8.0	6.1	-1.5	1.6
Natural gas	991	2679	7318	12	17	27	5.1	5.2
Nuclear	713	2591	2998	8.7	17	11	6.7	0.7
Hydro	1719	2632	3941	21	17	14	2.2	2.0
Geothermal	14	50	140	0.2	0.3	0.5	6.7	5.3
Other renewables	14	185	589	0.2	1.2	2.1	13.7	6.0

of urbanization accompanying economic growth. The natural gas share in Asian primary energy consumption is predicted to rise from 10 per cent in 2000 to 13 per cent in 2020, but the natural gas shift would be slower than in North America and Europe.

Consumption of coal is forecast to rise from the order of 1.049 billion oil-equivalent tons in 2000 to 1.811 billion tons in 2020, for an average annual increase rate of 2.8 per cent. It is estimated that China will account for about 70 per cent of the increase, and India, about 20 per cent. By sector, about 90 per cent of the increase should derive from power generation, and the remaining 10 per cent, from industry. While its share of primary energy consumption is forecast to slip from 43 per cent in 2000 to 40 per cent in 2020, coal should retain the single-largest share of the primary energy supply in Asia.

Outlook for Other Fuel Consumption

In Asia, consumption of power generated by nuclear power plants is forecast to increase at an annual average rate of 3.2 per cent, from 132 million oil-equivalent tons in 2000 to 247 million tons in 2020. Almost all of the corresponding global increase should come from Asia. There are good prospects for expansion in China and in countries with few domestic reserves of energy resources, such as Japan, Korea and India. China is predicted to account for about 50 per cent of the nuclear power increase in Asia. The nuclear share in primary energy consumption should remain around 5 per cent over the period in question. The share occupied by renewable energies (for example, hydropower, geothermal energy and new energy) is expected to increase from 3 per cent in 2000 to 4 per cent in 2020. It should be noted, however, that energy consumption is forecast to expand rapidly in the region, and this will make quick response to assure a stable supply of energy a matter of the highest priority. These circumstances would act to limit utilization of renewable energies, whose supply can be unstabilized by natural conditions (except for hydropower and geothermal energy). Nevertheless, installation of new energy systems with low environmental loads will continue to be a key agenda item.

Outlook for Final Energy Consumption

In Asia, fast-paced economic growth is being linked to an upgrading of the industrial structure, rise in the standard of living and rapid increase in the consumption of electrical power. Power consumption increased at an average annual rate of 5.9 per cent from 1980 to 2000, and is forecast to increase at

Table 13.5: Primary Energy Consumption in Asia

Primary energy consumption	Millions of toe			Share (%)			AAGR(%)	
	1980	2000	2020	1980	2000	2020	1980-2000	2000-20
Total	1054	2423	4570	100	100	100	4.2	3.2
Coal	469	1,049	1,811	44	43	40	4.1	2.8
Oil	485	938	1720	46	39	38	3.3	3.1
Natural gas	52	237	598	4.9	10	13	7.9	4.7
Nuclear	25	132	247	2.4	5.4	5.4	8.6	3.2
Hydro	20	38	91	1.9	1.6	2.0	3.3	4.4
Geothermal	2.6	16	52	0.2	0.6	1.1	9.4	6.2
Other renewables	0.4	13	52	0.03	0.6	1.1	19.8	7.0

Table 13.6: Final Energy Consumption in Asia

Final energy consumption	Millions of toe			Share (%)			AAGR(%)	
Sector	1980	2000	2020	1980	2000	2020	1980-2000	2000-20
Total	755	1511	2826	100	100	100	3.5	3.2
Industry	393	708	1118	52	47	40	3	2.3
Transportation	133	346	786	18	23	28	4.9	4.2
Residential/Commercial	208	416	863	27	28	31	3.5	3.7
Non-energy, etc.	21	41	60	2.8	2.7	2.1	3.3	1.9
Energy source								
Total	755	1511	2826	100	100	100	3.5	3.2
Coal	302	346	427	40	23	15	0.7	1.1
Oil	333	763	1471	44	50	52	4.2	3.3
Natural gas	25	94	240	3.3	6.2	8.5	6.9	4.8
Electricity	88	276	619	12	18	22	5.9	4.1
Heat	7.5	28	64	1	1.9	2.3	6.9	4.2
Other renewables	0	3.7	4.4	0	0.2	0.2	-	0.9

4.1 per cent over the forecast period. By sector, the rate of increase is expected to be the highest in the residential/commercial sector at 4.8 per cent. By region, China has the highest corresponding rate at 5.5 per cent, followed by India at 5.2 per cent. Against the backdrop of steady motorization, the share of the final energy demand occupied by petroleum products is forecast to expand from 50 per cent in 2000 to 52 per cent in 2020. Similar to that of home electrical products, the diffusion of the automobile is one of the most symbolic indicators of a tangible rise in the standard of living, and the general trend of motorization is bound to deepen.

Outlook for the Generation Structure

In Asia, many countries have abundant reserves of coal, and coal-fired power plants accounted for about 50 per cent of the region's generated output in 2000, the remainder being accounted for by natural-gas-fired plants, nuclear power and hydropower. Oil-fired power plants generated about 10 per cent of the supply. Over the forecast period, the structure should shift to natural gas along with increased installation of combined-cycle generation systems fuelled with it, but coal-fired power generation should also continue to increase in line with policy for effective use of domestic resources. With expanded utilization in China, India and Indonesia, the coal-fired share is predicted to increase from 51 per cent in 2000 to 54 per cent in 2020 as such plants acquire even more weight as the majority source. Meanwhile, the natural-gas-fired share is anticipated to experience a corresponding expansion from 13 to 17 per cent. The installed capacity of nuclear power is projected to increase in countries including China, South Korea and India, but its share in the generated output for the region as a whole is forecast to fall from 13 per cent in 2000 to 11 per cent in 2020.

Outlook for CO_2 Emissions

As fossil fuels should be the source for about 90 per cent of the primary energy consumption in the world as a whole over the forecast period, CO_2 emissions, which were about 6.5 billion (carbon-equivalent) tons in 2000, are forecast to reach a level of about 9.9 billion tons in 2020. They would consequently expand at an average annual rate of 2.1 per cent, about the same as that for primary energy consumption, and multiply by a factor of about 1.5. About 70 per cent of this increase would come from non-OECD countries, and about 30 per cent, from China alone.

Outlook for Motorization

In Asia and other largely developing regions, consumption of gasoline, gas oil and other transportation fuel is rapidly expanding. Among the developed countries, motorization has already run its course and the demand is more or less saturated. The developing countries of Asia, in contrast, are now at the threshold of motorization, which is anticipated to gather momentum over the coming years as standards of living rise. The expanded consumption of oil associated with motorization in Asia should be a major factor characterizing the structure of energy supply and demand in the region over the medium and long terms. In 2020, the ownership volume in China is forecast to reach about 120 million vehicles (about 1.5 times as many as in Japan today), but this would amount to a diffusion rate of only about 8 per cent, which would still be low as compared to the average in developed countries (53 per cent in 2000). In other words, China would still have margin for further motorization after 2020, and the diffusion of ownership there may be expected to have a tremendous impact on the international oil market.

Crude Oil and LNG Supply and Demand in Asia

In the three countries in Northeast Asia (Japan, China and South Korea), the rate of oil dependence on the Middle East should deepen steadily. Specifically, in 2020, it is forecast to reach about 90 per cent in Japan and 80 per cent in South Korea. In China, too, it is forecast to jump from 15 per cent in 2000 to about 50 per cent in 2020 due to the sharp increase in oil demand and the levelling off of domestic production. In the process, the corresponding rate of dependence of Northeast Asia as a whole on the Middle East may be expected to rise from 58 per cent in 2000 to approximately 70 per cent in 2020 along with the quantitative expansion of consumption in China. If the three countries begin to import crude oil produced in Siberia (in quantities totalling about 100 million tons per year), the corresponding rate could possibly be lowered by about 11 per cent.

In North Asia (consisting of Japan, China, South Korea and Taiwan), import of liquefied natural gas (LNG) should be in the range of 120-150 million tons in 2020, considering the commencement of natural gas import from Irkutsk and Sakhalin. At present, plans extending to 2010 would increase the LNG supply capacity to the Asia-Pacific market in that year to about 110 million tons, and this could be increased further to about 180 million tons with the execution of additional projects now under study. Assuming that LNG development moves steadily

Table 13.7: Power generation in Asia

Electricity generation	(TWh)			Share (%)			AAGR(%)	
	1980	2000	2020	1980	2000	2020	1980-2000	2000-20
Total	1193	3966	8985	100	100	100	6.2	4.2
Coal	301	2037	4896	25	51	54	10.0	4.5
Oil	470	384	420	39	10	5	-1.0	0.5
Natural gas	91	519	1486	7.6	13	17	9.1	5.4
Nuclear	97	505	949	8.2	13	11	8.6	3.2
Hydro	231	480	1057	19	12	12	3.7	4.0
Geothermal	3.0	18	60	0.2	0.4	0.7	9.4	6.3
Other renewables	0	22	116	0	0.6	1.3	-	8.6

ahead in the second half of the forecast period from 2010, potential for supply to the region should be sufficiently high in 2020.

Implications

While the long-term holds the prospect of a deepening dependence on the Middle East for the supply of oil in Asia, the region should have an ample supply capacity for natural gas and coal. The simultaneous attainment of energy security, market rationalization and environmental preservation in Asia demands the construction of the 'best mix' of energy sources in each country, considering its situation with regard to its amount of energy reserves, geographical conditions and stage of economic development. Further, the formation of an analogous 'best mix' in the region as a whole would require extensive utilization of coal and nuclear power alongside natural gas while assuring the stability of the oil supply.

Ensuring Energy Security in Asia

Strong economic growth and progressive motorization are going to expand the demand for energy in Asia. As noted above, the dependency on the Middle East for supply of oil should deepen, because the regional oil supply would not be able to keep pace with the swift expansion in demand. While it is naturally important for the individual countries to make efforts to secure their own energy supplies, there is also a possibility that excessive pursuit of national interest by any single country could damage the energy security of the rest of the region. Consequently, it is becoming increasingly important for the issue to be treated as one in which all countries in the region have a common stake.

To this end, it is imperative for the Asian countries that are net consumers of energy to collaborate with each other in pursuit of the following four major tasks: a) fuller exercise of bargaining power given their collective position as a massive regional consumer of oil, and strengthening of ties of dialogue and cooperation as equal partners with net oil producers; b) construction of a shared reserve scheme for responding to emergencies and effective use of the existing infrastructure to deal with short-term crises such as supply suspensions; c) promotion of cooperative resource development and procurement inside and outside the region; and d) conditioning of international oil markets to give the supply and demand structure more flexibility.

Pursuit of Energy Diversification

Pursuit of the best energy mix is another agenda item to be tackled by each country in accordance with its circumstances with respect to energy demand attributes, amount of resource reserves, level of technology and economic merit. However, it is also vital to retain the perspective of optimizing the mix for the region as a whole, based on cooperation between the net consumers and net suppliers.

Coal has excellent economic merit but also entails a high environmental load, and its utilization in developed countries could stop expanding as a result. In Asia, there are abundant reserves of coal in countries including China, India and Indonesia, and the region's utilization of coal is expected to expand, especially in the power sector. This would further heighten the importance of environment-friendly utilization, harnessing high-efficiency technology. As viewed from the perspective of energy security and economic merit, it is crucial for Asia to make better use of its abundant coal deposits, and Japan can play a pivotal role in this connection as a technologically advanced country.

Utilization of natural gas is also projected to expand in Asia, especially in the power and civil sectors. This points to a need for improvement of its economic feasibility. The Asia-Oceania region has a fully sufficient supply potential for natural gas in the long term, and the net consumer countries must collaborate in efforts to heighten the economic merit, for example, by exercise of stronger bargaining power. Gas prices have thus far been set through linkage to crude oil prices because of the competition with oil, but competition with coal is going to carry increasing weight in the future.

In the developed countries of Europe and North America, construction of additional nuclear power plants has essentially been halted, and the installed capacity is expected to decline. As a result, Asia should be the site of almost all additional nuclear power plants. Many Asian countries have a relatively low level of domestic natural resources, and nuclear power has a major role to play in the assurance of supply stability and conquest of environmental problems. There is also a need for intra-regional cooperation encompassing the aspects of operation and management in this area.

At any rate, it is vital to have various options for energy supply sources. This would be linked not only to higher levels of energy security but also a stronger position in price negotiations for competing fuels.

Responding to Global Environmental Problems

The trend of rapid increase in CO_2 emissions in China and other developing Asian countries underscores the limited effectiveness of Japan's emission countermeasures within its borders. As such, a far larger overall benefit would be delivered by mitigation of environmental load through transfer of technology to other countries in Asia and other regions with a burgeoning energy demand.

Japan should regard this role not merely as a variety of assistance to fulfill its obligations as a developed country but also as a precious opportunity for the development of a promising business deriving from the environment. China and other developing Asian countries have immense potential for energy conservation, and offer enormous margin for technical assistance through the Clean Development Mechanism (CDM) and other schemes. Japan is at the vanguard worldwide in respect of energy conservation and environmental technology. With its dearth of natural resources, it is crucial for Japan to support the advancement of its economy through extensive use of its undepletable resource—its technology.

Table A13.1: World Primary Energy Consumption (by Region)

(millions of toe)

	Actual		Forecast		AAGR (%)			
	1990	2000	2010	2020	2000/ 1990	2010/ 2000	2020/ 2010	2020/ 2000
North America	2137	2555	2863	3196	1.8	1.1	1.1	1.1
	(27.4)	(28.2)	(25.9)	(23.5)				
Central and South America	382	526	710	980	3.2	3.0	3.3	3.2
	(4.9)	(5.8)	(6.4)	(7.2)				
OECD Europe	1624	1764	1953	2116	0.8	1.0	0.8	0.9
	(20.8)	(19.5)	(17.7)	(15.6)				
Non-OECD Europe	1468	1001	1197	1385	-3.8	1.8	1.5	1.6
	(18.8)	(11.1)	(10.8)	(10.2)				
Africa	201	259	336	455	2.5	2.7	3.1	2.9
	(2.6)	(2.9)	(3.0)	(3.4)				
Middle East	224	385	492	703	5.6	2.5	3.6	3.0
	(2.9)	(4.3)	(4.5)	(5.2)				
Asia	60	2423	3335	4570	3.9	3.2	3.2	3.2
	(21.2)	(26.8)	(30.2)	(33.6)				
China	673	932	1406	2063	3.3	4.2	3.9	4.1
	(8.6)	(10.3)	(12.7)	(15.2)				

Table A13.1 continued

Table A13.1 continued

	Actual		Forecast		AAGR (%)			
	1990	2000	2010	2020	2000/1990	2010/2000	2020/2010	2020/2000
Japan	439	525	543	561	1.8	0.3	0.3	0.3
	(5.6)	(5.8)	(4.9)	(4.1)				
India	187	322	452	684	5.6	3.4	4.2	3.8
	(2.4)	(3.6)	(4.1)	(5.0)				
Other Asian countries	361	644	934	1263	6.0	3.8	3.1	3.4
	(4.6)	(7.1)	(8.4)	(9.3)				
Oceania	102	129	149	166	2.4	1.4	1.1	1.3
	(1.3)	(1.4)	(1.3)	(1.2)				
Other regions	14	15	18	22	0.9	1.7	1.9	1.8
	(0.2)	(0.2)	(0.2)	(0.2)				
OECD country total	4517	5317	5981	6633	1.6	1.2	1.0	1.1
	(57.8)	(58.7)	(54.1)	(48.8)				
Non-OECD country total	3293	3740	5073	6961	1.3	3.1	3.2	3.2
	(42.2)	(41.3)	(45.9)	(51.2)				
World total	7811	9057	11053	13593	1.5	2.0	2.1	2.1
	(100.0)	(100.0)	(100.0)	(100.0)				

Note: Figures in parentheses indicate percentage shares of totals.
Source: Based on data from *Energy Balances of OECD Countries* and *Energy Balances of Non-OECD Countries*, IEA; forecast figures prepared by the IEEJ.

Table A13.2: Primary Energy Consumption in Asia (by Region)

(millions of toe)

	Actual		Forecast		AAGR (%)			
	1990	2000	2010	2020	2000/1990	2010/2000	2020/2010	2020/2000
China	673	932	1406	2063	3.3	4.2	3.9	4.1
	(40.5)	(38.5)	(42.2)	(45.1)				
Japan	439	525	543	561	1.8	0.3	0.3	0.3
	(26.4)	(21.7)	(16.3)	(12.3)				
South Korea	93	191	262	303	7.5	3.2	1.5	2.3
	(5.6)	(7.9)	(7.9)	(6.6)				
India	187	322	452	684	5.6	3.4	4.2	3.8
	(11.3)	(13.3)	(13.6)	(15.0)				
Indonesia	52	98	144	209	6.5	3.9	3.8	3.9
	(3.1)	(4.1)	(4.3)	(4.6)				
Taiwan	48	83	110	132	5.6	2.9	1.9	2.4
	(2.9)	(3.4)	(3.3)	(2.9)				
Singapore	13	25	36	48	6.3	4.0	2.9	3.4
	(0.8)	(1.0)	(1.1)	(1.1)				
Malaysia	20	47	74	110	8.7	4.6	4.0	4.3
	(1.2)	(1.9)	(2.2)	(2.4)				

Table A13.2 continued

Table A13.2 continued

	Actual		Forecast		AAGR (%)			
	1990	2000	2010	2020	2000/ 1990	2010/ 2000	2020/ 2010	2020/ 2000
Philippines	18	33	57	96	5.9	5.6	5.5	5.5
	(1.1)	(1.4)	(1.7)	(2.1)				
Thailand	29	58	89	145	7.3	4.4	5.0	4.7
	(1.7)	(2.4)	(2.7)	(3.2)				
Vietnam	5.8	14	33	54	9.5	8.7	5.2	6.9
	(0.3)	(0.6)	(1.0)	(1.2)				
Hong Kong	11	15	18	20	3.8	1.7	1.1	1.4
	(0.6)	(0.6)	(0.5)	(0.4)				
Other Asian countries	71	80	111	144	1.2	3.4	2.6	3.0
	(4.3)	(3.3)	(3.3)	(3.2)				
Asia total	60	2,423	3,335	4,570	3.9	3.2	3.2	3.2
	(100.0)	(100.0)	(100.0)	(100.0)				
Developing Asia	21	1 8	2792	4010	4.5	3.9	3.7	3.8
	(73.6)	(78.3)	(83.7)	(87.7)				

Note: Figures in parentheses indicate percentage shares of totals.
Source: Same as in Table A13.1.

14

Regional Cooperation for Asian Energy Security

Vipul Tuli

Introduction

The global energy industry is on the threshold of some very exciting changes and Asia is at the centre of these changes. Energy decision makers in Asia have the power to shape the future of the world's energy landscape. This chapter attempts to convey three key messages: First, interdependence in energy among Asian countries is vital for the economic development of key Asian countries. Second, there are several key impediments to increasing Asian interdependence; addressing these impediments is critical. Finally, the chapter presents some ideas on opportunities for Asian nations to find common ground on energy security, stability and sustainability. The ideas described are not exhaustive, and there are several other areas of cooperation that Asian economies can pursue. The author believes that Asia is well-positioned to shape the future of the world's energy landscape.

Why Regional Cooperation Within Asia is Vital

Why is Asian cooperation vital for both consuming and supplying nations? In general, the term Asia is used in its widest sense, including the Middle East, South and Southeast Asia and the Far East. When it comes to specific issues, though, the chapter will refer to the relevant sub-region such as the Middle

East, or to individual countries. There are four main reasons why Asian cooperation is vital.

First, Asia is likely to become a dominant consumer in both the global and regional energy industry. Major Asian buyers already account for about 50 per cent of global coal demand, 20 per cent of global oil demand and 6 per cent of global gas demand. As can be seen from Figure 14.1 over the next 20 years, Asian demand is likely to be the primary growth engine—accounting for 38 per cent of global oil demand, 14 per cent of global gas demand and 60 per cent of global coal demand in 2025. Asian demand for oil, gas and coal is expected to increase to 57 million barrels per day (mb/d), 34 trillion cubic feet per year (tcf/y) and to 2930 million tons per year by 2025 respectively.

Figure 14.1: Asia: Dominant Consumer of Oil, Gas and Coal

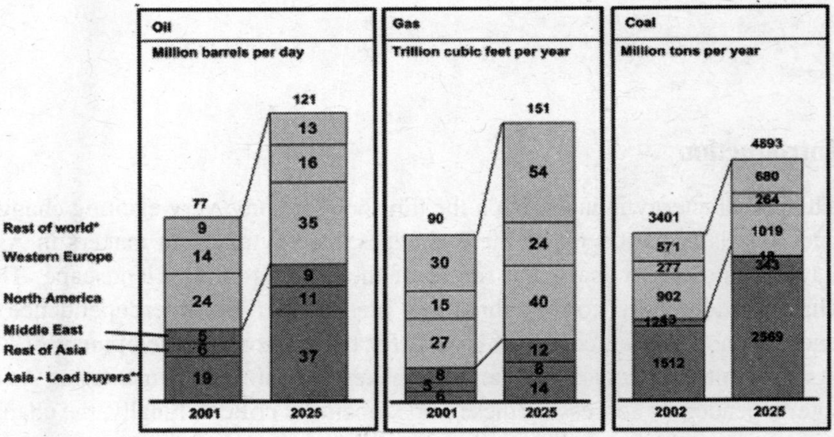

Notes: * Includes Africa, Eastern Europe, New Zealand, Australia and former Soviet Union countries.
** India, China, South Korea, Japan.
Source: International Energy Outlook, IEA.

The implications of this are dramatic—by 2010, Asian oil demand will be higher than that of North America. By 2025, it will be two and half times the size of Western European demand, with China, India, South Korea and Japan being the primary consumers. India alone will become the fourth largest oil consumer and the third largest coal consumer in the world.

Second, much of Asia's oil and gas production is already consumed within the region, driven by economic logic. As can be seen from Figure 14.2, in the year 2003, 55 per cent of crude oil was consumed within the region. The major consumers are Japan, South Korea, India and China and the major regional suppliers are the Gulf Cooperation Council (GCC) countries such as Saudi Arabia, Kuwait, UAE, Oman, Qatar; others Yemen, Iran, Iraq; and some Southeast Asian countries like Indonesia, Malaysia and Brunei. This interdependence between consumers and producers in Asia is driven by the geographical setting and economic fundamentals of demand and supply, factored by the favourable transportation costs.

Figure 14.2: 55 per cent of Asian Crude Currently Consumed within Asia, 2003

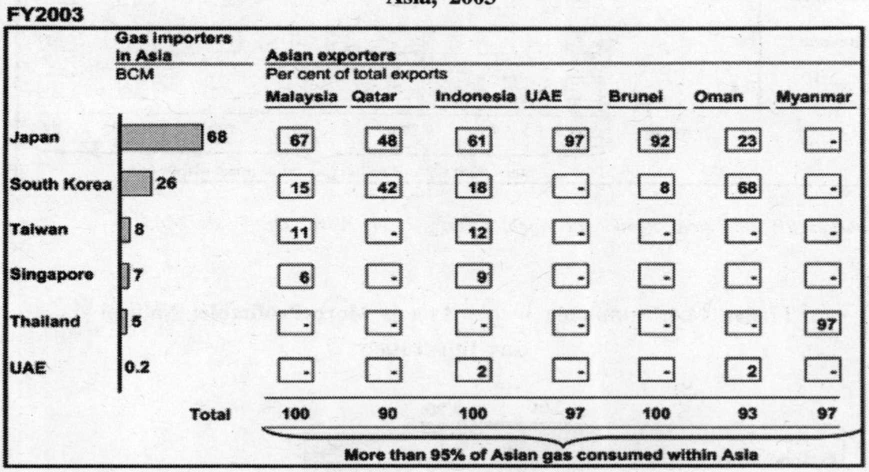

Note:* Indonesia, Malaysia, Brunei.
Source: BP Statistical Review of World Energy 2004; *World Oil Trading 2003*.

Moreover, for gas, as can be seen from Figure 14.3, this picture is even more extreme: 95 per cent of Asian gas is currently consumed within Asia. Therefore, maintaining or even increasing the inter-Asia supply interdependence makes economic sense.

The conventional economic principle underlying the supply of gas suggests that supplying gas from the Middle East to China (or India) could result in higher netbacks for producers relative to the US due to lower transport costs, assuming that longer term market prices for gas tend to be similar across regions. The same argument also applies to crude oil.

Figure 14.4 depicts one such illustration. As is evident, the disaggregation of the components of gas supplying costs gives a differential of US$0.90 per one million metric btu (mmbtu) of gas supplied from Qatar to US and the

Figure 14.3: More than 95 per cent Asian Gas Production is Consumed within Asia

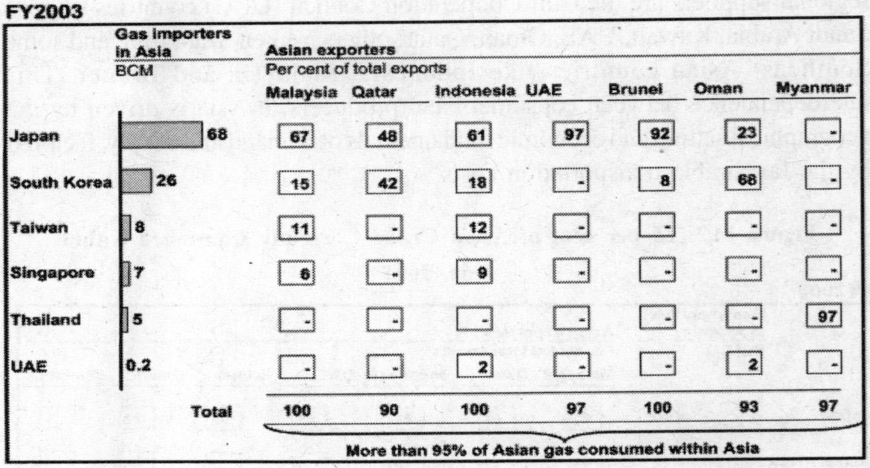

Source: BP Statistical Review of World Energy 2004; World Oil Trade 2003.

Figure 14.4: Supplying within Asia is More Profitable: Natural Gas Illustration

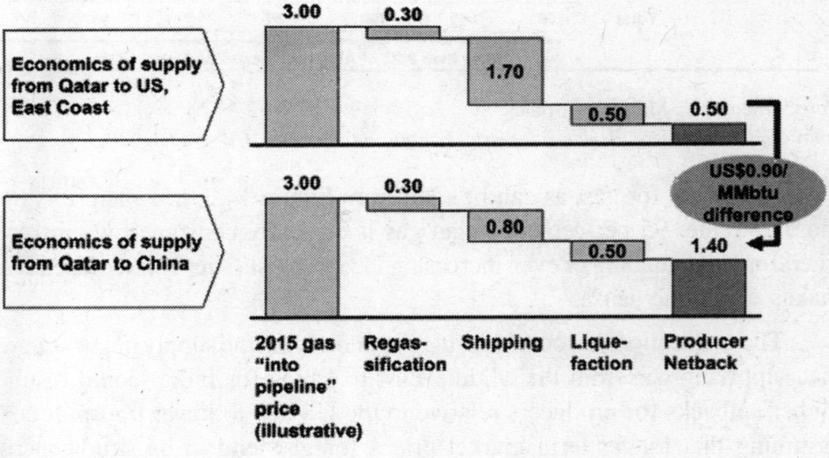

Source: McKinsey Global Gas Model.

same quantity supplied to China in Asia. However, other concerns such as diversity in supply and terrorism are increasingly influencing the choice of supply source. For example, a terrorist attack in the straits of Malacca could disrupt supplies to the Far East.

Third, improved Asian linkages are critical for Middle East and Southeast Asian suppliers to increase their share in global energy revenues. The development of world energy markets is at a critical juncture. To illustrate this, we would like to share two key scenarios distilled from McKinsey's extensive research on the future of energy markets. These scenarios are developed on the basis of the transformation of the global oil and gas market as a result of world economic reorganization where Asian emerging markets have become the main consumers of oil and gas exported from the major suppliers in the region, as their previous world market share has decreased and is being reorganized.

McKinsey's research on the 'Future of Energy Markets' envisages two broad scenarios. In the first scenario, OPEC and non-OPEC nations follow a 'balanced approach', keeping capacity addition in line with demand growth, and maintaining, current market shares. The second scenario is a 'boom-bust scenario', where supply tightness drives up prices, triggering significant non-OPEC supply and market share growth for non-OPEC countries. This market dynamic, in turn, could induce aggressive capacity building by OPEC, a pattern seen in the 1980s; this would help OPEC regain share, but at the cost of lower oil prices and significant revenue loss.

Figure 14.5 shows that the balanced world approach will lead to higher economic growth, higher demand for oil and a larger share and size of OPEC production. The size of the prize is large.

We argue that a boom-bust scenario can cause substantial damage to supplier nations by slowing down investments targeted at improving social infrastructure, for example education and health care. As per McKinsey estimates, the annual oil revenue for OPEC is expected to be US$295 billion in the balanced scenario and only US$166 billion in a boom-bust scenario. This implies that there is a huge gap in the form of revenue needed for social sector investment in the OPEC supplying countries, thereby signifying the importance of market stability for the producers.

Moreover, there is an additional reason why Asian linkages are critical for major producers. Figure 14.6 shows that crude slate from the Middle East is getting heavier and sourer and Asia has low availability of complex refining capacity to process such crudes. Therefore, additional investments will be

Figure 14.5: Balanced Approach Increases Share and Volumes

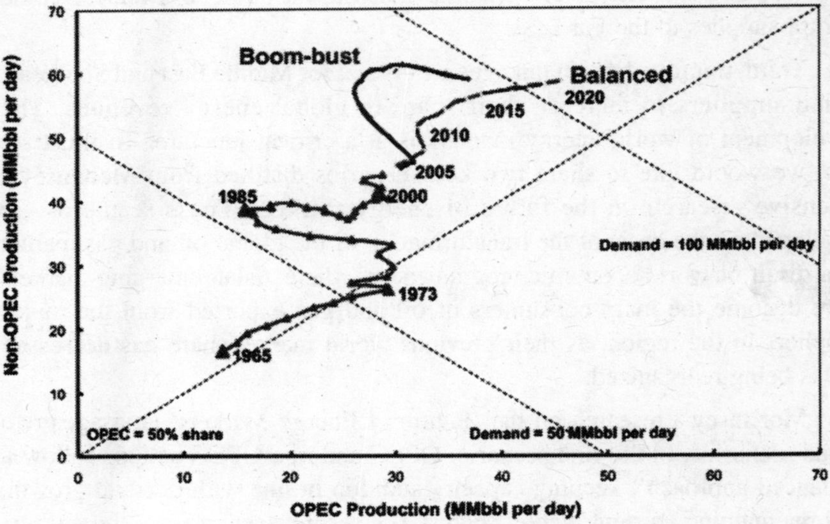

Source: McKinsey Global Oil Model

Figure 14.6: Huge Investment Requirement for Complex Refining

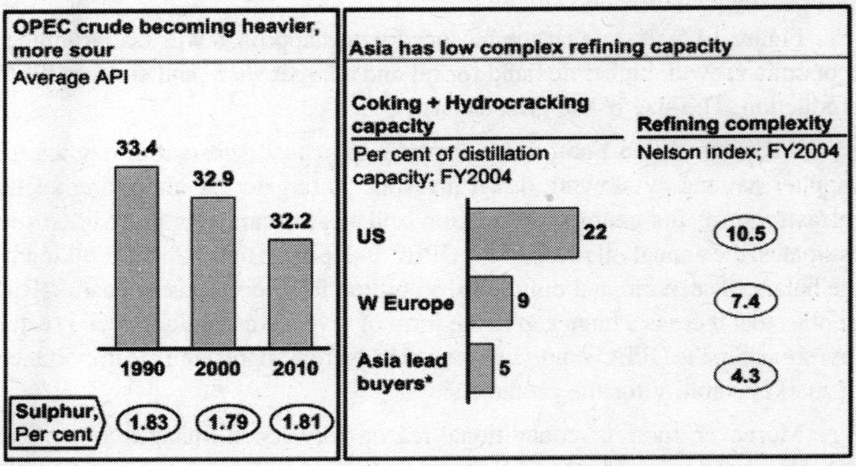

Note: * China, Japan, India and South Korea.
Source: FACTS.

required in consuming nations to realize the full economic value of the Middle Eastern crudes.

Fourth, greater interdependence is also critical for Asian consuming nations to reduce energy market volatility and to ensure greater stability. Continued economic development of consuming countries hinges on stable energy prices. For example, as Table 14.1 shows, domestic and international experts believe that volatility in energy prices can easily shave off 5-10 per cent of China's potential GDP growth, and is the second largest potential shock to growth.

Thus, clearly, the potential for both upside and the downside cooperation for all Asian countries is very high.

Table 14.1: Importance of Market Stability for Consumers: Example of China

Type of shock	Lost GDP growth (per cent)
Financial	
• Local Liquidity Crisis	
• Local non-performing loan Implosion	10-20
Energy	
• Input price shock	
• Distribution Shock	5-10
Natural Disaster	
• Grains Shortage (Floods)	
• Destruction of Major Cities or transportation Hub	2
Public Health	NA
• Infectious Disease	

Source: Mckinsey.

Impediments to Greater Asian Cooperation do exist today

There are the key issues that will need to be addressed to clear the way for true Asian cooperation. The first set of issues pertains to Asian interdependence in oil. We believe that three issues currently hinder oil interdependence in Asia:

The first issue is that oil supply is projected to remain tight and large; risky investments are needed to increase supply. While supply is expected to remain tight, we believe significant options still exist to increase future production. In the longer term, most supply growth will need to come from OPEC, Russia and unconventional sources. However, realizing these production increases will entail significantly higher investments. Figure 14.8 shows that

Figure 14.8: Annual Upstream Capital Investment Requirements in Supplying Countries (US $ billion)

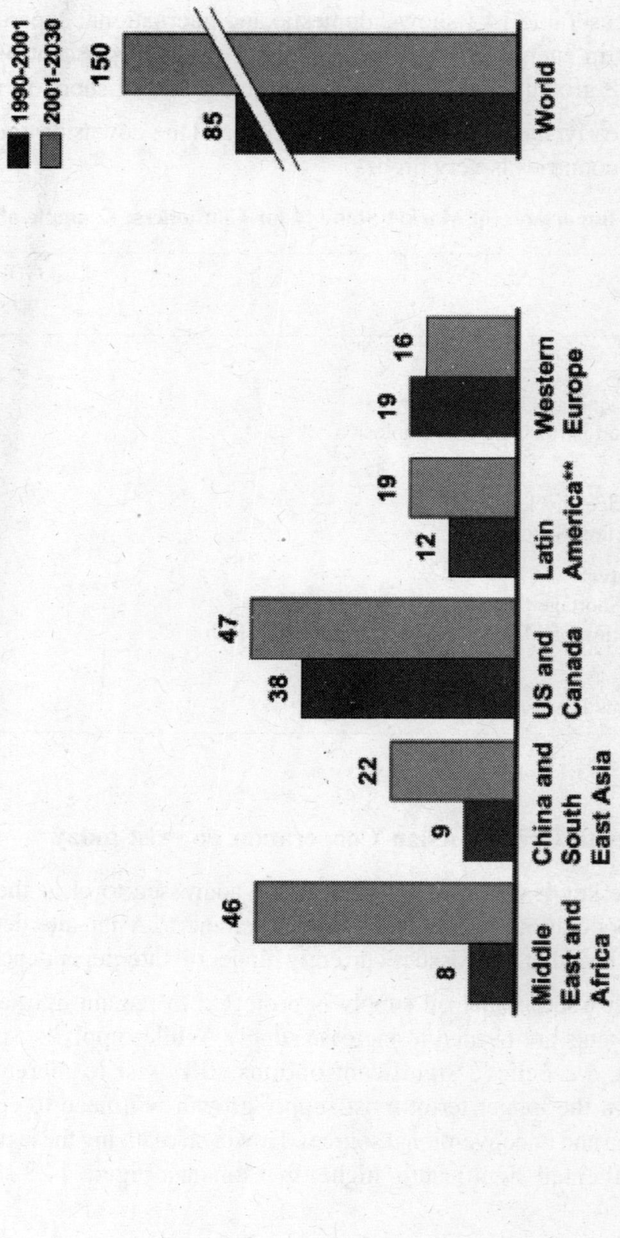

Note: Both oil and gas—Oil includes investment for E&P, non-conventional oil and refining; natural gas includes E&P, transmission storage, LNG and distribution; ** Includes Mexico.

Source: IEA World Energy Investment Outlook 2003; Worldwide Petroleum Industry Outlook.

investments for increasing supply will be larger and more risky. For the Middle East and Africa alone, capital investment will need to increase from $8 billion per annum in the last decade to $45 billion per annum for the next three decades.

Moreover, despite their strong financial position—due to the higher oil prices in recent years—supplier countries are likely to require external funding to sustain such large capital investments, if they are to ensure adequate focus on social investments and nation building, assuming an oil price of $30/barrel. Figure 14.9 shows the external funding requirement of OPEC member countries reflected through the widening gap between government revenue and government expenditure plus Capex requirements for the period 2005-20, assuming an oil price of $30/barrel. Thus, a subject for consideration is whether collaboration within Asia could help bridge this investment gap.

The second issue is that significant downstream investments are needed in consuming nations to meet Kyoto commitments. To meet the environmental standards specified in the Kyoto protocol, substantial desulphurization and coking investments are needed. Therefore, another area for discussion is the relative economics for consuming nations between desulphurization investments in refining vs upstream investments in securing sweeter crudes from regions other than the Middle East.

Third, Asian energy markets are currently neither deep nor transparent, relative to the developed markets in North America and Europe. To start with, Asia as a whole has lower levels of crude storage compared to North America and Western Europe. Except for Japan and Korea, which are members of the International Energy Agency (IEA) members and have 161 and 100 days of crude storage capacity (measured in days of consumption), other big countries such as China and India have only 13 and 6 days of reserves in storage, respectively.

Moreover, the oil market in Asia falls short on all the key elements that characterize an efficient market. First, there is no Asian market with the active backing of key demand and supply centers and sophisticated financial markets. Second, the markets are not backed by adequate storage and delivery facilities that can control excessive speculation. Third, appropriate regulatory mechanisms need to be put in place, for example, clear settlement, clearance and arbitration processes. Finally, the market doesn't have adequate scale to offer participants liquidity. Such an underdeveloped market results in buyers not being able to hedge risks and heightens supply security concerns. Sellers also lose out as they leave significant money on the table because of the 'noise' caused by volatility in marker crudes that do not reflect physical trades in

Figure 14.9: External Funding requirements in Supplying Countries Example of OPEC

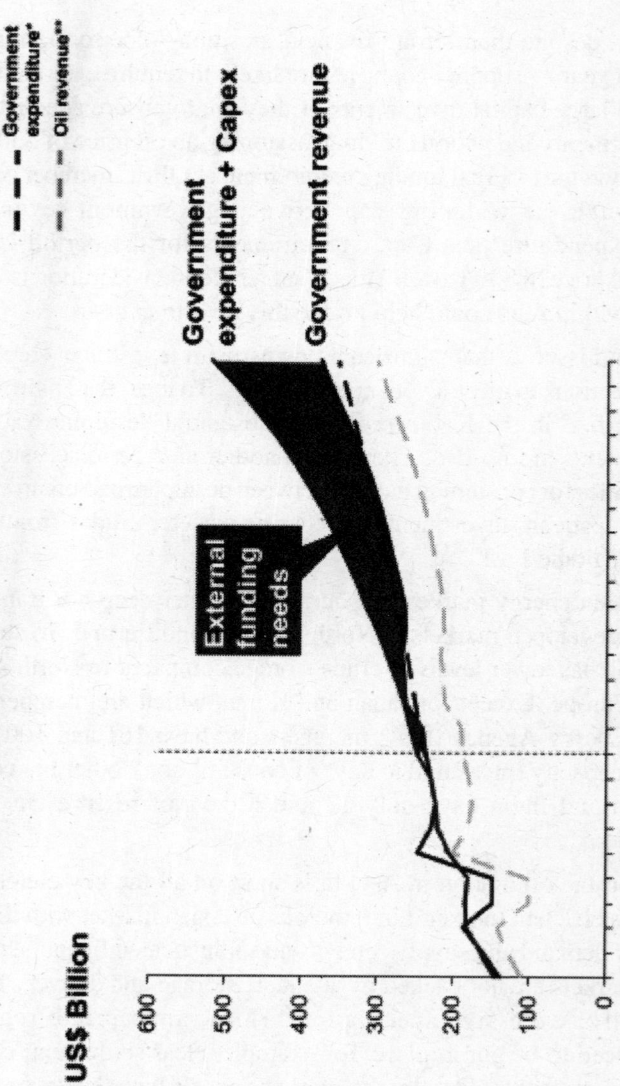

Notes: * Projection based on 2004 expenditure and demographics; ** Assumes oil price of US$30/bbl.
Source: BP Statistical Review; Goldman Sachs; McKinsey Global Oil Model; McKinsey analysis.

Figure 14.10: Asian Gas market—Third largest Margin Pool in the World

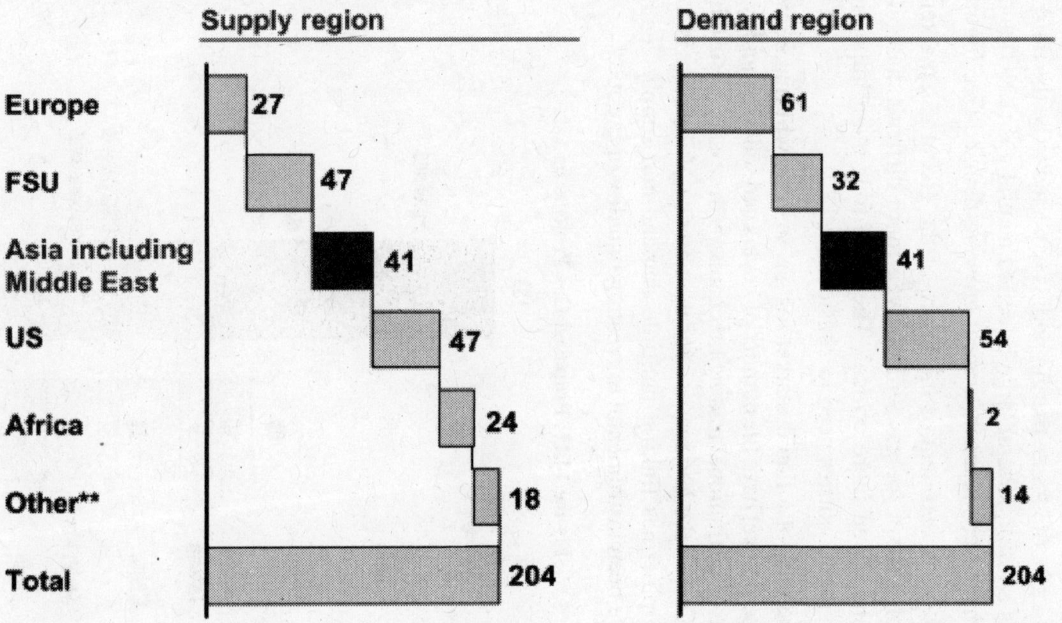

Notes: * Margin defined as total net-back in chain, that gas price in demand region minus re-gas, shipping, liquefaction and production cost; ** Latin America (including Mexico), Canada, Australia and New Zealand.
Source: McKinsey Global Gas Model.

Asian markets. Putting in place the building blocks for creating a vibrant Asian market would be another topic to consider.

The second set of issues pertains to Asian interdependence in gas. Asia offers a large margin pool for investors in gas over the next 10 years. In fact (see Figure 14.10), the Asian margin pool is expected to be the third largest in the world. As a result, several large liquefied natural gas (LNG) and pipeline investments have been planned to meet growing demand (see Figure 14.11).

McKinsey's assessment of the future of the global gas market suggests that the Asian market for gas will be even more difficult than oil, making interdependence even more critical. There are four main impediments for collaboration that countries need to consider:

First, the lack of a liquid market for gas in Asia will make investments risky. Asia does not yet have the number of buyers and sellers, liquidity, physical infrastructure or institutional trading mechanisms necessary to sustain a traded gas market. One of the key reasons for the absence of liquidity is the lack of cross-border pipelines linking multiple demand and supply centres. Such pipelines have been instrumental in creating liquidity in Europe.

Figure 14.11: Proposed Gas Projects in Asia

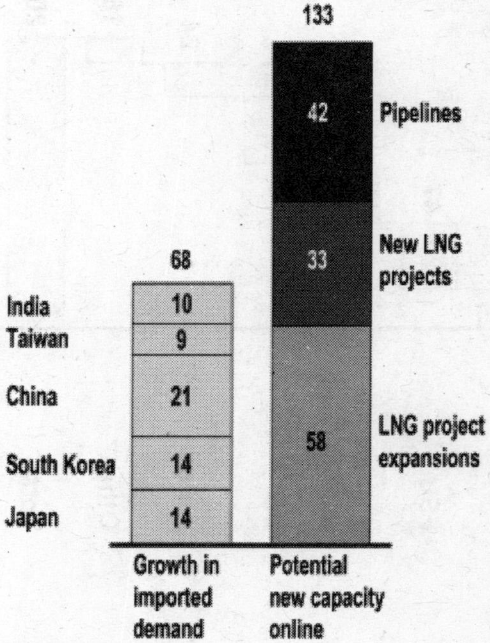

Note: New capacity includes Asia-Pacific countries, Oman, Qatar, UAE and Russia.
Sources: BP Statistical Review 2001; Energy Information Administration; Press Research.

Second, gas investment plans, particularly in India and China, will need to factor in competition from coal in power generation. As evident from Figure 14.11, with some of the largest reserves of coal in the world available in the Asian region, Asian power generators are unlikely to be able to pay much more than about US$3 per mmbtu on a sustainable basis.

Third, LNG and pipeline projects will compete for markets. In comparison to the 1980s, the relative economics of LNG and pipelines are changing, with pipelines becoming competitive over longer distances. LNG, however, will continue to offer advantages over longer distances, over politically risky routes, and for market seeding.

Fourth, gas pipelines inherently require nations to work together. Already, gas pipelines from the Middle East to India, from Southeast Asia to India, and within Southeast Asia appear economically viable.

Therefore, creating a vibrant gas market and accelerating these various gas infrastructure projects will require a high level of collaboration and orchestration amongst countries.

The third set of issues pertains to Asian interdependence in coal. Asia offers a large market for coal over the next 10 years. In fact (see Figure 14.13), the Asian region could be the largest consumer and producer of coal in the world by 2010. A drop in coal demand in Europe due to Kyoto could potentially accompany this increase in Asian demand. Therefore, Asian countries need to make substantial investment in coal mining and development of clean coal technology (CCT).

McKinsey's assessment of the coal industry suggests that the opening up of the coal sector in countries like India is critical to attract the required investment and technology. The three main reasons for this are discussed below:

Closed Nature of the Coal Mining Sector

The coal mining sector in India and China is dominated by government-owned mining companies, and private investment (either domestic or foreign) is limited to certain types of investors. There is little competition in the coal market and as a result, mining costs are higher, despite lower labour costs. This prevents transfer of skills through joint ventures (JVs) and partnerships from large coal exporters like Australia, South Africa and Indonesia.

Figure 14.12: Coal vs Gas in Power Generation in Asia

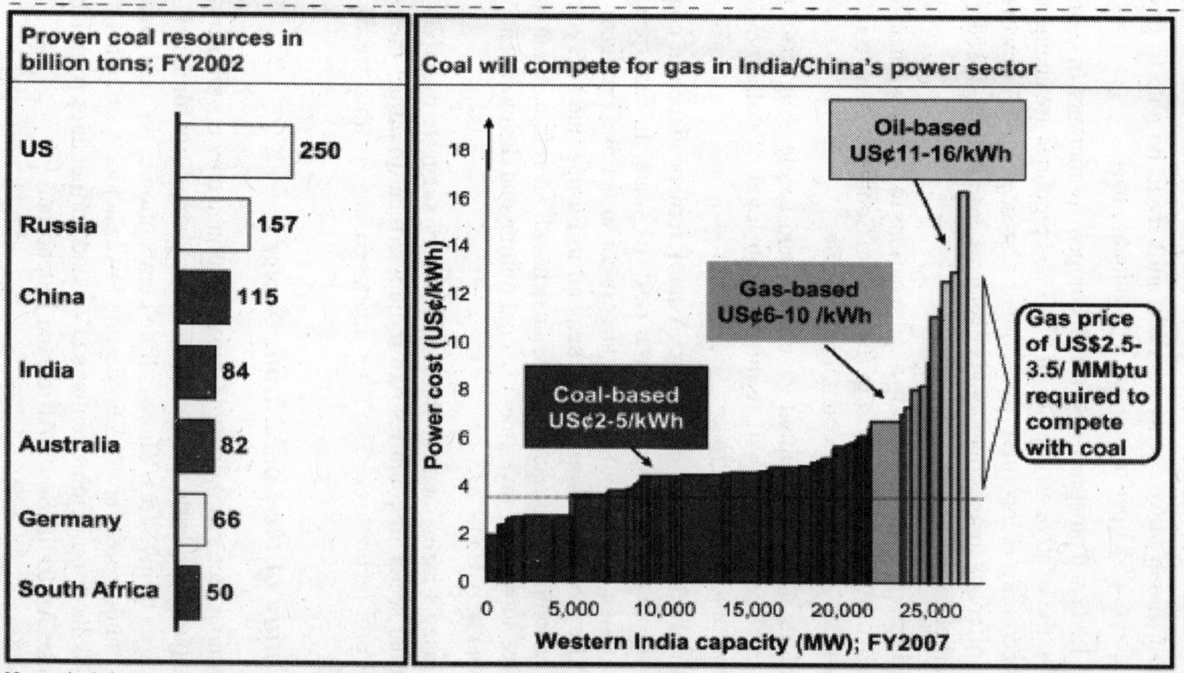

Note: * Assumes gas price of US$4/MMbtu.
Source: International Coal Handbook; *BP Statistical Review*; McKinsey analysis.

Figure 14.13: Coal Production and Consumption in Asia, 2001-25

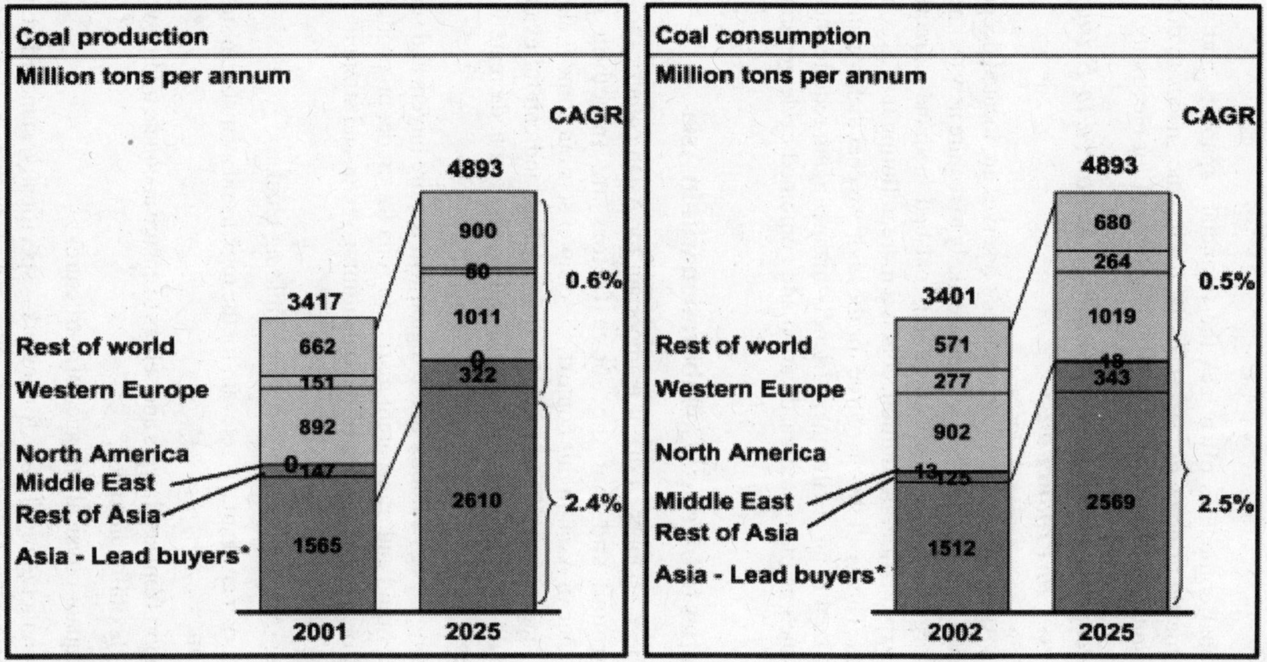

Note: * Japan, Taiwan and Korea.
Source: *International Annual Outlook* (IEA).

Weak Financial and Execution Capability of National Coal Companies

Incumbent coal companies often lack the financial capability and skills to bring the domestic reserves to market. India, for instance needs to double its coal production by 2012 to meet the growing demand for electricity.

Limited Access to Alternative Technology Required to Bring Deep Coal Reserves to Production

Moreover, in Asia a large part of the untapped reserves are located deeper than proven reserves (see Figure 14.14). They are likely to require new technologies such as underground coal gasification and coal bed methane extraction for economical exploitation. In addition, coal is a more polluting fuel as compared to natural gas. This is all the more true for the high ash coal that is available in India. Using coal in an environment-friendly manner again requires access to technology such as integrated gasification and combined cycle generation.

Opportunities to Increase Collaboration within Asia

It has been established that it is important for Asian countries to pursue common ground and that the above factors are impeding greater interdependence in Asia. In this context, the chapter sets out some preliminary ideas to consider. Most of these ideas require debate and careful evaluation, but they could possibly help move the dialogue forward and create win-win opportunities.

Increasing energy stability in the region will require buyers and sellers to build a deep, liquid and transparent market in Asia for crude, oil products and gas. In addition, a liberalization of the coal mining sector and strengthening of national coal companies is essential.

A strong Asian market requires five building blocks

- A marker crude that is relevant for the region and available in sufficient volume;
- Support from key buyers and sellers to ensure adequate trading volumes and flexibility in trades;
- Adequate physical storage infrastructure;
- A conducive regulatory framework—specifically, standard contracts, settlement and eligibility processes and arbitration mechanisms; and

Figure 14.14: Asian Prospective Coal Reserves

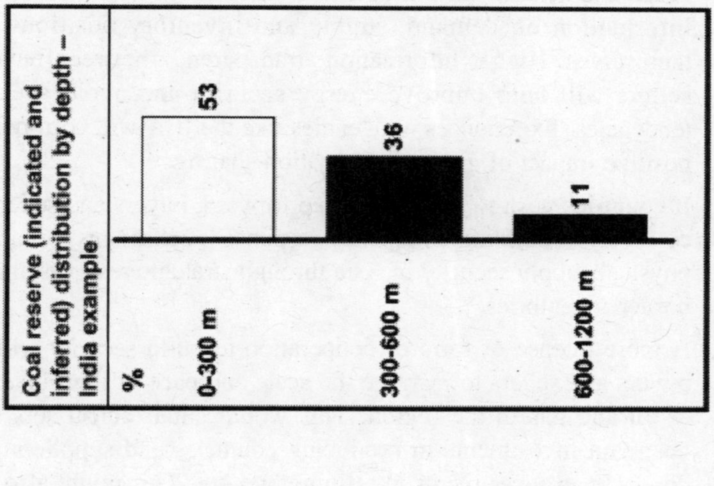

Source: Industry interviews.

- Robust financial markets to support hedging and trading.

Creating a vibrant oil and gas market in the region will go a long way in addressing the stability concerns of both buyers and sellers. To build energy security in the region, there is a wide range of options such as the following:

- Asian and Middle Eastern countries should start with sharing detailed information on demand, supply and inventory positions among themselves. Higher information transparency between buyers and sellers will help improve energy security and avoid speculative tendencies. Experiences of agencies like the IEA will corroborate the positive impact of greater information sharing.
- If countries wish to take this a step forward, buyers and sellers could co-invest in building emergency response mechanisms by increasing physical supply security in Asia through strategic reserves and cross-border inventories.
- A more intense of form of cooperation to build security will be for buyers and sellers to increase the scale and pace of joint investments in oil and gas in the region. This would entail consumers making upstream investments in producing countries and suppliers making downstream investments in refining and gas. This might also require some longer term price and volume agreements to underpin the investments.
- On another front, major coal bearing countries could reform the coal mining sector to allow the entry of private and foreign investment in this critical sector. This will enable them to reduce dependence on other countries for their energy requirements, thereby enhancing their energy security.
- Finally, an enduring mechanism to improve energy security in the region will be to create a pan-Asian gas grid linking multiple demand and supply sources.

Ensuring sustainability will require building enduring multilateral partnerships. Specifically, the following steps need to adhered to:

- Pursue longer-term multilateral projects to strengthen cooperation, such as joint research on energy technologies relevant to Asia, jointly addressing key environmental priorities like standardizing specifications for gasoline and diesel across Asia and broader sharing of mutual capabilities, including human resource development. In addition, there could be joint research on technologies for cleaner utilization of Asian coal reserves like underground coal gasification, integrated gasification combined cycle generation and coal liquefaction (developed by Sasol in South Africa).

- Similarly, in the coal mining sector, India and China can allow coal mining companies from Asia and other regional economies such as Indonesia, South Africa and Australia to invest in commercial coal mining. Apart from bringing in the much-needed investment, this will enhance the transfer of new skills and technology to the host countries.
- Strengthen national oil companies and national coal companies in the region through further corporatization, permitting JVs with regional coal companies and far-reaching regional cooperation.

Part VI
Epilogue

15

An Agenda for the East Asia Summit

Editors

The developments of the past few years have led to an Asian resurgence with the emergence of China and India as engines of growth, recovery of Japan from a decade old recession, rise of the Asian middle class as source of final demand and increasing resilience of Asian countries to external shocks such as oil price rise, etc. Over the past decade Asian countries have also integrated themselves within the region as is evident from the high and growing proportion of intra-regional trade and investments. Besides the growing economic interdependence, Asian countries also face shared vulnerabilities to external shocks and natural disasters such as the Tsunami.

There is also an attempt to build on this 'functional' or market-driven cooperation and growing interdependence to more formal institutionalized cooperation as is clear from the numerous sub-regional or bilateral free trade arrangements.

ASEAN has played an important role in evolving a framework for broader cooperation by bringing together the major Asian countries such as Japan, China, India and South Korea as dialogue partners. These dialogue partners are all working on ASEAN+1 FTAs. China, Japan, Korea and India are also studying bilateral FTAs between themselves. Through the emerging web of FTAs a virtual Asian economic community is evolving.

There is a need for building on these sub-regional and bilateral attempts to form a broader regional framework that would provide a seamless market, facilitating more effective exploitation of synergies. The studies conducted by RIS and ADB have shown that broader regional integration in Asia has the potential of generating billions of dollars of new output and puting Asia on a high growth path.[1] Furthermore, it has been shown that Asian economic integration will benefit the rest of the world as it implies more trade creation rather than trade diversion. Hence, it is a case of win-win for both Asia as well as the world economy. Regional economic integration is also likely to bring about a convergence in the levels of development and hence could be an important instrument in the region's fight against poverty.

A number of Asian leaders and statesmen had spoken of the importance of broader regional cooperation in Asia asserting the Asian identity. However, Asia lacked a forum for dialogue for such cooperation. The launch of the East Asia Summit (EAS) in Kuala Lumpur on 14 December 2005, attended by the leaders of ASEAN-10, Japan, China, South Korea, India, Australia and New Zealand, provided to the region a much needed forum for such a dialogue.

The new forum, that is, EAS, could have far reaching consequences for promoting broader regional cooperation in Asia. By giving to the leaders of the largest and most dynamic economies of Asia a much needed annual forum for dialogue, the EAS is expected to facilitate the cause of community building in Asia. It is likely that future Summits will take steps towards concretizing Asian regional cooperation in a number of areas, thereby hastening the re-emergence of Asia as the centre of gravity of the world economy.

A key priority consideration for future EAS would be to create a comprehensive pan-Asian framework for regional economic cooperation and integration.The comprehensive economic partnership arrangement combining the EAS partners could be subsequently expanded to include other Asian countries to evolve into a truly Asian Economic Community (AEC) which could be an 'arc of advantage, peace and shared prosperity' in the words of the Indian Prime Minister, Dr Manmohan Singh.

EAS members together account for more than a fifth of global output and trade, half of world's population and more than two- thirds of global foreign exchange resources. EAS provides the basis of a major grouping that could become the third pole of the world economy after NAFTA and the EU. By providing a seamless market to the EAS (or Asian) businesses and industry such an arrangement will help in efficiency-seeking restructuring of Asian industry and could emerge as an engine of growth. RIS studies have shown that integration of EAS economies has the potential of generating substantial welfare gains.

There is some debate on whether ASEAN+3 is a better forum for evolving a broader scheme of economic integration in Asia than EAS. However, research has shown that EAS has the greater potential to generate welfare gains for all the partners as compared to ASEAN+3. Also EAS will be able to benefit from the dynamism and other strengths of India, Australia and New Zealand for mutual benefit. With a US$1000 billion economy growing at 9 per cent per annum, and a 300 million strong middle class, India is emerging as the third largest economy in the world. Its software and services dominated economy complements well with the hardware and manufacturing driven economies of the other East Asian countries. With booming demand for infrastructure investments, that are projected to be over US$500 billion, India can provide a huge market for East Asian investors and underutilized construction and engineering capacities. Rapid integration with East Asia as a part of the Look East Policy (LEP) followed by India since 1991 has made the region the largest trade partner of India, ahead of the EU and the US. India is increasingly getting integrated with East Asian production chains, especially in the more critical knowledge-based segments such as R&D and product design. India is already evolving an FTA with ASEAN (besides individual countries such as Singapore and Thailand), South Korea and Japan, and considering such arrangements with China and is hence very much a part of the growing web of FTAs linking the East Asian countries. With its excellent trading and transport links and emerging preferential trading arrangements with South Asian countries, GCC and other West Asian countries, India could act as a bridge for East Asia for the markets in South, West and Central Asian countries. Finally, it can be argued that an EAS based grouping will be more balanced than an ASEAN+3 based community.

The EAS comprehensive economic partnership arrangement could target to liberalize regional trade and investment regimes in a phased manner by 2020 with provisions for safeguards for sensitive products, special and differential treatment for countries at different levels of development and dispute resolution. Agricultural trade liberalization should be attempted on a separate track from that of industrial goods to allow supremacy to considerations of food security as well as livelihood issues.

Care must be taken in designing the programmes of regional economic integration such that they keep equity, employment generation, balanced regional development and necessary social transformation and social safety nets for the vulnerable sections of the society at their heart so that they represent regionalism with an 'Asian Face'. By balancing the interests of efficiency and equity, the Asian arrangement could well emerge as a role model for trade liberalization in multilateral as well as regional contexts in the whole world.

The other adjuncts of the EAS comprehensive economic cooperation arrangement could include an Asian monetary architecture of EAS countries for facilitating intra-regional trade and exchange rate stability within the region by pooling reserves, creation of an Asian Currency Unit (ACU) as a unit of account, setting up an Asian Investment Bank, an Asian Energy Forum to pursue regional cooperation for energy security and a cultural foundation for evolving an Asian identity.

To conclude, the launch of EAS as a forum for dialogue between Asian leaders represents a landmark development in the direction of regional cooperation in Asia. In the coming years, it will hopefully prove to be an important vehicle for charting the agenda for broader regional cooperation and integration for realizing the Asian dream!

Asian Leaders on the Asian Economic Community

The RIS proposal for broader regional cooperation in Asia by forming an AEC in a phased manner with Japan, ASEAN, China, India and South Korea (JACIK) as its core was first presented and discussed at the High-level Conference on Asian Economic Community organized by RIS in New Delhi in March 2003 in collaboration with the Malaysian Institute of Economic Research and the Centre for Strategic and International Studies, Jakarta. Since then a number of Asian Statesmen and leaders have spoken on the relevance of an AEC as an inclusive grouping of JACIK, among other countries, as a way forward for regional economic cooperation in Asia, as excerpted below. Subsequently, the EAS was launched as a forum for dialogue on Asian cooperation in December 2005 in Kuala Lumpur covering all the JACIK countries and Australia and New Zealand.

'If the 14 of us (viz. ASEAN-10, India, Japan, China and South Korea) combine into a broader Asian Economic Community, it can promote our overall competitiveness and create a new engine of growth for the entire region'.

— *Prime Minister Shri A.B. Vajpayee at the ASEAN-India Summit, Bali, October 2003.*

'It is only inevitable that we seek to take the existing India-ASEAN relationship to a higher level, where we envision an Asian Economic Community, which encompasses ASEAN, China, Japan, Korea and India. Such a community would release enormous creative energies of our people. One cannot but be captivated by the vision of an integrated market, spanning the distance from the Himalayas to the Pacific Ocean, linked by efficient road, rail, air and shipping services. This community of nations would

Box continued

Box continued

constitute an "arc of advantage", across which there would be large-scale movement of people, capital, ideas, and creativity. ....This is an idea whose time is fast approaching, and we must be prepared for it collectively'.

— *Prime Minister Dr. Manmohan Singh at the Third India-ASEAN Business Summit, 21 October 2004.*

'In time, [India-Singapore Comprehensive Economic Cooperation Agreement] CECA can eventually lead to an Asian Economic Community linking South Asia, Southeast Asia and Northeast Asia. Such a Community will result in a strong and prosperous Asia, with India as one of the key pillars'.

— *Prime Minister Goh Chok Tong of Singapore while accepting the Jawaharlal Nehru Award for International Understanding in New Delhi, July 2004.*

'There is the emerging ASEAN+3+India, and that will be a formidable regional grouping that can negotiate then with the European Union, the Americas, Africa and such regional economic groupings'.

— *President Gloria Macapagal Arroyo, Republic of the Philippines at the ASEAN Business Summit, Vientiane, Laos, 28 November 2004.*

'India should join in [East Asian Community], as ...it will expand the market, force more specialization, division of labour, and India has some thing to contribute in economic, political, diplomatic as well as the security fields. So I believe it is to the advantage of the ASEAN countries that any such East Asian Community should include India'.

— *Singapore's Minister Mentor Lee Kuan Yew's address to the Foreign Correspondents Association of Singapore, reported in The Straits Times, 22 December 2004.*

'Recognising the need for concerted efforts among Asian countries to translate the positive developments into an 'Arc of Advantage and Prosperity' involving growth, prosperity, stability and closer integration in Asia, the two leaders acknowledged the responsibility that the two countries have in this new emerging Asian era and thus committed to work together to promote the vision of an Asian Economic Community'.

— *India-Japan Joint Statement issued during the visit of Prime Minister Koizumi to India during April 2005.*

'We feel confident that in the next few years, we may see the rise of a Pan-Asian Free Trade Area covering all major Asian economies, including India, Korea, China, Japan, ASEAN and possibly extending to Australia and New Zealand. This could be the third pole of the world economy after the European Union and the North-American Free Trade Area and will open up new growth avenues for all our own economies'.

— *President Dr. A.P.J. Abdul Kalam of India addressing the Major Business Chambers of Korea, Seoul, 7 February 2006.*

Box continued

Box continued

'An East Asia Summit (EAS) FTA by 2020 can be envisaged... and the region is likely to become a major driver of the global economy sometime in the first half of this century'.

— *Singapore's Minister for Foreign Affairs, Mr. George Yeo at Boao Forum for Asia Annual Meeting, 22 April 2006.*

'The proposed Asian trade zone (consisting of the 10-member ASEAN, plus Australia, China, India, Japan, New Zealand and South Korea) would benefit from having a population of three billion people and current economic activity of nine trillion dollars.... We are certain it will be to the benefit of all the countries of the region'.

— *Mr. Toshihiro Nikai, Minister of Economy Trade and Industry, Japan, after Meeting with ASEAN Trade Ministers in Kuala Lumpur, as reported in the International Herald Tribune, 24 August 2006.*